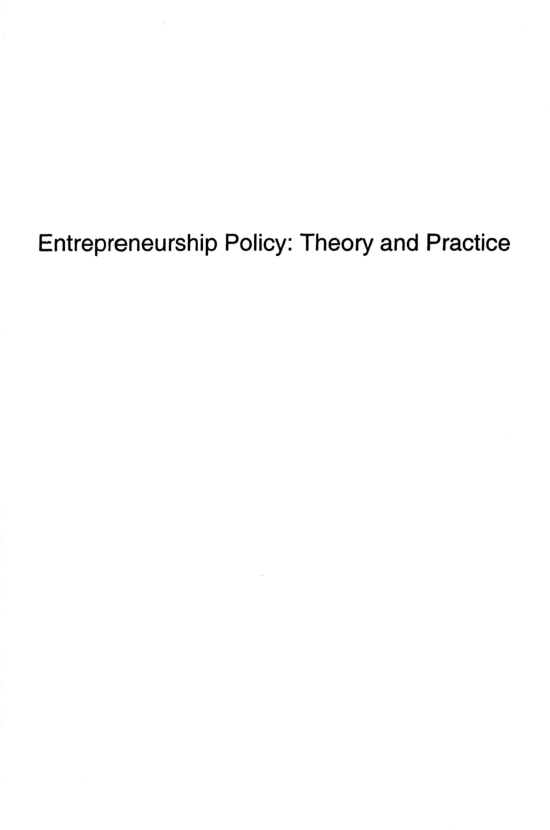

Entrepreneurship Policy: Theory and Practice

INTERNATIONAL STUDIES IN ENTREPRENEURSHIP

Series Editors:
Zoltan J. Acs
University of Baltimore
Baltimore, Maryland USA

David B. Audretsch
Indiana University
Bloomington, Indiana USA

Entrepreneurship Policy: Theory and Practice

by

Anders Lundström
Swedish Foundation for Small Business Research, Örebro, Sweden

Lois Stevenson
Wilford White Fellow and Fellow of the IC² Institute, Ottawa, Canada

 Springer

Library of Congress Cataloging-in-Publication Data

A C.I.P. Catalogue record for this book is available
from the Library of Congress.

ISBN 0-387-24140-X   e-ISBN 0-387-24202-3   Printed on acid-free paper.

Printed in the United States of America.

9 8 7 6 5 4 3 2 1   SPIN 11333562

springeronline.com

About the Authors

Prof. Lois Stevenson is a former Director, Entrepreneurship Development with the Atlantic Canada Opportunities Agency and former Director, Policy and Liaison in the Entrepreneurship and Small Business Office of Industry Canada. In 2002, she served as Deputy Executive Director, Industry Canada's Innovation Secretariat, and leads the Practice of Innovation Initiative, profiling highly innovative firms and their CEOs. Prior to joining the Government of Canada in 1990, she spent ten years as a university professor teaching and researching in the areas of entrepreneurship and small business management. She has authored (or co-authored) seven books and has over 40 papers published in refereed journals and conference proceedings. She is a Past-President of the International Council for Small Business (ICSB) and the Canadian Council for Small Business and Entrepreneurship (CCSBE); a member of the Entrepreneurship Of The Year Institute; a Fellow of the Price-Babson Fellows Program; a Fellow of the IC^2 Institute of the University of Texas at Austin; and a Wilford White Fellow. Ms. Stevenson is a member of the International Reference Council of the Swedish Foundation for Small Business Research (FSF) and during 2000-01 was a visiting researcher with the Foundation leading an international study of entrepreneurship policy. She holds three degrees from universities in Canada and the UK and lives in Ottawa, Canada.

Prof. Anders Lundström is Founder and President of The Swedish Foundation for Small Business Research (FSF), with offices in Örebro and Stockholm, Sweden and Brussels. He is responsible for the FSF research programme concerning the effects of small business and entrepreneurship policy programmes and has conducted many studies on the problems and possibilities for SMEs and related policy issues. Dr. Lundström was Deputy-

Director at NUTEK, Sweden's Business Development Agency, and prior to that, the Research Director at SIND, the Swedish National Industrial Board. He founded FSF in 1994, acting as the chair of its Board of Directors until assuming the role as President in 1997. He also founded the FSF-NUTEK award, the International Award for Small Business and Entrepreneurship Research, and chairs FSF's International Reference Council. Dr. Lundström has written over 20 books and numerous articles in the field of small business and entrepreneurship. His current research interests are in the field of SME and entrepreneurship policy. In 2002-03, he led the research project to examine entrepreneurship policy approaches in the five Nordic countries. He is a Past President of the International Council for Small Business (ICSB) and chaired the ICSB World Conference in Stockholm in 1996 and the 2001 International Small Business Congress (ISBC) World Conference in Stockholm. He is a Professor at the Business School of Mälardalen University and Assistant Professor at the Gothenburg Business School, where he obtained his PhD in Business Administration in 1976. He has also authored a novel and a book of poetry. He lives in Stockholm.

Contents

Preface

During 2000-01 we undertook a study of what governments in ten countries were doing at the national policy level to stimulate entrepreneurial activity. This research was sponsored by the Swedish Foundation for Small Business Research (FSF) with funding support from NUTEK, the Swedish Business Development Agency, and the Swedish Ministry of Industry, Employment and Communications. This was followed in 2002-03 by a second study in five Nordic countries (two of which were included in the first study). Case study descriptions of the government policies affecting the development of entrepreneurship in these countries were compiled in Stevenson and Lundström (2001) and Lundström (ed.) (2003) as part of the FSF's Entrepreneurship Policy for the Future project.

The inspiration for the Entrepreneurship Policy for the Future project came directly from two sources: (i) the work of Stevenson (1996)[1] who elaborated an entrepreneurship development framework that formed the basis for the design and implementation of entrepreneurship policies and programmes in an underdeveloped region of Canada throughout the early 1990s, and (ii) the work of Boter, Hjalmarsson and Lundström (1999) who were exploring different small and medium enterprise (SME) policy frameworks within the context of Sweden.

At the time we started our international research, entrepreneurship policy was an emerging area of economic policy development that was not well developed. Interest in the role of entrepreneurship in economic development and growth by international organisations, such as the Organisation for Economic Cooperation and Development (OECD) and the European Union (EU), as well as by the research community (e.g., the Global Entrepreneurship Monitor initiative) began to intensify in the late 1990s, but limited knowledge existed at that time about entrepreneurship as a policy area or about how to strategically design and implement such a policy area. In fact, there appeared to be considerable confusion around what constituted policies to stimulate the development of entrepreneurship versus the traditional and well-entrenched set of policies to promote small and medium-sized enterprises (SMEs).

Based on both our analysis and experience, we held the view that the set of policies necessary to increase entrepreneurial activity levels were qualitatively and quantitatively different than those being implemented to protect and strengthen the SME sector. Although entrepreneurship was emerging as a policy issue, we believed that, as a policy domain, it suffered from a lack of clarity and specificity. If entrepreneurship policy was to stand as a distinct policy field, it would need better definition and articulation. What were its policy parameters? How did it differ from SME policy? How were governments approaching the development of policies to support higher levels of entrepreneurship? What were they specifically doing in this area? We decided to explore these questions by examining the practices of national-level governments in a set of diverse, yet developed countries. Lessons learned from an analysis of the experiences in this group of countries would enable a more concrete elaboration of the entrepreneurship policy field and be helpful in guiding other countries wishing to pursue an entrepreneurship policy focus.

The ten countries for the first study were selected on the basis of diversity: Australia, Canada, Finland, Ireland, the Netherlands, Spain, Sweden, Taiwan, the United Kingdom and the United States. The situation in each of these countries was detailed in Stevenson and Lundström (2001). Although all were economically developed countries, among them, we included countries with large and small populations; higher and lower per capita GDP levels; high and low unemployment rates; high and low labour force participation rates for women; and reportedly high and low levels of entrepreneurial activity, as measured by Reynolds et al. (1999) in the 1999 GEM report. The countries also differed in their cultural and socio-economic contexts (Asian, European and North American countries) and in the government's apparent focus on entrepreneurship as an economic development vehicle.

The main purpose of the study was to address gaps in the existing knowledge base about entrepreneurship policy. Based on an examination of what governments were actually doing, our intent was to develop an operational definition for entrepreneurship policy; articulate its policy framework and programme parameters; map out the dimensions of each area of the framework; and identify good practice policy development approaches, measures and implementation structures. In our initial study of practices in 10 countries, we discovered a number of examples of policy measures to stimulate and support the emergence of entrepreneurship, but only three countries with, what we termed, a "holistic" entrepreneurship policy approach. In most cases, policies to stimulate entrepreneurship were "added-on" to existing SME policies or, to a lesser degree, incorporated within innovation policy frameworks.

The second study explored entrepreneurship policy development in the five Nordic countries: Denmark, Finland, Iceland, Norway and Sweden (Lundström (ed.), 2003). This time the selection of countries was based on their perceived similarity, particularly in terms of cultural, political and social contexts. We wanted to examine whether a set of countries with similar "contexts" would produce similar entrepreneurship policy approaches. The study found that these countries were not as similar in context as initially anticipated; however, their governments shared a lot of similarity in the choice of policy measures to promote entrepreneurship, even if their micro-policies were not exactly the same in detail. One of the explanations for the similarity in approaches could be the number of opportunities Nordic policymakers have to exchange what they are doing, a process which encourages the adoption of each other's "good practices". However, what may produce good outcomes in one country may well not be the most appropriate in another without taking into consideration their differing "contexts". This issue of context and policy focus is one we explore further in this book.

As a direct outcome of our studies, we mapped out a coordinated and integrated process that could lead to the establishment of entrepreneurship policies appropriate to a country's idiosyncratic contextual realities. We also identified a number of challenges related to the effective design and delivery of entrepreneurship policy that are in need of further examination, including development of appropriate performance indicators and evaluation measures and national and regional level implementation structures.

It is now over four years since we started our work of defining and describing the development of entrepreneurship policy in these countries. Since the FSF first published our preliminary findings in 2001 (Lundström and Stevenson, 2001), there has been a rapid increase in the level of interest in entrepreneurship policy. Developments have accelerated much faster than we could have imagined. By mid-2004, we found evidence that governments in more of the 13 countries have set objectives to strengthen the entrepreneurial culture and to increase the level of entrepreneurial activity and business entry rates. They are supporting these objectives as a strategic priority with concrete policy measures and targets. An increasing amount of attention is being paid to areas of the entrepreneurship policy framework defined in our first study, for example, the integration of entrepreneurship in the education system and policies targeted to defined segments of the population, especially women and innovative entrepreneurs. Growing emphasis is being given to entrepreneurship development in regional development strategies with more actions being taken at the regional and local levels. In other words, entrepreneurship policy is evolving as more of a distinct policy field. There are now programmes and policies for this area in almost every developed country, as well as formulations by the Commission of the European Communities, the OECD, the Asia-Pacific Economic Cooperation (APEC) and the United Nations. Interest in the public policy implications of fostering entrepreneurial activity has also been growing within the research community (Hart, 2003; Acs and Audretsch, 2003; Audretsch et al., 2002) and the importance of entrepreneurship as a tool for improving the economic and social situations in developing economies has escalated (UNDP, 2004; Kantis, 2002).

In spite of these recent developments, many compelling questions and policy dilemmas persist. These relate to the nature of the causal relationship between entrepreneurial activity levels and economic growth, the setting of policy targets, the application of policies in different contexts, management of policy development and implementation processes, and evaluation issues. Remaining questions and issues of note include:

- What is an entrepreneurial society/economy and how does a country/region become one?
- If a government's goal is to create a business and policy environment that encourages entrepreneurship, employment opportunities and sustainable growth, what should that environment look like?
- Do higher entrepreneurial activity rates contribute significantly to economic growth and if so, how? What difference can policy actions make? What policies would have the most desired impact?
- How does a government determine its priorities and actions within the entrepreneurship policy framework; what needs to be done given their context?
- Why do different national governments adopt the approaches they do?
- What is the relationship between the SME policy and Entrepreneurship policy domains?
- How does one manage the transition from SME policy to Entrepreneurship policy or the interface between them?
- How does the ministry responsible for small business and enterprise development manage the horizontal interface with other relevant ministries and regulatory agencies, for example, with ministries of education to integrate entrepreneurship education in the school system?
- How does a government know if its entrepreneurship policy is working? How does one measure the outcomes of entrepreneurship policies, programmes and initiatives?
- What are the appropriate performance indicators?

- Can a country/region have too many entrepreneurs? Is there an optimal level of business ownership in a society? How does one attain the optimal level? What is the cost of not moving to the equilibrium point, if one exists?

In this book, we present the salient findings from our studies of entrepreneurship policy in a total of 13 countries, including our definition of entrepreneurship policy and its policy foundations; our entrepreneurship policy framework; the entrepreneurship policy typology; and a roadmap for adopting an entrepreneurship policy approach. We also discuss conceptual issues related to the quantification and measurability of entrepreneurship policy inputs and outcomes; the relationship between a country's contextual make-up and the appropriate choice of entrepreneurship policy options; and several issues concerning the evaluation of entrepreneurship policies and programmes. We introduce an entrepreneurship policy comprehensiveness index that may be useful to governments in taking stock of their current policy orientations and to better enable the assessment of entrepreneurship policy across countries. We conclude with a discussion of how to approach the development of an integrated entrepreneurship policy approach and the future implications of this for policymakers, researchers, and economic development agents.

This book will be useful to government policymakers, international organisations, researchers and educators. It is a tool to assist policymakers in making the transition to an entrepreneurship policy approach; a guide for international organisations in sorting out the clearer separation of initiatives targeted to increasing the level of entrepreneurial activity versus strengthening the environment for SMEs; a base for the research community in identifying key entrepreneurship policy issues worthy of further examination; a curriculum resource for the education community in designing new courses in entrepreneurship policy to complement existing courses on new venture creation and the management of entrepreneurial firms; and a source of confirmation for early champions of an entrepreneurship policy approach.

In Chapter 1, we discuss why entrepreneurship policy is important, highlight recent developments in research knowledge about the factors affecting entrepreneurial activity levels and explore the current state of development of entrepreneurship policy frameworks. In Chapter 2, we present our definition of entrepreneurship policy, discuss differences between SME policy and entrepreneurship policy, introduce the entrepreneurship policy comprehensiveness index and highlight practices of the 13 governments in each area of our entrepreneurship policy framework. In Chapter 3, we present our typology of entrepreneurship policy, categorise the 13 governments using the typology as a framework, and highlight recent trends in policy developments, for example the rapid emergence of policy for innovative entrepreneurship. Chapter 4 discusses the relevance of context to entrepreneurship policymaking and how policy choices might be made to produce more optimal performance outcomes given a country's context. In Chapter 5, we expand on our conceptual model of the underpinnings of entrepreneurship policy, stressing the complexities involved in trying to determine how to increase the supply of entrepreneurs in an economy given the difficult-to-measure array of forces influencing an individual's propensity to start a business. Chapter 6 goes into more detail about the problems of evaluating SME and entrepreneurship policies and programmes and, finally, Chapter 7 concludes with an integrated framework for entrepreneurship policy analysis and development using the building blocks presented in the earlier chapters of the book. It points to the way forward for both policymakers and for the research community.

---

[1] The objectives of the strategy described in Stevenson (1996) (OECD/ACOA) were to increase the pool of people who had the motivation, skills, abilities, and desire to start their own businesses and to increase the level and extent of appropriate community-based support for new venture activity at every stage of the entrepreneurial process.

Foreword

Entrepreneurship is first and foremost a mindset. To seize an entrepreneurial opportunity, one needs to have a taste for independence and self-realisation. But one also has to be prepared to handle the uncertainty that is inherent to entrepreneurship. And entrepreneurs need to be able to transform opportunity into economic value, by blending their creativity and knowledge with a strategic vision and sound management.

Entrepreneurs, as the vehicle for the commercial exploitation of innovative and creative ideas, have a key role in the Lisbon agenda that the European Union has set itself to boost competitiveness and dynamism.

The European Union is not fully exploiting its entrepreneurial potential. The 2003 Eurobarometer revealed that almost half of Europeans said to prefer entrepreneurship over employment, yet only 17 percent tactually realise their ambitions. Europeans are also relatively risk-averse. US entrepreneurs appear to test the market and, if successful, expand rapidly. In Europe, many business ideas never come to the market as their viability is already questioned before they can be tested in the market place. Indeed the Eurobarometer showed that 44 percent of Europeans agreed that *'one should not start a business when there was a risk of failure'* against only 29 percent in the US.

In February 2004, the European Commission presented its agenda for entrepreneurship. This action plan sets the priorities for fostering entrepreneurial performance in the European Union. It emphasizes in the first place the need to encourage more business start-ups, by fuelling entrepreneurial mindsets and reviewing the balance between risks and rewards related to entrepreneurship. It also highlights the importance of encouraging businesses development and growth and the key role of finance in realising this. Finally, entrepreneurs need to be able to operate in a facilitating regulatory and administrative framework.

Successfully raising entrepreneurial activity depends on a complex set of mutually interacting framework conditions, attitudes and skills. In order to make tangible progress, the Action Plan identified a first list of measures to be taken both at EU level and within the Member States. But further work is needed. In addition, countries and regions each have a unique mix of strengths and weaknesses affecting their entrepreneurial culture and business environment. These require specific responses as well.

To complete the entrepreneurship agenda, there still is a way to go. The book in your hands provides a structure to the complex relations between all factors influencing entrepreneurship. This makes the book a reliable guide for policymaking on the road to entrepreneurship.

I am very pleased to recommend this book as a true reference to everyone who is, either professionally or personally, concerned with entrepreneurship and policy-making.

Olli Rehn

Member of the
European Commission

Acknowledgements

It is our privilege to acknowledge the contributions of many people and organisations to the completion of this book and to thank them for their support and assistance. First and foremost, we extend a great deal of gratitude to our editors, Zoltan Acs, Distinguished Professor of Entrepreneurship and Innovation, Professor of Economics, and Director of the Entrepreneurship Program at the Robert G. Merrick School of Business, University of Baltimore, Maryland and David Audretsch, Ameritech Chair of Economic Development, Director of the Institute for Development Strategies and Director of the Center for West European Studies, Indiana University, for inviting us to prepare this manuscript and for encouraging us in its pursuit. Their belief in the value of this contribution to a better understanding of entrepreneurship policy and their helpful comments on an earlier draft of this book have been invaluable to us.

In addition, we would like to thank the following:

Carina Holmgren, Research Assistant with the Swedish Foundation for Small Business Research (FSF), for her help in compiling updated statistical data on each of the countries in the study; Britt-Marie Nordström, Communications/Marketing Officer with FSF, for supporting various phases of the preparation of the manuscript; Judi Macdonald for the endless hours spent working with us during the final stages of editing and proofreading; Irmeli Löfstedt-Rosén of IR Skrivbyrå for her highly professional and tireless commitment to the task of preparing the final formatted version of the manuscript; Kimmo Eriksson, Professor of Mathematics at Mälardalen University for his insightful and useful comments on the methods and models presented in Chapters 4 and 5; Timo Summa, Director for Entrepreneurship and SMEs and SME Envoy, European Commission and

Floor Van Houdt, Administrator, D-G Enterprise, European Commission for their useful comment; and Industry Canada and the FSF for supporting us with the management time necessary to complete the final version of the book.

Anders Lundström
Swedish Foundation for
Small Business Research
Örebro, Sweden

Lois Stevenson
Wilford White Fellow
and Fellow of the IC^2
Institute
Ottawa, Canada

Chapter 1

INTRODUCTION

In this book, we provide a systematic framework for formulating entrepreneurship policy. This is based on conclusions from our three-phase examination of entrepreneurship policies in 13 countries. We discuss our definition of entrepreneurship policy, the foundations on which such a policy is based, the framework of entrepreneurship policy measures, the parameters of entrepreneurship policy vis-à-vis small and medium enterprise (SME) or small business policy and our entrepreneurship policy typology. We share instruments and tools we have developed that will be helpful to policymakers in identifying gaps as well as opportunities for future policy actions and we lay out a systematic process for arriving at an integrated entrepreneurship policy platform.

However, we argue that policymaking in the entrepreneurship field is complex and messy. Many areas of government policy affect levels of entrepreneurial activity – regulatory policies, trade policies, labour market policies, regional development policies, social policies, and even gender policies. This means governments must adopt more horizontal structures for developing and implementing an integrated policy approach. The mix of policy options will depend on a number of factors, including the prevailing attitudes of the population towards entrepreneurship, the structure of the labour force, the size and role of government, the prevalence of existing SMEs (i.e., SME density) and the existing level of entrepreneurial activity. We will argue that this "context" matters, which is one reason why it is not always appropriate to replicate the "good practice" policy measures of governments in other countries. We will also discuss the complexities of assessing the existing state of "entrepreneurial capacity" in a country, given the problems of measuring and influencing the motivations and skills of the population towards entrepreneurship as an occupational choice. Finally, we highlight some of the major challenges faced by governments in evaluating the impact of policies and measures geared towards producing higher levels of entrepreneurial activity and discuss the potentially conflicting perspectives of entrepreneurs, policymakers and service providers. This work advances knowledge in the field of entrepreneurship policy development and lays out a path for policymakers to follow.

THE IMPORTANCE OF ENTREPRENEURSHIP POLICY

Interest in entrepreneurship policy has been escalating over the past five years. One of the compelling driving forces behind this interest is the growing body of research on the relationship between entrepreneurship and economic growth (Carree and Thurik, 2003; OECD 2001b; Kirzner, 1982), the essential contribution of new firms to employment growth and economic renewal (Audretsch and Thurik, 2001b; Kirchhoff, 1994; Friis, et al., 2002), and influences on the differing rates of business ownership and entrepreneurial activity across nations (Carree at al., 2002; Reynolds et al., 2004). These bodies of work point to, and reinforce, the critical contribution of new firms to job creation, innovation, productivity and economic growth in an economy.

A number of factors have been identified in the research literature as being associated with the level of entrepreneurial activity in a country or region, acting as either promoters or inhibitors. In our review of this literature, we identified at least 41 multi-faceted and varied influencers, including social and cultural factors; attitudinal factors (e.g., positive attitudes towards entrepreneurship; fear and "stigma" of failure; risk-taking); taxation and ease of business entry and exit factors; population, immigration and GDP growth factors; labour market and regulatory factors; the relative size of the public to the private sector; the density of small firms/business owners in the population; and the prevalence of entrepreneur role-models, just to mention a few. We provide a summary of this list of factors and findings in Annex 1-1 at the end of this chapter.

These studies and their findings provide a great deal of important input to our understanding of the factors influencing entrepreneurial behaviour in a society; however, most studies examine the impact or influence of only a small set of variables on entrepreneurship activity levels. Given the large number of possible influencers, it is difficult to ascertain the precise impact of any one factor on a country's level of entrepreneurial activity. There have been very few attempts to model the complexity of variables. In addition, there is very little understanding of how these factors and influencers,

individually or in combination, work to produce
entrepreneurial activity relative to another country
combination of those factors and influencers. One of t¹
our studies is that in making entrepreneurship policy, ____
matters. We also conclude that it is difficult to find simple correlations
between the level of entrepreneurial activity and, for example, economic
growth. So how are policymakers to cope with sorting through this vast
array of factors believed to influence the emergence of entrepreneurship,
especially if they are trying to determine what to do within the parameters of
their own context?

No one field of research by itself has produced the definitive answer to
such questions as: what can be done to increase the level of entrepreneurial
activity within an economy or what is the precise role of government in that
process? There is no straightforward answer as to which framework
conditions are the most essential for entrepreneurship and boosted growth.
Although there is widespread agreement among the leading experts who are
working on this problem that provisions bearing on business entry and exit
dynamics – venture spirit, administrative burden, advisory services,
financing, taxation, and commercialisation of research results – are central to
any effective and focused entrepreneurship policy, there is limited clarity as
to which combination of policy measures will produce the desired result in
any particular country. The answer appears to lie somewhere in the complex
interplay between dimensions of the individual (the entrepreneur), the
enterprise and the environment.

Lots of policy prescriptions have been produced listing what *should* be
done to produce higher levels of entrepreneurial activity, but limited
knowledge exists about how entrepreneurship policy is constructed – what it
actually looks like, what policies characterise its make-up and how
policymakers make decisions about the mix of these policies. More
knowledge about this will be very important for governments to have in light
of rapidly changing industrial and economic policy paradigms where
entrepreneurship is becoming a recognised force in the attainment of positive
economic outcomes.

The first attempt to examine entrepreneurship policy on an international
scale, based on what governments are actually doing, is the research we
completed in 2001 (Lundström and Stevenson, 2001; Stevenson and
Lundström, 2002). The purpose behind our research was to learn more about
the construction of entrepreneurship policy by examining what national-level
governments in a number of diverse countries were doing – their policy
objectives, their policy measures, the weighting of their focus on different
policy measures and their rationale for doing so. Through this research we
were attempting to explore such questions as: if entrepreneurship policy is a

olicy domain, what does it look like; what does it consist of; what indicators are appropriate to measure the performance of policy implementation; and how does the configuration of entrepreneurship policy reflect the economic, social, political and cultural circumstances idiosyncratic to a country or region? A summary of our methodological approaches to the three phases of the research is presented in the Appendix at the end of this book.

The first phase of the study, which involved 10 countries, was exploratory in nature. Through it, we were attempting to define, establish the parameters of, and articulate a framework for entrepreneurship policy. We found that the entrepreneurship policy situation differed from one country to another, some being more advanced than others. They had different macro-economic starting points, different levels of experience with SME policy, some dating as far back as the 1950s and 60s and others to the mid-to-late 1990s, and sought to solve different economic problems by encouraging higher levels of entrepreneurship. In the second phase, the objective was to apply the framework in a set of countries with similar contexts (Lundström (ed.), 2003). The five Nordic countries were selected. In the third phase, we built on what we had learned about entrepreneurship policy in the first two phases by developing a measure for assessing the extent of a government's entrepreneurship policy comprehensiveness. This index enables a more systematic approach to identifying policy actions in the entrepreneurship area, assessing both what is currently being done and where policy gaps may exist.

EXPLORING ENTREPRENEURSHIP POLICY FRAMEWORKS

Apart from the work of the European Union (EU) and the Organisation for Economic Cooperation and Development (OECD), few researchers have focused on the topic of entrepreneurship policy until very recently. The work being done draws from a number of disciplines, such as economics, sociology, psychology, management, and geography (Acs and Audretsch (eds.), 2003). Audretsch and Thurik (2001a) explain the rise in entrepreneurship policy formulation as a necessary response to fundamental industrial and economic restructuring – a shift from the "managed economy" to the "entrepreneurial economy". Several frameworks for analysing the determinants of entrepreneurship have been proposed (Reynolds et al., 1999; Verheul et al., 2001; Audretsch et al., (eds.), 2002). Prescriptions about what entrepreneurship policy *should* be have been derived either from the development of these theoretical, conceptual frameworks or from findings of research on the experiences and needs of entrepreneurs.

Wennekers and Thurik (1999), Verheul et al. (2001) and Audretsch et al. (eds.) (2002) propose an eclectic theory of entrepreneurship that weaves together into an integrated framework aspects of culture, occupational choice, the resources available to entrepreneurs, and the extent of entrepreneurial opportunities in the economy. This framework is intended to provide insights to policymakers striving to promote entrepreneurship. These researchers suggest a number of possible roles for government policy in influencing the level of entrepreneurship at the country level. They distinguish between the supply side and the demand side of entrepreneurship and highlight the different sets of policy interventions available to governments depending on which view is taken vis-à-vis the determinants of entrepreneurship. Influencing the demand side are factors such as the demographic composition of the population, the resources and abilities of individuals and their attitudes towards entrepreneurship. The supply side is influenced by opportunities for entrepreneurship created by new technologies, the differentiation of consumer demand and the industrial structure of the economy. Carree et al. (2002) further introduce the concept of actual versus equilibrium rates of entrepreneurship, suggesting the possibility of a predictable relationship between the level of business ownership in a country and its level of economic development (GDP/capita). Verheul et al. (2002) suggest that the process by which the actual rate of entrepreneurship is established involves both micro and macro components. On the demand side, entrepreneurial opportunities are created by market demand for goods and services, whereas the supply side generates (potential) entrepreneurs that can seize the opportunities, provided they have the resources, abilities and preferences to do so.[1] The actual rate of entrepreneurship is determined by occupational choice decisions and may deviate from the equilibrium rate due to demand-side forces, such as changes in market structure and technological developments. The discrepancy between the actual rate and the equilibrium rate is expressed through a surplus or lack of entrepreneurial opportunities, which will then lead to either the entry or exit of entrepreneurs. Actual and equilibrium rates can be mediated through market forces, but governments may also choose to intervene through selected policy measures.

Verheul et al. (2001) outline five types of policy interventions that could have an impact on entrepreneurial activity levels. Type 1 interventions impact on the demand side of entrepreneurship (affecting the type, number and accessibility of entrepreneurial opportunities); Type 2 interventions impact on the supply of potential entrepreneurs (immigration policy, regional development policy); Type 3 interventions affect the availability of resources and knowledge for potential entrepreneurs (advice and counseling, direct financial support, venture capital and entrepreneurship education); Type 4 interventions shape entrepreneurial values in society (through the education system and the media); and Type 5 interventions alter the risk-reward profile of entrepreneurship by directing interventions at the decision-making process of individuals and their occupational choices (e.g., taxation, social security arrangements, labour market legislation, bankruptcy policy).

Wennekers and Thurik (1999) conclude that there is room for two types of policy interventions – one aimed at promoting the creation of technology-based firms in selected industries and the other aimed at promoting newly-created firms, regardless of sector, by providing better access to the financial, organisational and technological resources needed to grow. They suggest a role for government in stimulating cultural or social capital and creating the appropriate institutional framework at the country level to address the supply side of entrepreneurship, i.e., focusing on the number of people who have the motivation, the financial means and the skills to launch a new business.

The GEM research team employs a combination of research approaches in their formulation of the key framework conditions for entrepreneurship (Reynolds et al., 1999). To arrive at their prescriptions for entrepreneurship policy, they examine a number of economic measures, survey a random selection of nascent and new entrepreneurs, and interview a small number of experts in participating countries. Their model brings together the Conventional Model of Economic Growth and the Model of Entrepreneurial Processes Affecting National Entrepreneurship Growth into a detailed framework of the factors and conditions giving rise to entrepreneurship.[2] In the Conventional Model, major established firms are assumed to be the primary focus of economic growth and smaller firms are given a lower priority. The Entrepreneurial Process Model focuses on the entrepreneurial sector itself, the conditions that shape it and its direct economic consequences. Reynolds et al. (1999) stress it is important to properly understand both views of the economic growth process. In their refined economic growth model, they introduce Entrepreneurial Framework Conditions (elements of environment, opportunities, motivation and capacity) to the Conventional Model and replace the primary focus on major established firms with a more contemporary emphasis on Business Churning (births, deaths, expansions, contractions of firms) as the driver of growth. The 1999 GEM report (Reynolds et al., 1999) proposed that a policy focus on entrepreneurship was very important for three major reasons:

- there is a strong positive relationship between new firm start-up rates and measures of economic prosperity, particularly changes in GDP;

- new ventures are contributing substantially to both gross and net employment growth, while large firms are shedding jobs;
- the ability of a country to replenish the stock of businesses and jobs and to accommodate the volatility and turbulence in the small business sector will enable it to be best positioned to compete effectively in the global economy (i.e., as an economy becomes more dynamic, new firm creation will be vital).

With the inclusion of several new countries from lesser-developed parts of the world in 2001, GEM researchers are able to differentiate between "opportunity" and "necessity" entrepreneurship. The 2001 Executive Report (Reynolds et al., 2001) stresses the importance of the following major policy implications based on their research findings:

- enhance general and entrepreneurship-specific education;
- lessen the regulatory burden on new and small firms;
- strike a balance between the need to protect the unemployed with the need to encourage higher levels of individual self-sufficiency;
- facilitate greater levels of female participation in business ownership;
- compensate for gaps in the population age structure in cases where there is a projected decline in the 25-44 year old age cohort, the group with the highest propensity for becoming entrepreneurs; and
- encourage tolerance of diversity in personal income and wealth.

Kantis (2002) derives his recommendations for entrepreneurship policy actions in four South Asia and five Latin American countries from empirical studies of the behaviours, activities and barriers faced by entrepreneurs, particularly at the start-up stage, in each of these nine countries. Besides noting several differences in the environment for entrepreneurs in each region, he draws a number of policy implications from his analysis of the entrepreneurial process experience of new entrepreneurs. He specifically recommends policies aimed to:

- broaden the base of future dynamic entrepreneurs by boosting entrepreneurial capacity (e.g., disseminate information about role models through mass media; stimulate and motivate young people to start new businesses through the education system);
- promote entrepreneurial networks and create settings and incentives for building entrepreneurial teams;
- shorten the inception period for new enterprises by promoting innovative systems, strengthening connections among existing entrepreneurs and potential ones, and facilitating the range of preparatory activities needed to launch a business (e.g., information, networks, access to resources and assistance);
- reduce barriers to the creation and development of new companies by reducing bureaucratic costs and red tape, as well as lack of finances

and high transaction costs in highly imperfect markets (financial, labour, technical and professional services markets) and by building a solid infrastructure of venture finance; reducing red-tape and compliance costs associated with start-ups; helping entrepreneurs resolve their initial start-up problems; and modifying existing incentives for SMEs to meet the specific needs of new businesses (tax credits, tax rebates);

- strengthen the institutional context to promote entrepreneurship; and
- involve participation of a wide range of institutions, the make-up of which varies depending on the specific conditions of each country. Universities, as well as private foundations, chambers of commerce, and civic organisations have a key role to play.

According to Kantis, the role of government, at various levels, is to act as a catalyst. They are the agents who must plan the strategy, build the vision, mobilise key players, and commit resources to promote the emergence and development of new entrepreneurs and dynamic enterprises.

Each of these somewhat different approaches to deriving policy recommendations contributes to the advancement of our knowledge. But neither Kantis (2002), GEM researchers, nor the Verheul et al. (2001) team examined what governments were actually doing to stimulate entrepreneurship or the extent to which they were doing it. Although Audretsch et al. (eds.) (2002) did apply the "eclectic theory" framework to their description of entrepreneurship policy initiatives in five countries, the reader is left to discern precisely how the framework played out in their different country contexts.

Recently, there have also been attempts to benchmark entrepreneurship policy. Paramount in this area are the Enterprise Scoreboard project (European Commission, 2003a, 2003b) and the Danish Entrepreneurship Index Initiative (Danish National Agency for Enterprise and Housing et al., 2004). The Enterprise Scoreboard tracks countries' performance against a range of quantitative indicators deemed to influence higher levels of entrepreneurial activity (e.g., the number of patents per inhabitant, the level of early-stage venture capital as a percentage of GDP, and the number of tertiary graduates per 1,000 population), or to reflect higher entrepreneurial activity levels (e.g., the gross birth rate of enterprises and the female self-employment rate). The Scoreboard rates the enterprise performance of participating EU countries based on their rankings against each of these indicators and identifies where they are both weak and strong. Governments in these countries can draw implications from the findings regarding changes to policy emphasis to improve their rankings. Development of the Danish Entrepreneurship Index, which is based on a conceptual model consisting of a comprehensive set of variables relating to policy, is still in very experimental stages. Data comparing the seven participating countries in phase one of the project were collected from country experts using online surveys supplemented with interviews. Although the framework purports to measure entrepreneurship policy, the study itself does not actually examine what governments in the countries are doing in the entrepreneurship policy area.

THE RISING INTEREST IN ENTREPRENEURSHIP

Research findings continue to confirm that entrepreneurship is important to economies in several ways. One of the earliest compelling arguments for the importance of small business to the economy was its role in job creation, first uncovered by David Birch (1979). Birch's research revealed that most of the jobs in the United States were not only being generated by small firms, but by new and rapidly-growing young firms. Research in other countries confirmed the job creating contribution of new and small firms.

Governments in developed countries are paying more recent attention to entrepreneurship policies because of the need for renewal of their economic performance. As part of the restructuring of the "old economy", many large companies are still moving their production units (and jobs) to locations around the world with lower wage rates. This trend will likely continue over the coming years as pressure continues to bear on the reshaping of industrial structures. Further declines in the manufacturing sectors of developed economies will be accompanied by growth in the knowledge-based and services sectors where many low-barrier-to-entry opportunities exist for small firms and new start-ups to supply products and services. One of the effects of this restructuring will be a demand for new indigenous firms and growing small businesses to replace lost jobs and economic momentum.

Entrepreneurship is also seen as part of the solution to reducing unemployment levels and absorbing new labour force entrants. Since research confirms the important role of new and young firms in employment creation, future employment growth is likely to come from growth in entrepreneurial activity. Thus, governments are expressing more interest in how to stimulate start-ups and encourage more entrepreneurship.

Stimulating entrepreneurial activity requires a different set of policy imperatives than supporting the maintenance and growth of existing small and medium-sized enterprises. Governments and societies are eager to identify gaps in their existing policy frameworks or areas that are deficient in meeting the conditions for an environment conducive to entrepreneurship and seeking knowledge about, and a better understanding of, how to do this.

Recent Developments in the Field of Research Knowledge

A series of significant breakthroughs and recent developments has accelerated the knowledge base on entrepreneurship, making policymaking in the area more possible. The first among these is a dramatic improvement in the quantity and quality of statistical data on the SME sector. The ability of government statistical offices, specifically in developed countries, to capture data on new firm entries and to track the employment growth of new and existing small firms over time has significantly improved our understanding of the impact of new and small firms on the economy. We are able to see for the first time that underlying the small incremental net growth in the stock of firms and their net employment on an annual basis is a high level of turbulence. "Enterprise demography"[3] allows policymakers to see that business turnover and the entry and exit of firms merits their attention. One of the policy implications one can draw from an analysis of this enterprise demography data is that new firms are required to replace exiting firms and to create jobs to replace those lost due to exiting and downsizing firms. Hult (2003) reports that the mean annual rate of business entry and exit in nine European countries over the 1997-2000 time period was 8.5 percent and 7.9 percent respectively.[4] Although the average size of a newly-born enterprise was less than two employees, collectively, these new firms were responsible for creating almost 5.5 million jobs. Enterprise demography data has also uncovered wide variations in business dynamics both across countries (Hult, 2003) and within regions of single countries (Acs and Armington, 2003). The OECD (2002a)[5] points out that explaining this variation will contribute to an understanding of the policy factors that drive these differences, a task which remains to be done.

Governments also have greater capacity to measure self-employment rates in the population and to track the entries and exits into and out of self-employment on an annual basis (Picot et al., 1999; Branchflower, 2000; Cowling, 2003). Combining business registration and self-employment databases allows policymakers and researchers to examine the relationship between firms and individuals and to profile both firms and their owners.

The second major development in the area of entrepreneurship research and statistical analysis is the development of harmonised methodologies to measure the level of entrepreneurial activity across countries and make credible international comparisons. The Entrepreneurial Activity (TEA) Index, developed as part of the Global Entrepreneurship Monitor (GEM) project, provides a standardised measurement of nascent entrepreneur rates, rates of new business entrants and young firm prevalence rates across countries. Data generated from 40 countries (Reynolds et al., 2004) is now being used by the research community to make predictions about the level of entrepreneurial activity in a country and its level of economic growth, to relate these entrepreneurial activity levels to other dimensions of the economy (e.g., level of income disparity, investments in R&D and venture capital), and to explain variances among countries (e.g., Cowling and Bygrave, 2003). Other research is also being done to harmonise cross-country data related to business ownership rates and to link these to GDP levels (van Stel, 2003; Carree et al., 2002).

The third significant development is the ability to study the behaviour of nascent entrepreneurs,[6] defined by Reynolds and White (1997) as a person who, alone or with others, is currently in the process of trying to start a business. This research not only enables, for the first time, an estimation of the extent of nascent entrepreneurial activity in a country/region, but an investigation of the characteristics of the adult population attempting to start a new business, the kinds of activities they undertake and the properties and characteristics of the start-up efforts that become infant firms, including gestation periods and reasons for not proceeding. The results of this research, which is being replicated in several countries, is intended to aid government policymakers in measuring the impact of existing SME and entrepreneurship policies and measures and in designing better informed and more effective instruments to foster a higher level of entrepreneurial activity.

The fourth significant development is the generation of country/regional studies of good practice in entrepreneurship-oriented policies and programmes (National Governors Association, 2004; European Commission, 2004a, 2004c, 2004e, 2003e, 2002c, 2001; Stevenson and Lundström, 2002; Audretsch et al., 2002; Kantis, 2002). Although this work is in its infancy stages, the good practice documents of the EU and the OECD, in particular, form the basis for developing benchmarks for the implementation of entrepreneurship policies and for tracking a country's performance in achieving targets. The OECD Bologna Charter on SMEs and the European Charter for Small Enterprises (European Commission, 2002a) lay out the strategic priority areas for member countries and States. Adoption of these charters by OECD member countries and by EU member States and acceding and candidate countries enables a process for future benchmarking in key areas of entrepreneurship policy. Member countries and States are required to report progress against objectives on an annual basis. A series of good practice and BEST reports have already been published on top-level business support (European Commission, 2001), business angels (European Commission, 2003e), the administration of start-ups (European Commission, 2002c) and the promotion of female entrepreneurship (European Commission, 2002b). Policy dialogues are regularly held. These processes of policy dialogue, annual reporting, and documentation of good practices is moving countries towards more standardised approaches that are intended to be flexibly applied to individual country circumstances. The recent adoption of the European Agenda for Entrepreneurship can be expected to create further pull on entrepreneurship policy development from among EU member States (European Commission, 2004d).

Work on an entrepreneurship agenda in Latin and South American countries is at an earlier stage of development but the Inter-American Development Bank (IDB) has begun a process to examine the state of entrepreneurship in these countries, starting with research to compare the situation in Latin and South American countries with that in Asian and European countries (Kantis, 2002; Banco Interamericano, 2004). The Asia-Pacific Economic Cooperation (APEC) has produced a series of reports on policies oriented to entrepreneurship development in Asia-Pacific countries and APEC Ministers have released a joint statement regarding the centrality of a vibrant "entrepreneurial society" to the growth of APEC economies (APEC, 2003a).

The United Nations, which has been supporting micro and small enterprise development activity in developing parts of the world for several decades, is also focusing more acutely on the entrepreneurship agenda. In this developing country context, entrepreneurship is seen as a major vehicle for eradicating poverty and helping countries meet the Millennium Development Goals set by the United Nations. The United Nations Development Programme report on entrepreneurship (UNDP, 2004) states that the foundations for entrepreneurship are not yet in place in the developing parts of the world and that the three pillars of entrepreneurship are too often missing – a level playing field; access to financing; and access to skills and knowledge. Of course, the challenge is quite different for developing countries. They often have very high levels of entrepreneurial activity, but mostly "necessity-driven" (see Reynolds et al., 2004). Because there are limited employment options and very weak social security systems, the majority of people must become self-employed in order to generate an economic livelihood. Complex, bureaucratic and costly business registration processes mean that most enterprises in the economy remain in the informal sector, unable to access business support and financial resources, and constrained in their growth.

The final critical development has been the phenomenal increase in the number of opportunities to exchange knowledge about the entrepreneurial process and in the dissemination of research findings. In the early 1980s, there were only three academic journals focused on small business and entrepreneurship research: the *Journal of Small Business Management* (JSBM), the *American Journal of Small Business* (AJSB), and the *European Small Business Journal* (ESBJ). *Frontiers of Entrepreneurship Research* (Babson College) and the proceedings of conferences such as the

International Council for Small Business (ICSB), the International Small Business Congress (ISBC) and the Small Business Institute Directors' Association (SBIDA) were the other major sources of research knowledge at the time. By 2003, there were more than 44 academic journals (Katz, 2003), including those focused on business venturing, entrepreneurship theory and practice, entrepreneurship and regional development, entrepreneurship education, enterprising culture, and entrepreneurial behaviour. Starting in 1992, there has been a growing interest in small business and entrepreneurship from the mainstream economics community, facilitated largely by the *Journal of Small Business Economics*, which has created a forum for economists to publish articles and research papers, further legitimating the role of entrepreneurship within economic theory. There are now also a large number of national and international conferences providing venues for the sharing of research findings, policy and practice.

THE STATE OF THE RESEARCH ON ENTREPRENEURSHIP

Informed policy is based on research, on what is known about the critical factors affecting the policy target and where opportunities exist to influence certain elements to produce a desired outcome. In the field of entrepreneurship policy, this is quite complex. Although mention of entrepreneurship has existed in the literature for several decades, the field of entrepreneurship is a relatively recent area of research and, thus, so is its policy development. Entrepreneurs exist in every society and entrepreneurship is part of the fabric of every economy. It exists in environments that support it or not and independent of whether government policies specifically focus on it. As Lowrey (2003) points out, countries with low levels of individual entrepreneurship often achieve long periods of economic growth, using the examples of Russia, Korea and others. In fact, the emergence of entrepreneurship is often a by-product of government policies and, for years, this was even the case in the United States (National Commission on Entrepreneurship, 2002). However, entrepreneurship appears to flourish in environments where it is supported.

Research in three areas comes together to influence policy thinking in the area of entrepreneurship and small business development: (A) research on the entrepreneur; (B) research on the enterprise: and (C) research on the environment for entrepreneurship (see Figure 1-1).

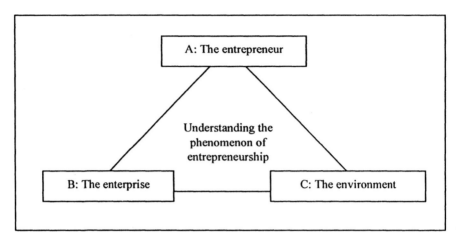

Figure 1-1. Streams of entrepreneurship research

We next briefly outline the evolution of the three key streams of entrepreneurship research.

A: Research on the Entrepreneur

With respect to the entrepreneur, initially, the prevailing research approach was to look for the traits that seemed to differentiate entrepreneurs from non-entrepreneurs in a society. If it is desirable to have more entrepreneurs in the economy, what can be done to identify people with the set of traits exhibited by entrepreneurs, or to instil the set of essential traits in non-entrepreneurs? Basically, this research stream attempted to address the "are entrepreneurs born or made" question. Is there a single spring that can be triggered in individuals to increase their propensity to become entrepreneurs? This stream of research was heavily stimulated by the work of McClelland (1961) who made a compelling case that if an individual's achievement motivation could be increased, then a country could affect an increase in the level of economic development. Over the next couple of decades, researchers studied populations of entrepreneurs looking for the salient traits and characteristics, such as risk-taking propensity (Brockhaus, 1979) and internal locus of control (Kets de Vries, 1977).

Failing to produce definitive results, another group of researchers started to ask another question. If it isn't a set of personal innate traits, then what factors predict whether someone becomes an entrepreneur? Kets de Vries (1977) hypothesised that deprivation in a person's background was a major influencing factor (various forms of emotional, economic, and social impoverishment). Shapero (1984) and Shapero and Sokol (1982) proposed that the decision to become an entrepreneur is heavily influenced by situational factors related to family background, work experience (dissatisfaction) and life conditions, and that it is the complex interaction of these familial, sociological, economic, and situational forces, and an individual's reaction to them, that determines whether one becomes an entrepreneur. They concluded that it is how a person interprets the desirability and feasibility of the entrepreneurial event given their expectations, objectives and personal life circumstances that determines her/his predisposition towards entrepreneurship. Some people will react to a set of situational forces by starting a business, while others might not. Still we didn't know why this was the case.

Chell (1985) provides a good summary of this body of earlier entrepreneurship research.

Gartner (1988) asserted that researchers were again asking the wrong question and proposed that it would be more fruitful to examine the behaviours of entrepreneurs, what is it that entrepreneurs do. He believed that it is their behaviours that matter, not the characteristics of entrepreneurs themselves. The creation of an organisation is the principal outcome of entrepreneurial behaviour; it is the exercise of certain behaviours that produces organisations. A detailed discussion of this stream of research is presented in Gartner and Carter (2003).

Other researchers started to produce findings on the demographic make-up of entrepreneurs, noting differences based on sex, age, ethnic background and educational level. This opened up research on the challenges and barriers of women entrepreneurs (Hisrich and O'Brien, 1982; Stevenson, 1986; Holmquist and Sundin, 1988), ethnic minorities (Waldinger et al., 1990; Rettab, 2001) and, later, of young entrepreneurs (Branchflower and Meyer, 1994; Branchflower, 1998). Researchers also noted different kinds of entrepreneurs based on their objectives and motivations for going into business. This led to categorisations of lifestyle entrepreneurs, necessity entrepreneurs (Reynolds et al., 2001) and high-growth entrepreneurs, or "gazelles" (Birch, 1987).

The work of Reynolds and White (1997) took the research into another new direction. If we wanted to know more about how people made the decision to start a business, what influences them and the steps they take, they believed we should study people who are currently in the process, what they referred to as "nascent entrepreneurs". This work led to the launch of the Panel Study of Entrepreneurial Dynamics (PSED), a systematic longitudinal survey of individuals in the process of starting a business. Replication of the nascent entrepreneurs study is now going on in a number of countries.

In the meantime, economists were more interested in the set of functions and roles that entrepreneurs performed in an economy. Neoclassical economic growth theory rejected the notion that entrepreneurial behaviour is the foundation of economic behaviour, proposing instead that economic growth is achieved through capital accumulation and exogenous technological progress, so the entrepreneur's essential economic motive was overlooked (Carree and Thurik, 2003; Lowrey, 2003). The emergence of endogenous growth models in the early 1990s has repositioned the role of entrepreneurial activity, and thus, of the entrepreneur, as a major variable in the economic growth of a region or nation (Carree and Thurik, 2003).

B: Research on the Enterprise

Another group of researchers focused on the firm as the focus of study. One stream of this body of research studied the nature and characteristics of small firms. What role do small firms play in the economy? What opportunities exist for the emergence of small firms in a country, given its industrial structure, concentration of industries, and market opportunities? What needs do small firms have that make them different from large firms and what impact does that knowledge have on formulations of policy to address any unique barriers and challenges? Welsh and White (1981) introduced the notion of "resource poverty". Churchill and Lewis (1983) concluded that small firms and their owners have different needs at different stages of growth. Others noted the negative impact of information asymmetries and pointed out various market failures. Another stream of the research explored small business management issues. What key factors in the management of small enterprises are essential to their survival and growth? How do owners of firms acquire the skills in financial management, sales and marketing, and production management they need to improve the performance of their enterprises?

A third, and more recent area of study, is of the role played by the small firm in economic development and growth, e.g., employment creation, innovation, and productivity improvements (Birch, 1979; Acs and Audretsch, 1990; OECD, 2001b, 2001c). Better statistical means with which to study the dynamic of the small firm sector and to track business entry, survival, growth, and exit rates over time has enhanced our knowledge about the importance of small firms to economic growth, as well as the specific importance of new firms and growth firms to employment growth and renewal.[7] Kirchhoff (1994), Storey (1994), and Acs et al. (1999), among others, have made significant contributions to our understanding of the dynamic of business start-up and exit rates. Each year, in every country, there is evidence of a great deal of turbulence in the SME sector – new firms are being formed and existing firms are expanding, contracting and disappearing. This dynamic underlies only small net changes reported in the total stock of firms and jobs on an annual basis. In the past, this volatility was seen as a negative feature; this process of creative destruction is now seen as a positive force in long-term job creation and economic growth. Take Canada as an example. Of the total stock of employer firms in Canada at the end of 1984, 77 percent no longer existed in 1999 (Parsley and Dreessen, 2004). With them, these exiting firms took almost 38 percent of the private sector jobs (measured on the 1984 base). Firms that existed in 1985, but that had declined in size by 1999, resulted in the loss of another 18 percent of the 1984 job count. Large firms with over 500 employees accounted for 71 percent of the total employment loss. Over the 1985-1999 period, these firms and jobs were more than replaced by new firm entries and growing SMEs (in a diverse range of sectors[8]), clearly demonstrating that small businesses were the principal engine of growth. The net effect of the churning resulted in the creation of 1.3 million jobs. Parsley and Dreessen conclude that: (a) business start-ups and new firms are an enormously important source of employment and wealth creation; (b) it is important to understand the barriers and special needs faced by new firms if government action is to have a decisive impact; and (c) if conditions that promote the growth of firms could be identified, government interventions could be targeted more effectively.

New firms are also critical to innovation activity and productivity improvements. Baldwin (1999) found that new entrants exhibit a high level of innovation behaviour and argues that new firms contribute to innovation by constantly offering consumers new products and higher levels of service. He suggests that the experimentation associated with entry and exit is the key to a dynamic market-based economy. Acs and Armington (2002) state that in most cases new entrants represent agents of change in the market. Audretsch and Thurik (2001b) argue that entrepreneurs, not firms, should be the starting point for theories of innovation. Recent research also points to the importance of new entrants to a nation's overall labour and multi-factor productivity growth and the contribution of firm entry and exit activity to aggregate productivity growth (Scarpetta et al., 2002; Bosma and Nieuwenhuijsen, 2000). Scarpetta et al. (2002) ascribe approximately 25 percent of productivity growth in OECD countries to the turnover of companies – the establishment of new companies and the closure of the inoperative. Bartelsman et al. (2003) conclude that this process of creative destruction warrants the attention of policymakers because firm turnover depends on regulations and institutions affecting start-up costs and the financing of new ventures, as well as on market characteristics (e.g., concentration, diversification) and that policies fostering market competition, entrepreneurship and appropriate bankruptcy rules play a role within this context of dynamism.[9]

Hall (2002a) indicates that across APEC countries, there is a new firm entry rate of about eight percent a year and an exit rate of seven percent, and argues that, at the general policy level, the business environment should encourage the start-up, growth and exit of firms. Purrington and Bettcher (2001) point out that the formation of new industries and the development of most new technologies are highly dependent on the creation of new firms – this has been true for hardware and software development, the Internet, biotechnology, fast food restaurants, discount retailing, package delivery services and so on. Building on this, Reynolds et al. (2002) state that lessons from entrepreneurial history make it clear that the businesses most likely to drive the economy in the next 25 years will come from the efforts of nascent entrepreneurs starting today.

This body of research brings us back to the perennial question of how to ensure a steady supply of new entrepreneurs to create this future growth. Where will they come from? How will they acquire the skills and knowledge they need? What environment will be most conducive to their emergence?

C: Research on the Environment (for entrepreneurship)

At the same time earlier researchers were looking at the entrepreneur and the small firm as the units of analysis, another group was theorising about the role of the environment on the emergence of entrepreneurship (Wilken, 1979; Hjalager, 1989; and myriad of others). Why do certain environments produce more entrepreneurs and what are the elements of those environments that make the difference? Wilken (1979) identified the legitimacy of entrepreneurship in a society as a major predictor of its emergence – the more legitimate it was seen, the higher its levels. Social mobility was a factor, especially for marginalised groups within a society. If marginal groups did not have access to mainstream mobility channels, then entrepreneurship was seen as the only mechanism for them to pursue economic livelihoods. The role of culture was also explored, some cultures found to be more supportive of entrepreneurship than others. Using Hofstede's indices of power distance and uncertainty avoidance,[10] Wildeman et al. (1999) found a relationship between culture dimensions and levels of self-employment in 23 OECD countries. De (2001) discusses the role of social acceptance of entrepreneurs and the importance of this "social capital" in a person's decision to start a business. Casson (2003) argues that the demand for entrepreneurship is partly created by entrepreneurs themselves, those who perceive opportunities that they are personally equipped to exploit, but that a culture which emphasises norms supportive of entrepreneurship will stimulate this perceptual process. Other studies revealed the importance of a range of other environmental factors – the political environment; the economic and labour market structure of an economy; the regulatory environment; and the interplay of a number of other policy domains that could affect the emergence of entrepreneurship, for example, regulations affecting the entry and exit of firms; social security regulations and policies; fiscal and monetary policies; competition policies; and structure of the banking and financial systems; to name a few.

Finally, there is a growing body of literature on the links between entrepreneurship levels and economic growth and development. Wennekers and Thurik (1999) examined the relationship between business ownership rates and GDP per capita across a number of OECD countries and Reynolds et al. (1999, 2004) examined the relationship between entrepreneurial activity levels and economic growth rates. The task of relating a country's business birth rate to its economic growth rate is a complex one, but Reynolds et al. (2004) observe that countries with high levels of entrepreneurial activity have above average levels of economic growth and that no country with high entrepreneurial activity levels among the 40 in the 2003 study has low economic growth. However, there are a number of intervening variables and linkages between economic conditions and entrepreneurial propensity on the one hand, and between entrepreneurship and economic growth on the other hand, so simple causal relationships cannot be determined.

One factor may be the level of a country's economic development. In their study of the long-term relationship between a country's business ownership rate and its level of economic development, measured in GDP per capita, Carree et al. (2002) have found a U-shaped curve relationship, with declining business ownership rates as GDP per capita increases until this reaches about US$18,000, at which point, business ownership rates start to increase with increases in GDP per capita. They suggest that countries falling above or below the U-shaped curve may have either too few or too many business owners. Countries with too many business owners, usually developing economies, may not be benefiting sufficiently from economies of scale and scope, with too many marginal enterprises. Countries falling below the curve may not have enough entrepreneurial activity, meaning that opportunities for innovation and competitive undertakings may be underdeveloped. In both cases, there is a penalty – either too few or too many business owners will lead to lower economic growth rates. Hall (2002b) estimates that 50-70 million new SMEs need to be created in APEC countries over the next two decades if their developing countries are to contribute fully to overall growth of the APEC region and to achieve international competitiveness.

The first GEM report (Reynolds et al., 1999) concluded that high levels of entrepreneurial activity in a country are positively associated with: (i) the degree to which members of its population perceive "opportunity" and have the capacity to pursue it, both in the areas of motivation and capacity (skill and education); (ii) infrastructure suitability (capital, professional services, R&D transfer and flexible labour markets); (iii) population growth; (iv) higher education levels; and (v) a positive cultural attitude towards entrepreneurship. Other factors which influence the level of entrepreneurial activity (positively or negatively) were identified as: "social safety nets"; attitudes towards the importance of large firms; immigration policies (i.e., impacts on population growth; immigrants tend to be disproportionately self-employed); general perception of risk; and a society's overall support for entrepreneurship.

Research also points to high levels of regional variation in entrepreneurial activity rates within countries. Using 1991 data for US Labour Market Areas (LMAs), Acs and Armington (2002) found that business ownership rates (as a percentage of labour force population) varied from a low of 9.9 percent to a high of 44.8 percent across LMAs around the national average rate of 20.5 percent. Similar regional variations are found in the UK, Canada, and other countries. The same type of regional variation is found in business birth rates. Acs and Armington (2002, 2003) found that variations in regional economic growth rates are closely associated with the regional variation in new firm start-up rates. In other words, the level of entrepreneurial activity matters to growth.

Influences on Entrepreneurial Activity Levels - Summary of the Research Findings

The OECD projects that, in the future, governments will orient their policies and programmes more towards fostering entrepreneurship; however, their assessment in 2000 was that entrepreneurship remained a mysterious process.[11] Measuring the level of entrepreneurship is still difficult due to the imprecise ability in many countries to measure start-up and exit rates and knowledge is still being created about the factors giving rise to entrepreneurship in an economy.

In Figure 1-2, we illustrate our categorisation of the many interacting dimensions appearing to have an influence on entrepreneurial activity levels. They fall into five groupings: (A) demographic, macro-economic and structural dimensions; (B) cultural dimensions; (C) human dimensions; (D) SME density and entrepreneurial dynamic dimensions; and (E) policy dimensions. The summarised detail of research findings in each of the groupings appears in Annex 1-1. Amid all of this complexity of interacting dimensions, at least three things appear to be clear:

- Low barriers to the entry and exit of businesses are necessary conditions for the creation of economic dynamism and renewal. This entrepreneurial vitality drives turbulence within the SME sector (e.g., the dynamic caused by firm birth, expansion, contraction, and exit) and fuels growth (Wennekers and Thurik, 2001; Reynolds et al., 1999). If new firm entry is so important to the economy, this suggests that public policies should be more oriented towards removing barriers to business entry (and exit) and stimulating the supply of future entrepreneurs.
- A number of economic, social, cultural and political factors influence entrepreneurship, although we do not know precisely how. We also know there is a great deal of regional variation in the entrepreneurial attitudes and skills of the population in most countries, and barriers discouraging entrepreneurship are found within the education and training system, the regulatory environment and institutional arrangements.
- The country's context matters.

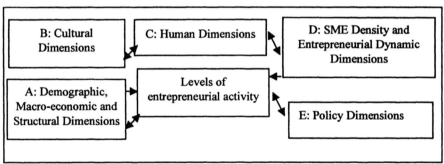

Figure 1-2. Dimensions influencing entrepreneurship activity levels

INTRODUCTION TO THE COUNTRIES IN OUR STUDY

The analysis on which the rest of this book is based comes from our examination of the entrepreneurship policy practices of national-level governments in 13 countries: Australia (AU), Canada (CA), Denmark (DK), Finland (FI), Iceland (IS), Ireland (IE), the Netherlands (NL), Norway (NO), Spain (ES), Sweden (SE), Taiwan (TW), the United Kingdom (UK) and the United States (US). The methods we used in this three-phase exploration of entrepreneurship policy included a combination of interviews with country officials, an analysis of their policy documents and programme information, and a review of country economic indicators.

We will unfold the story of entrepreneurship policy development in these countries in the next chapters of this book but before doing that, we briefly discuss general influences on their economic policy development and then present some data on their levels of entrepreneurship.

Many contextual factors will influence a government's approach to its overall economic policy and its views on the importance of entrepreneurship development as part of that policy. Firstly, it will depend on the assumptions made about what drives economic growth processes. The dominant approach to development in the latter part of the 20th century was based on the assumption that a small number of large, established firms were the major source of economic growth and that this would produce a "trickle-down" effect on the economy, creating economic opportunity for small and medium-sized firms. Therefore, governments focused on efforts to ensure that "national firm champions" were as efficient and productive as possible (Reynolds et al., 1999). These efforts took the form of special legislation, tax incentives and protective regulations to reduce costs or competition for established companies. This model overlooked the role of new firms as a major source of innovation and job creation and ignored the role of the entrepreneur in the economic development process. Historically, entrepreneurship was rarely a stated economic policy objective – at best, it was a by-product of the economic policy development process. In fact, the Reynolds research team suggested that proposals to improve the global competitiveness of large, established firms (e.g., subsidising large firms, reducing internal market openness, and investing in refinements to established production technologies) actually discouraged the emergence of new firms and, therefore, innovation, economic renewal and overall country competitiveness. Audretsch and Thurik (2001) concur. Governments in our case countries may still focus some policy attention on "national firm champions" but they have all shifted more of the policy emphasis towards development of new and small firms.

A government's approach will also depend on its views about the role of government in the economy. Should the State be actively involved in the market place? Should it own and control enterprises? Should government privatise state-owned enterprises? Should it assume a laissez-faire approach and let market forces prevail? What should be maintained in terms of a balance between endogenous and exogenous growth, social and economic goals, foreign and domestic firms, large and small firms, and growth-oriented or new firms? Should special sectors, entrepreneurial groups or regions of the country be targeted with special efforts? The bottom line is that the whole area is not very precise and different governments make an array of policy choices, depending on the size of the country, its political orientation, and its economic and social priorities. The range of this diversity is displayed in the countries we have studied.

A government's approach could also be affected by its level of economic development. The evolution of industrial policy in our case studies suggests that at earlier stages of economic development, the focus was on building up the manufacturing sector. This started with import-substitution policies, moved to export development and possibly, direct foreign investment strategies, and then to a focus on technology development and R&D investment. At some point along the journey policymakers recognised the need to strengthen their indigenous small business base, particularly at the local, regional level. This often led to regional development policies and SME support measures to stimulate employment and growth. And finally, they came to the point of acknowledging the importance of entrepreneurs in bridging the gap between technology and R&D efforts and the commercialisation of innovation. That seems to be where most of the countries in this study are at the present time.

A number of different economic growth strategies have been employed by our case countries. Ireland's recent phenomenal growth has been driven by its success in attracting inward direct foreign investment from American and European multinationals and by its strong export performance. Finland has a large public sector with state-owned enterprises and a few large successful private sector firms. NOKIA along with its immediate suppliers has been responsible for over a third of growth in Finland's GDP.[12] While the development of a strong small business sector has been a central element of Taiwan's economic growth, export growth is also an important factor. The point is that differences in economic growth cannot be simply explained by a country's level of entrepreneurial activity because of the confounding effects of other economic policies and structures.

The increasing focus on policies to stimulate higher levels of entrepreneurship in the 13 countries is currently driven by a number of objectives – employment creation, social cohesion, economic renewal, enhancement of sector productivity and competitiveness, innovation, and wealth creation. A government's reason for pursuing entrepreneurship development objectives will vary according to its economic and social circumstances, as well as existing levels of business ownership and entrepreneurial vitality. Data from the 2002 and 2003 GEM reports, specifically the TEA Index and nascent entrepreneur prevalence rates, and standardised business ownership rates from the EIM COMPENDIA database, show much cross-country variation among the countries we have studied (see Figures 1-3, 1-4 and 1-5).

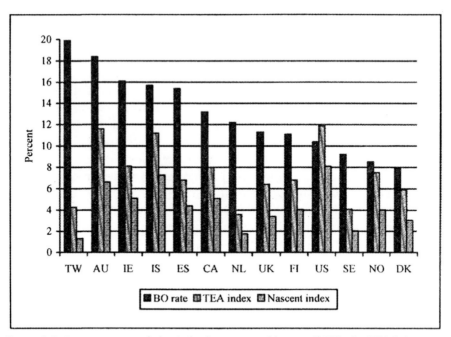

Figure 1-3. Cross-country variation in business ownership rates (2002), the TEA index
           (2003) and the nascent entrepreneur prevalence rate (2003)

Sources: Data for the TEA and nascent indices come from GEM 2003 statistics (based on
adult population); for the business ownership rate from the BLISS COMPENDIA data (EIM)
(based on labour force). The exception is data for Taiwan which is based on 2002 GEM
statistics and business ownership rates calculated from data in the *White Paper on Small and
Medium Enterprises in Taiwan 2003* (SMEA, 2003).

As we will demonstrate later, in countries with lower rates of business
ownership and entrepreneurial activity (as measured by the TEA Index),
governments have a greater tendency to adopt a more comprehensive
entrepreneurship policy approach. Governments in lower business ownership
rate or TEA index countries, such as Denmark, Norway, Sweden, Finland,
the UK and the Netherlands, want higher dynamics. As such, they have
adopted a more comprehensive set of policies to stimulate entrepreneurial
activity. Governments in Australia, Canada, Iceland, Ireland, and the US,
countries with high business ownership rates or higher TEA rates do not
appear to focus their policies on increasing overall entrepreneurship levels.

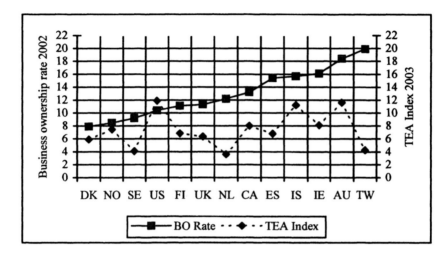

Figure 1-4. The business ownership rate (2002) to the TEA index (2003)
Note: The TEA index for Taiwan is based on 2002 data.

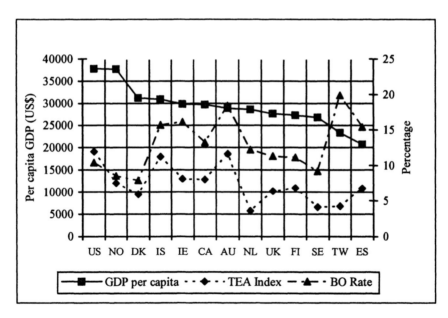

Figure 1-5. GDP per capita (2003), business ownership rates (2002) and the TEA index
(2003)
Note: The TEA index for Taiwan is based on 2002 GEM results.

This does not mean to say that the environment for entrepreneurship in
these countries is weak, as might be said about the set of countries with low

business ownership or TEA rates, but their governments are less likely to be concerned about overall business start-up rates than they are about trying to generate more economic activity from investments in R&D and firms with high-growth potential. In other words, they appear to be more interested in wealth creation than increasing the business entry and exit dynamic and, as we shall show in Chapter 3, score higher on "innovative entrepreneurship policy" than overall entrepreneurship policy. These also tend to be countries where it is easy to start a business and where there is fair and open competition, lower levels of government taxation and public sector employment, higher levels of employment in SMEs and so on. These contextual influences on a government's entrepreneurship policy orientation will be discussed in greater detail in Chapter 4.

In the next chapter, we describe our entrepreneurship policy framework, discuss the differences between SME and entrepreneurship policy, and begin to present our analysis of government practices in the 13 countries.

Annex 1-1. Influences on the level of entrepreneurial activity

A: Demographic, macro-economic, structural dimensions	Relationship to entrepreneurial activity levels	Policy Implications/Responses
Level of economic development	Inverse relationship between level of economic development and entrepreneurial activity levels (Reynolds et al., 2004). As GDP per capita increases, business ownership rate declines, then starts to increase again at about US$18,000 in per capita GDP (Carree et al., 2002).	
Population growth	Growing population leads to increased demand for products and services; increases the base for new business opportunities (Reynolds et al., 1999; Verheul et al., 2001). Regions with higher population growth rates have higher prevalence rates for nascent entrepreneurship (Reynolds et al., 2002).	More open immigration policy. In low population growth regions, increase the labour force participation rates.
Growth in the immigration rate	Immigrants have a high propensity to start businesses because of the "displacement" factor. Entrepreneurship is an option for labour market integration and social mobility (Verheul et al., 2001; Storey, 1994).	Immigration policy. Promote entrepreneurship among immigrant groups; translate business information and material into several languages; ethnic support services; immigrant entrepreneurial networks.
Growth in per capita GDP	Higher standard of living leads to increased prosperity. Higher incomes increase disposable income, increase opportunities for entrepreneurship (Reynolds et al., 1999).	Support efforts to raise productivity, innovation, employment and entrepreneurship levels.
Well-functioning, decentralised market economy	Open markets offer potential for new business entries. Regulated business environments increase start-up costs. (Davidsson & Henrekson, 2000; Fitzsimons et al., 2001; Commission of the European Communities, 2004).	Deregulation of industry sectors; privatisation of government enterprises; review of Competition Policy.

	Relationship to entrepreneurial activity levels	Policy Implications/Responses
A: Demographic, macro-economic, structural dimensions		
Age distribution of the population	Nascent entrepreneur prevalence rates are highest in the 25-34-age cohort of the population (Reynolds et al., 2004).	Focus attention on the nurturing of young people as entrepreneurs.
Household income	Higher household income is associated with higher propensity to be involved in start-up activities (Reynolds et al., 2004).	
Education level of population	People who finish high school and do some additional education are more likely to be involved in the entrepreneurial process (Reynolds et al., 2002). Higher levels of participation in tertiary education associate with higher levels of opportunity entrepreneurship (Reynolds et al., 2004).	Invest in higher education levels of population.
Sectoral shift from manufacturing to service industries	Business entry rates are higher in the service industries; lower cost and fewer barriers to entry. Outsourcing activity of large manufacturing firms leads to new firms in the services sector (Bosma et al., 2003).	Foster linkages between large and small firms.
Size of the public service	An oversized public service distorts competition and inhibits the creation of new firms (Arenius & Autio, 2001).	Privatise government-owned enterprise; reduce unfair competition between the public and private sectors.
Flexible labour markets and moderate non-wage labour costs	Flexible labour laws facilitate the flow into and out of self-employment. Stringent laws make it difficult for new firms to hire employees; high non-wage labour costs prohibit start-ups from hiring and stunt their growth (Davidsson & Henrekson, 2000; Reynolds et al., 2000). High hiring, firing and wage costs tend to discourage the entry of new firms into most markets (Scarpetta et al., 2002)	Revision of labour laws and employee contracting requirements; reduction of non-wage labour costs.

A: Demographic, macro-economic, structural dimensions	Relationship to entrepreneurial activity levels	Policy Implications/Responses
Unemployment rate	One percent rise in the unemployment rates correlates with a 0.11 percent rise in self-employment rate (van Stel & Carree, 2002). Unemployment is a push factor for self-employment (Evans & Leighton, 1989). Negative relationship between self-employment and unemployment rate (Branchflower, 2000).	Provide support for unemployed people to become self-employed.
Social security systems	High levels of social security can act as a disincentive to business entry decision (Verheul et al., 2001; van Stel et al., 2003. Countries where social welfare payments are more generous have lower necessity entrepreneurship rates (Cowling & Bygrave, 2003). Levels of welfare payments raise the reservation rate (the wage people are prepared to work for).	Reduce the risk-reward ratio associated with paid versus self-employment; provide incentives for under-and unemployed individuals to start businesses.
Taxation level	The overall taxation intensity of a national economy (tax revenue as a percentage of GDP) correlates negatively with all forms of entrepreneurial activity (Reynolds et al., 2004).	Review taxation policies and levels.
Marginal and average tax rates	Higher marginal tax rates reduce self-employment; higher average tax rates lead to an increase ((Robson & Wren, 1999).	Review taxation policies.
Presence of labour and employer unions	Strong unions result in high wage rates and low profit margins for businesses (Bosma at al., 2003).	
Political regime	Entrepreneurship is shaped by policies imposed by political regimes (Baumol, 1990; Lowrey, 2003).	

B. Cultural dimensions	Relationship to entrepreneurial activity levels	Policy Implications/Responses
Tolerance for income dispersion	Higher income dispersion allows accumulated savings required for investment in new firms; high-income individuals/households create demand for goods and services providing opportunities for new firms (Reynolds et al., 2000; Verheul et al., 2001).	Taxation policy. Reduce tax wedge. Reduce capital gains and wealth taxes.
Social and cultural norms that value and support entrepreneurship	Societies that value self-sufficiency, individualism and autonomy, and respect people who accumulate wealth are more predisposed to entrepreneurship (Reynolds et al., 1999; Verheul et al., 2001; Casson, 2003).	Create widespread awareness of the benefits of entrepreneurship to the economy and to society.
Positive media attention to entrepreneurship	Media attention to the entrepreneurial phenomenon tends to be a feature of countries with high rates of entrepreneurial activity (Fitzsimons & O'Gorman, 2003).	Profile entrepreneurship and entrepreneur role models in the media.
C: Human Dimensions	Relationship to entrepreneurial activity levels	Policy Implications/Responses
Positive attitudes towards entrepreneurship	Positive attitudes towards entrepreneurship will lead to positive intent to start a business (Various).	Promote entrepreneurship in the media and through high-profile activities.
Perception of opportunity	People who perceive a high level of opportunity are more likely to become entrepreneurs (Hindle & Rushworth, 2003).	
Belief in "efficacy"	People who believe they have the necessary skills to be an entrepreneur are many times more likely to become entrepreneurs (various country GEM studies).	Implement initiatives to expose more people to entrepreneurship education, training, and mentoring.

C: Human Dimensions	Relationship to entrepreneurial activity levels	Policy Implications/Responses
Fear and "stigma" of failure	A person's perception of the costs of business failure can act as a disincentive to entrepreneurship (Vesalainen & Pihkala, 1999; The Ministry of Economic Affairs, 2000b; Small Business Service, 2000).	Develop "rescue" culture. Revise Bankruptcy rules. Provide counseling and advisory services to troubled firms.
Dissatisfaction	Dissatisfaction in a "push" factor into business ownership (Shapero & Sokol, 1982). Countries with people who are more dissatisfied with the society in which they live have a higher proportion of self-employed (Noorderhaven et al., 2003).	
Exposure to entrepreneur role-models	Exposure to role models has a demonstration effect on others; recognition of role models serves to increase social legitimacy of entrepreneurship (Reynolds et al., 2000; Hindle & Rushworth, 2003).	Introduce awards programs for successful entrepreneurs and entrepreneurial behaviours; promote entrepreneurs in the media.
D: Dimensions of SME density and entrepreneurial dynamic	Relationship to entrepreneurial activity levels	Policy Implications/Responses
Density of business owners and SMEs	The higher the SME density, the more exposure to entrepreneurial activity. The more exposure to entrepreneurship, the higher the propensity to become an entrepreneur. This is impacted by growing up in an entrepreneurial family, working for an entrepreneur, knowing other entrepreneurs from personal and business networks. SME employment is an incubating environment. (Various).	Promote local role models; facilitate networks; encourage apprenticeships in small firms; support the development of more small businesses.

D: Dimensions of SME density and entrepreneurial dynamic	Relationship to entrepreneurial activity levels	Policy Implications/Responses
Women's participation in business ownership	Countries with the highest levels of business ownership by women also have higher levels of entrepreneurial activity, increased participation of women as entrepreneurs will contribute to economic growth (Reynolds et al., 2004; APEC, 1999).	Encourage more women to become entrepreneurs.
Regional dynamics	Regions with higher growth rates have higher start-up and exit rates (Acs & Armington, 2003).	
E: Policy dimensions	**Relationship to entrepreneurial activity levels**	**Policy Implications/Responses**
Exposure to entrepreneurship through education	Students of entrepreneurship courses have a higher propensity to start businesses (Charney & Libecap, 2000); education can play a key role in fostering entrepreneurship (OECD, 2001b; European Commission 2004d).	Introduce entrepreneurship at all levels of the education system, across disciplines. Provide lots of opportunities to learn entrepreneurial skills and gain experience.
Ease of business entry	Excessive regulation and high compliance costs in the registration of a new business can act as impediments to entrepreneurship. Reducing legal barriers to entry leads to more start-ups. (OECD, 2001; Ministry of Economic Affairs, 2000a; Djankov et al., 2000; Carree & Nijkamp, 2001; Scarpetta et al., 2002). Perceived administrative complexity has negative impact on the long-term level of business ownership (van Stel & Stunnenberg, 2004).	Reduce start-up procedures and compliance costs; simplify licensing and permit requirements; one-stop shops; revise Incorporation Laws.

E: Policy dimensions	Relationship to entrepreneurial activity levels	Policy Implications/Responses
Ease of business exit	Stringent bankruptcy laws discourage risk-taking; failed entrepreneurs may be prohibited from starting another business (Micronomics, 1998; OECD, 2001a).	Review Bankruptcy rules and laws (insolvency procedures, discharge periods, restrictions on firms), reduce restrictions on bankrupt entrepreneurs to restart after failure.
Positive, supportive climate and infrastructure for entrepreneurship at the regional level	Entrepreneurship activity levels are highest in regions that provide lots of support for new and growth-oriented entrepreneurs. Entrepreneurship is an important dimension of regional policies in the "entrepreneurial economy" (Birch et al. 1999; OECD, 1997; National Commission on Entrepreneurship, 2001).	Include an entrepreneurship focus in regional development polices. Provide programmes and services for new entrepreneurs; incubators, web-portals, advisory services, one-stop shops, mentoring, networking, etc; identify and encourage regional growth companies.
Government support for entrepreneurship at the margins	Higher levels of entrepreneurial activity can be stimulated within economically disadvantaged and minority groups and economically disadvantaged regions through targeted government efforts (Zacharakis et al., 2000).	Include entrepreneurship development as part of regional development policy. Target policy measures at groups of the population under-represented as business owners.
Access to capital needed to start and grow new firms	The inability to access financing is a barrier to the new firm creation process (Reynolds et al., 2000 and various others).	Enhance possibilities for new and growth firms to raise capital. Loan funds, guarantee funds, venture capital funds and angel networks. Tax relief for investments in new and early-stage firms. Reduce asymmetry of information - financing databases, matchmaking services.

E: Policy dimensions	Relationship to entrepreneurial activity levels	Policy Implications/Responses
Public sector procurement	As a major buyer of products and services, government is a possible lucrative market for new firms (Davidsson & Henrekson, 2000).	Procurement policies so new and small firms can compete for government contracts.
Favourable capital gains tax	A high capital gains tax poses barriers to investors in high-growth firms; acts as a barrier to the continuance of family enterprises (Davidsson & Henrekson, 2000; Ministry of Economic Affairs, 2000a; NFIB, 2000).	Reduction of Capital Gains Tax and inheritance and estate taxes.
Inequities in the tax treatment of self-employment income versus paid employment income	Higher tax rates on self-employment income act as a disincentive in a person's decision to leave paid employment to start a business (Davidsson & Henrekson, 2000; Ministry of Economic Affairs, 2000b).	Tax reform; tax relief for new starters; reduce corporate tax rates on business profits; offer start-up tax allowances and exemptions.
Inequities in the tax treatment of the income of unincorporated versus limited liability companies	Taxation of business income at the higher personal tax rate reduces valuable cash flow for reinvestment in the growth of the business (Ministry of Economic Affairs, 2000b; NFIB, 2000; Arenius & Autio, 2001).	Tax reform. Revisions to the taxation of sole proprietorships.
Entrepreneurial networks	Entrepreneurship is stronger in regions where entrepreneurial networks are widespread (Harding, 2003; Kantis, 2002).	Foster entrepreneurial networks, clusters, entrepreneurs' associations.
Entrepreneurship advocates	Most government departments are not well versed in the needs of entrepreneurs and small firms. This acts as a barrier to governance in the interests of the small business sector. (The SBA Office of Advocacy; the UK Small Business Service; and the National Commission on Entrepreneurship are examples of advocacy organisations). Entrepreneurship policy requires government "champions" (Fitzsimons et al., 2001).	Appoint entrepreneurship advocate within government to better inform other government departments, regulators, etc. Establish private-sector entrepreneurship advocacy organisation.

[1] Verheul et al. (2001), p. 15.

[2] Reynolds et al. (1999), p. 10 - 12.

[3] See "Enterprise Demography: Examining Business Dynamism in OECD Countries," in *OECD Small and Medium Enterprise* Outlook, OECD (2002), pp. 31-41.

[4] For the year 2000, entry rates ranged from a high of 9.7 percent in Spain to a low of 6.8 percent in Belgium. Exit (or death) rates also varied from a 1999 high of 10.2 percent in the UK to a low of 6.1 percent in Portugal.

[5] *OECD Small and Medium Enterprise Outlook 2002*, p. 39.

[6] The Panel Study on Entrepreneurial Dynamics (PSED) is the first national database to offer systematic, reliable and generalisable data on the process of business formation by nascent entrepreneurs.

[7] See *OECD Small and Medium Enterprises Outlook* 2004, p. 32 for an outline of the key problems associated with calculating entry and exit rates for cross-country comparisons.

[8] This study discovered that hyper and strong growth firms were not sector or industry dependent. The top job-creating industries included Transportation; Grocery Stores and Pharmacies; Restaurants, Take-out Food, Taverns and Bars; Shoe, Fabric & Yarn Stores; and Food Industries, not those traditionally viewed as high technology industries. Since no one industry is predisposed to growth, targeting industry clusters of firms may fail to produce desired wealth creation outcomes.

[9] Bartelsman et al. (2003), p. 25.

[10] See G. Hofstede (1980). *Culture's Consequences: International Differences in Work-Related Values*. Beverly Hills: Sage Publications.

[11] See the OECD *Small and Medium Enterprise Outlook,* 2000 Edition (2000).

[12] Reynolds et al. (1999), p. 55.

Chapter 2

ENTREPRENEURSHIP POLICY – DEFINITIONS, FOUNDATIONS AND FRAMEWORK

"ENTREPRENEURIAL" DEFINITIONS

In this chapter, we elaborate on our entrepreneurship policy framework, but before doing that, we briefly explain what we mean when we refer to the "entrepreneur", the "entrepreneurial process", "entrepreneurship", and "entrepreneurial culture". We also review our definition of entrepreneurship policy and the foundations model on which it is based.

What is an Entrepreneur?

Academics continue to debate what defines an entrepreneur, often using the terms self-employed, small business owner, small business owner/manager, and entrepreneur interchangeably. Arguments persist about whether every business owner is an entrepreneur or whether only innovative and growth-oriented business owners merit the label "entrepreneur". There is no unified definition. Baumol (1993) aptly describes two uses of the word. One use refers to the entrepreneur as someone who creates and then organises and operates a new firm, independent of whether there is anything innovative in the act, while the other use refers to the entrepreneur as an innovator, someone who transforms inventions and ideas into economically viable entities, independent of whether in the process he/she creates or operates a firm. Lowrey (2003) defines the entrepreneur as an economic agent and argues that both types of Baumol's entrepreneurs are significant for the performance of the economy, although they differ profoundly in their roles, the nature of their influence, and the type of analysis their roles require. One type focuses on the management of survival, routine and the status quo, and the other on creation for advancement, for growth and for dynamics. Lowrey (2003) further defines the entrepreneur as an individual with a perpetual desire for achievement.

Summarising the debate about the definition of an entrepreneur goes beyond the scope of our discussion, but at the end of the day, we believe it is more useful to adopt a process perspective. First of all, we associate business start-up, ownership and management of an owned-business with our use of the word entrepreneur. Beyond that, we take the view that entrepreneurs are people who, at different stages of life and at different stages of starting, managing and growing their own businesses, are at different stages of the entrepreneurial journey. They move along a continuum that includes nascent entrepreneurs, solo-entrepreneurs, micro-entrepreneurs, lifestyle-entrepreneurs, technology-entrepreneurs, high-growth entrepreneurs, and innovative entrepreneurs. Some start small and stay small, some start a series of progressively larger businesses over time, and some make the transition from micro-entrepreneur to high-growth entrepreneur as life and business circumstances change. Having said that, researchers and even governments will likely continue to differentiate between these typifications and debate the significance of each one to society and to the economy. But, by trying to categorise entrepreneurs into static "types", one ignores the diversity of entrepreneurship, the dynamism of the entrepreneurial process and the reality that people "become" entrepreneurs and develop over time.

For the purposes of policy, governments in our different case countries also use different labels. In Taiwan, a very entrepreneurial nation, its entrepreneurs are referred to as "SMEs". Until very recently, the word "entrepreneur" was generally avoided in Ireland, Australia, and to some extent, the UK[1], because it had negative connotations in society. In the past, it was more common in these countries to refer to entrepreneurs as small business owners or owner-managers. On the other hand, the word "entrepreneur" is used widely in the US and Canada and has become more accepted in the Netherlands, Spain and the Nordic countries.

What is the Entrepreneurial Process?

In line with the above perspective, we define the entrepreneurial process as "the process whereby individuals become aware of business ownership as an option or viable alternative, develop ideas for businesses, learn the processes of becoming an entrepreneur, and undertake the initiation and development of a business.... Entrepreneurship can be found in both the initiation and growth of businesses".[2] The process of increasing the supply of capable entrepreneurs within an economy requires attention to all activities leading to the creation of an enterprise, in particular, awareness, career orientation, new enterprise creation, self-employment, business survival and growth and stimulating an entrepreneurial spirit in the community.

What is Entrepreneurship?

There are two streams of research when it comes to defining entrepreneurship. In the management literature, entrepreneurship is defined as something that entrepreneurs "do" or in relationship to aspects of an individual's entrepreneurial behaviour. Reynolds et al. (1999) define it as any attempt at new business or new venture creation, such as self-employment, a new business organisation or the expansion of an existing business by an individual, a team of individuals or an established business. Hindle and Rushworth (2002) state that entrepreneurship is based on the availability, perception and conversion of opportunity. Gartner and Carter (2003) define it as "an organisational phenomenon and, more specifically, as an organising process".[3] The European Commission (2004d) defines entrepreneurship as the mindset and process needed to create and develop economic activity, blending risk-taking, creativity and/or innovation with sound management within a new or an existing organisation. Carree and Thurik (2003) define it as a behavioural characteristic of persons.[4] Shane and Eckhardt (2003, p. 163) define entrepreneurship as the discovery, evaluation and exploitation of future goods and services. They suggest that the study of entrepreneurship incorporates the sources of opportunities, the processes of discovery, evaluation and exploitation of opportunities and the set of individuals who discover, evaluate and exploit them. They view entrepreneurship as a sequential process.

Another stream of research defines entrepreneurship more in terms of an economic dynamic or a societal phenomenon. Morris (1996), for example, defines entrepreneurship as the relationship between entrepreneurs and their surroundings and the role government plays in creating the economic, political, legal, financial, and social structures that characterise a society (and the environment for entrepreneurs). Lowrey (2003) defines entrepreneurship as an economic system that consists of entrepreneurs, legal and institutional arrangements, and governments. Governments are important because they have the ability to adjust the economic institutions that work to protect individual entrepreneurs and stimulate their motives to achieve so economic development and growth can be fostered. McGrath (2003) asserts that the study of entrepreneurship has fundamentally to do with the study of economic change.[5]

Operationalising a definition for the purposes of developing policy, the Swedish government, as an example, views entrepreneurship "as an expression of the activities undertaken by individuals when ideas are generated and turned into something of value. Entrepreneurship can be seen as a process that arises in a social context. Entrepreneurship is an integral part of society – existing businesses and organisations, the public sector, associations, schools and the social economy.... Entrepreneurship results in new businesses and the development of existing businesses" (NUTEK, 2003, p. 13).

We adopt the broader definition of entrepreneurship – it isn't just something that entrepreneurs "do", it is a social phenomenon that emerges within the context of a broader society and involves many actors.

What is an Entrepreneurial Culture?

Many governments are seeking to develop a culture for entrepreneurship or an entrepreneurial society, but what is that? Gibb (2001) concludes that there is no absolute agreement on the definition of enterprise (entrepreneurial) culture. He explains that to some it means maximising the potential for individuals to start businesses and to others it means maximising the potential for individuals in all kinds of organisations and in all aspects of life to behave entrepreneurially. He argues that it is important for policymakers to recognise that entrepreneurial behaviour arises from the need of all kinds of individuals and organisations to cope with and enjoy high levels of uncertainty and complexity as a means of self-fulfilment. The overall challenge of an entrepreneurial society, according to Gibb, is to ensure that there are abundant role models for individuals to follow, wide opportunities for the practicing of entrepreneurial behaviour, local empowerment to enable things to happen, a belief in "trust" as a guideline for regulations to be minimised, and the encouragement of initiative at all levels.

In answer to the question, what would an enterprise culture look like, the UK government states the following: "The government's vision is of a nation in which all sections of society are better equipped to respond positively to change and new opportunities, to create and implement new ideas and ways of working, and make reasonable assessments of risk and rewards and act upon them. The spread of these skills will enable all to manage a flexible career, and help create a business environment supportive of becoming involved in enterprise" (Small Business Service, 2004a).

The European Commission (2004d) asserts that stimulating an entrepreneurial culture implies the need to focus on fuelling a more positive attitude towards entrepreneurship and risk-taking, on encouraging more people to become entrepreneurs and on supporting them to develop and grow by addressing issues such as entrepreneurship education, the balance between risk and reward and promoting entrepreneurial growth. It also implies providing an enabling environment for entrepreneurs with a sufficient flow of financing and a friendly regulatory and administrative framework.

In their 2003 Ministerial Statement, APEC Ministers state: "Entrepreneurs are products of their environments... policymakers are in part responsible for fostering an environment conducive to the growth of the entrepreneurial spirit. The entrepreneurial environment is directly affected by regulatory and tax burdens; labour market legislation; competition policy; and legal conditions.... Policymakers have a role to play to foster entrepreneurial activities through education and training... (and) to publicly highlight entrepreneurship as a valuable way of life that enriches the community as a whole" (APEC 2003a, p. 2-3). APEC Ministers further state that the strength of an entrepreneurial society is manifested through the number of business start-ups and the sustainability of SMEs and micro-enterprises.

DEFINING ENTREPRENEURSHIP POLICY AND ITS FOUNDATIONS

If entrepreneurship is a system that includes entrepreneurs (and potential entrepreneurs), institutions and government actions, and the desired policy outcome is an increased level of entrepreneurial activity, then the role of institutions and governments is to foster environments that will produce a continuous supply of new entrepreneurs[6] as well as the conditions that will enable them to be successful in their efforts to start and grow enterprises. In order to do this, the system of entrepreneurship must logically focus on all parts of the individual entrepreneurial process from awareness of the entrepreneurship option to early stage survival and growth of an emerging firm.

Existing knowledge about what is critical in influencing the entrepreneurial actions of individuals suggests that people are more likely to become entrepreneurs if: (1) they are aware of the option and perceive it as a societally desirable one; (2) they perceive opportunity exists and that they will have, or could gain, support to pursue a business idea; and (3) they have confidence in their own ability to do it. In other words, there will be higher levels of entrepreneurial activity in economies where people are aware of entrepreneurship as a feasible and viable option and willing to explore it (Motivation); have access to opportunities to gain the knowledge, skills and ability to be able to pursue it (Skills); and can gain ready access to the start-up supports they need, such as information and ideas, counseling and advisory services, business contacts, capital and encouragement, in an enabling regulatory and policy environment (Opportunity). These, the foundations of entrepreneurship policy, are modelled in Figure 2-1.

To operationalise "Motivation" we include the social value placed on entrepreneurship and its desirability and feasibility as a career and employment option. The level of these elements could be heightened through awareness, information, exposure, role models and actions to increase social legitimacy. "Skills" is operationalised in terms of technical, business and entrepreneurial skills and know-how. The acquisition of entrepreneurial skills and know-how could come through the education system, training programmes, experience working in a small business, hands-on experience in starting and running an enterprise or through peer and professional networks. Most entrepreneurs learn to do what they do through trial and error so there is considerable scope to create formal learning opportunities that will better enable future entrepreneurs. "Opportunity" is operationalised in terms of the support environment for entrepreneurship – the availability of information, advice, capital, contacts, technical support and business ideas, as well as the ease of access to these resources. It also encompasses the regulatory environment and processes of government administration. In order to create more Opportunity conditions, governments can reduce or eliminate obstacles in the regulatory, administrative, legislative and fiscal systems that may act as inhibitors to business entry. They can also reduce the penalties associated with bankruptcy, and the resulting "stigma of failure". In addition, labour market and social security policies and systems may impose hidden barriers or "quiet disincentives" to the self-employment versus paid employment decision; these must also be examined.

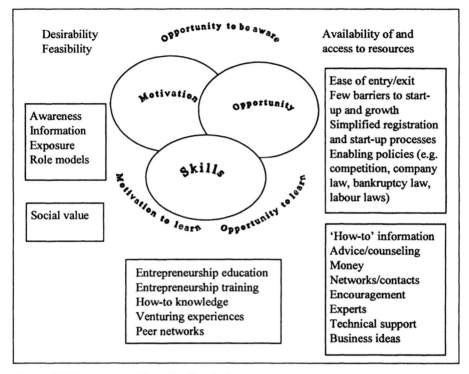

Figure 2.1. Entrepreneurship policy foundations

Source: Taken from Stevenson and Lundström (2002), p. 26.

According to our view, governments must address each of these areas of Motivation, Opportunity and Skills using an integrated entrepreneurship policy approach.

We define entrepreneurship policy as that which is:

- aimed at the pre-start, the start-up and early post-start-up phases of the entrepreneurial process,
- designed and delivered to address the areas of Motivation, Opportunity and Skills,
- with the primary objective of encouraging more people in the population to consider entrepreneurship as an option, move into the nascent stage of taking actions to start a business and proceed into the entry and early stages of the business.

Governments will likely have some difficulty determining their role in some of these areas, which is not surprising due to the complexity of trying to understand precisely how to influence an individual's propensity to pursue entrepreneurship or the population's entrepreneurial efficacy level. As we will discuss in Chapter 5, very little is known about how each of the components of Motivation, Opportunity and Skills interact to produce an entrepreneurial event, in spite of the growing body of literature on the motivations and behaviours of entrepreneurs and the potential impacts of government policy actions. However, one can conjecture at the macro-level about the likely outcomes on business entry of the existence of various combinations of high and low levels of Motivation, Opportunity and Skills

In Table 2-1, we speculate about the possible outcomes of various scenarios. For example, if members of the general population are not motivated to explore entrepreneurship, they will be unlikely to pursue it even in the face of an opportunistic environment. If there is a high level of motivation to start businesses, but the opportunity environment is weak, then it will be hard for people to acquire the resources they need and to overcome other start-up obstacles. This may lead to giving up on or abandoning their ideas. Or it may lead to a high level of marginal "necessity entrepreneurship," such as is the prevalent form in many developing countries (Reynolds et al., 2004). If people are highly motivated to start businesses, but have limited capability (a lack of entrepreneurial skills), then even if they have technical skills, the business is unlikely to grow beyond the fledgling stage, unless the environment is very supportive and nurturing. Of course, the optimal situation for a society would be to have high Motivation, high Opportunity and high Skills. One of the key challenges faced by governments is determining what policy levers will influence this combination.

Table 2-1. Possible interaction effects of high and low levels of Motivation, Opportunity and Skills

Motivation	Opportunity	Skills	Possible Interaction Effects
Low	Low	Low	Few, likely marginal, businesses will be started; few opportunities exist to gain know-how; limited chances for success. Indication of weak entrepreneurial culture; limited support for entrepreneurship.
Low	Low	High	Few businesses will be started; may be less marginal due to higher skill level, but will be "resource poor" (low support) and constrained by weak entrepreneurial culture.
Low	High	Low	Few businesses will be started because of lack of cultural support and know-how; will have higher chances of survival with the right support.
Low	High	High	May be able to "pull" some people into entrepreneurship depending on the incentive structure; chances for success are higher IF they can be motivated or compelled to actually take the step. A weak culture of entrepreneurship may exist. Unintentional deterrents, disincentives or barriers may exist in the social security or taxation system.
High	Low	Low	More people may try to start businesses but it will be difficult; likelihood of giving up because of lack of support and know-how. Even if businesses are started, they may have low chances of success due to the lack of support and assistance. An entrepreneur's personal determination and perseverance will be critical success factors.
High	Low	High	People are likely to start businesses but without access to a supportive environment will start on a small scale with their own resources and know-how; more likely to stay small. There could also be barriers to entry. Critical success factor will be the level of an entrepreneur's determination and capability.
High	High	Low	People will start businesses; with support such as mentoring and other forms of advice may be able to gain the know-how; critical success factor will be access to professional advice and peer networks.
High	High	High	Optimal chances for success both in terms of increasing start-up rates and firm survival and growth rates. Indication of a strong entrepreneurship culture, incentive system, entrepreneurship support and assistance, and opportunities to gain knowledge and experience.

In addition to creating the right conditions and support for the emergence of new entrepreneurs, entrepreneurship policy addresses their needs during the initial survival and growth phases of a business start-up. We use 42 months after start-up as the upper time limit for entrepreneurship policy for two reasons. Firstly, it reflects substantial research evidence that new firms are very vulnerable during their first three to five years in business (OECD, 2002a). A firm's chances of survival improve substantially after the first two years (Bartelsman et al., 2003). During this early period of experimentation, entrepreneurs benefit greatly from professional advice, mentoring, strategic networking and other important resources. Secondly, research reveals that high growth firms often start their growth trajectory in their early years of development. One of the goals of entrepreneurship policy is to enable a higher percentage of start-ups to grow rapidly by addressing growth obstacles during their early years. The 42-month limit is also consistent with the definition used in the Global Entrepreneurship Monitor (GEM) research.

We move next to a discussion of how entrepreneurship policy differs from SME policy.

SME POLICY AND ENTREPRENEURSHIP POLICY – A COMPARISON

SME policy has historically and traditionally focused on SME sector productivity and competitiveness issues (e.g., technology adoption, management skills, internationalisation) and heavily emphasised Opportunity measures (e.g., improving access to financial and information resources; reducing regulatory and administrative burden). Governments' direct efforts to create a level playing field for smaller businesses have been largely oriented towards addressing the needs of existing small firms once they are established. SME policies have pretty much ignored the entrepreneurial process perspective, particularly in addressing the motivation and skills needs of individuals in the awareness and nascent/pre-start-up phases.

When we first started doing our entrepreneurship policy research we noted that, in spite of the emerging presence of entrepreneurship-related policy statements (OECD, 1998; European Commission, 1998), the inventorying and comparative analysis of member countries' activities often lumped SME-oriented and entrepreneurship-oriented policies and measures together. A good example of this practice is illustrated in earlier versions of the *European Observatory on SMEs*. In the 1995 edition, the capstone "entrepreneurship" appears in the listing of SME policy lines along with SME financing, management skills, administrative burden, technology transfer and internationalisation (ESRN, 1995) and is used to capture any and all diverse measures oriented towards fostering entrepreneurial activity, including awareness and education activities, self-employment training initiatives, among others, but no attempts are made to further categorise these measures.[7] Entrepreneurship is inferred to be part of the SME policy prescription, but as we saw it, "tacked on" to the end of the list of the more traditional SME policy lines of action. We believed that entrepreneurship as a policy area would remain marginalised as a key component of industrial and economic development unless it was better articulated from a policy perspective.

We argue that entrepreneurship policy and SME policy are inter-related but at the same time distinctive. First of all, the two policy domains have quite different overall objectives. The over-riding objective of SME policy is to strengthen existing SMEs by ensuring they have a "level playing field" relative to large firms. Governments tend to intervene on the basis of neo-classical market failure arguments. The main objective of entrepreneurship policy is to stimulate higher levels of entrepreneurial activity by influencing a greater supply of new entrepreneurs. Although market failure arguments are still employed to justify government interventions, particularly in relationship to accessibility of start-up and early-stage financing, justifications for broader government actions are made on the basis of systemic and government failures, as well as cultural constraints. In entrepreneurship policy, it is insufficient to focus only on a favourable business environment; it is essential to also emphasise a favourable entrepreneurship culture and climate.

Apart from differences in the scope of their objectives and policy priorities, we propose four other major areas of divergence.

1. Entrepreneurship policy focuses on individuals, while SME policy focuses on firms.
2. Entrepreneurship policy focuses on supporting the needs of people as they move through the earliest stages of the entrepreneurial process from awareness to intent to pre-start-up and early post-start-up, while SME policy emphasises support to established firms that have acquired sufficient capacity to benefit from SME schemes and measures.
3. Entrepreneurship policy makes greater use of "soft" policy measures, such as mentoring and entrepreneurship promotion, while SME policy makes greater use of "hard" policy instruments such as financial subsidies to buy-down the cost of plant and equipment.
4. The implementation of entrepreneurship policy incorporates a broad set of institutional partners in the make-up of its "support environment" (e.g., educators, the media and a diverse set of government ministries), while SME policy is more likely to be

implemented through a narrower set of economic institutions (e.g., economic development agencies, financial intermediaries).

Because the development of entrepreneurship is affected by policies and actions in numerous areas beyond the sole scope of a ministry of economic affairs or industry, the implementation of entrepreneurship policy necessitates inter-ministerial, inter-governmental, horizontal approaches and strategies involving education ministries, labour and employment ministries, regulatory agencies, and even offices for gender equity. It also calls for the development of broad-based partnerships with community organisations, members of the media, and the business and corporate sector.

We summarise the key distinctions between the two policy areas in Table 2-2.[8]

One of the difficulties governments may have in the process of adopting entrepreneurship policy is not being able to identify precisely "who" the client is. In SME policy, the client is a firm, an existing entity that can be identified relatively easily. In entrepreneurship policy, the client is an individual who may not yet have an enterprise – they may be considering employment options, thinking about becoming an entrepreneur, or be in the process of taking some steps to start a business. As such, they are hard to identify. Existing SMEs are easier to deal with than nascent and start-up entrepreneurs because they already have a base, that is, some experience, knowledge and capital resources. Their owners are able to articulate, at least to some degree, their needs. Existing SMEs tend to be represented by SME associations, employer organisations or industry groups that can represent these needs to governments. Such organisations often do not represent the views of nascent and new entrepreneurs. Inadequate research on the population of potential entrepreneurs coupled with their lack of representative associations to lobby governments on their behalf or to be consulted by governments, means that their needs have been much lower on the policy radar screen. This situation is rapidly changing, as we saw in Chapter 1. A different set of performance indicators is also needed to measure the impact of governments' entrepreneurship versus SME policies.

Table 2-2. Characteristics of SME policy and entrepreneurship policy: a comparison

Characteristics	Traditional SME Policy	Newer Entrepreneurship Policy
Outcome	Firm growth, productivity growth.	Growth in entrepreneurial activity (i.e., in the number of business owners and firms).
General goal	Create a "favourable business climate" (e.g., tax regime; marketplace frameworks; reduced red tape).	Create a "favourable entrepreneurial climate and culture" (e.g., few barriers to entry, promotion of entrepreneurship in society).
Specific objective	To help individual firms modernise, expand or improve competitiveness.	To encourage more people to start their own businesses and provide opportunities for them to learn about the entrepreneurial process and develop the necessary skills.
Focus	On firms rather than individuals.	On individuals rather than firms.
Stage of business cycle	Primary focus is on support after the business has actually started.	Support is offered in the nascent stages as well as during the critical first years of a start-up.
Client groups and targeting	Existing firms. (Often) targets high growth sectors or high growth firms (i.e., "picking winners" approach).	Nascent and new entrepreneurs. Targets the general population and (often) segments within it (e.g., women, youth). Generally no sector targeting.
Policy priorities	Reduce red tape and paper burden for existing SMEs.	Reduce procedural, regulatory and taxation barriers to business entry.
	Improve access to financing.	Facilitate access to micro-loans, seed capital and other start-up financing.
	Improve SME access to information (provide business, economic, market, government regulatory and programme information).	Improve access to start-up information and advice, entrepreneurial know-how.
	Facilitate SME's access to domestic and international markets (e.g., tariff reductions, export subsidies).	Facilitate networking activities and exchanges to promote peer-learning, partnering and dialogue.
	Improve the competitiveness of small firms (e.g., management skills, strategic consulting).	Increase opportunities for people to learn the entrepreneurial process and skills for starting a business (e.g., education, training); enhance the quality of start-up support services.
	Foster R&D and technology adoption among SMEs (e.g., technology transfer).	Create awareness of entrepreneurship as a viable option (e.g., profile role models, influence public attitudes).
Primary policy levers	Use of financial/fiscal incentives to lever specific SME activities (e.g., R&D investment, exporting).	Greater use of non-financial levers (except in the case of start-up and seed financing).
Time period for results	More immediate (aims for results over a three-to-four year cycle).	More long-term (process perspective requires time).

Defining the Scope of the Two Policy Domains

According to our definition, entrepreneurship policy is about positively influencing the environment in favour of entrepreneurship and introducing measures that will enable more people to move through the entrepreneurial process. We divide this process into five phases: (i) awareness; (ii) pre-start-up (nascent); (iii) start-up; (iv) early post-start-up; or (v) maintenance and expansion. The process begins with becoming aware of entrepreneurship as an option and continues through to the early stages of survival and growth of a firm (the first three and a half years of business entry). SME policy is about creating good conditions for the improved productivity and competitiveness of a small firm once it is firmly established, applying more in the maintenance and expansion phase. However, in practical terms, there is overlap between the two policy domains. In Figure 2-2, we graphically illustrate where the points of this overlap are likely to be. Although the lines of the two policy wedges are somewhat arbitrary, we propose that the grey area between entrepreneurship and SME policy occurs in the areas of policy affecting start-ups and emerging growth firms. Entrepreneurship policy will play the predominant role prior to the late nascent phase and SME policy the predominant role when the business has survived its highly vulnerable post-start-up period.

The outer limit for SME policy attention, the open end of the SME policy wedge, will be firms below the maximum size level set by a government's "small and medium-sized enterprise" definition. This varies from country to country. In some countries, it is a business with up to 500 employees (the US and Canada), in others, less than 250 employees (the EU definition), and in others less than 100 employees (the Netherlands). The outer limit for entrepreneurship policy attention, the open end of its policy wedge, will be the general population. The dilemma is that we cannot know which individuals in the population are eventually going to become entrepreneurs or at what point they will make the decision. A country's future entrepreneurs are "doing something else" right now. They could be in school, out of the labour force, working for a large public or private organisation, working for a small firm, or officially unemployed. Some of these people will eventually start businesses, either alone or with others in a team, but likely unaware that this will be one of their future actions. So the beginning of entrepreneurship policy is triggering awareness among the population that the option of entrepreneurship exists as a possibility and creating positive attitudes regarding its desirability and feasibility.

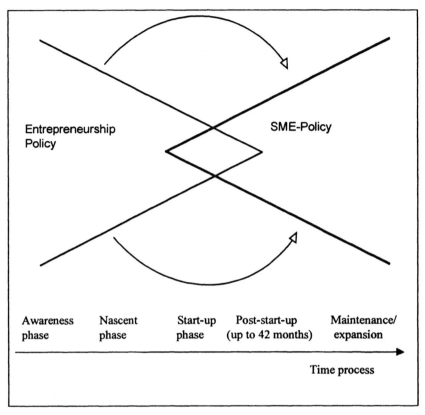

Figure 2-2. The interface between entrepreneurship policy and SME policy
Source: Lundström and Stevenson (2002).

As we see it, entrepreneurship policy is the base of SME policy and is needed to stimulate entrepreneurial activity and create the conditions for a high level of renewal (the "creative destruction" of entry and exit activity). Without efforts to foster the development of positive attitudes, motivated individuals, nascent entrepreneurs, start-ups, and young emerging firms, the foundation for an efficient SME policy will be limited.

We contend that the role and appropriate type of policy will change depending on which "failures" (i.e., market, systemic, cultural) government is aiming to address, at which phase of the entrepreneurial or SME development process, and that it is very important to weave this process perspective into entrepreneurship policy thinking. In Figure 2-3, we explore some assumptions about the role of different policy measures during the five different phases of the entrepreneurial process, proposing that Motivation, Opportunity and Skills measures will increase or decrease in importance over the cycle.

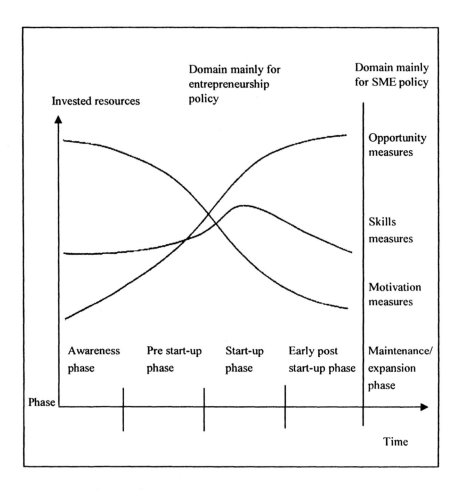

Figure 2-3. Weighting of general measures by policy domain

Our general proposition is that motivation-oriented measures will be more important during the awareness phase, diminishing in importance as the entrepreneur moves closer to the start-up phase. Opportunity measures will be of less importance in the awareness stage, but this will increase over time as the entrepreneur enters the start-up phase, perhaps becoming the most important type of measures in the SME policy domain. Skills-oriented measures become very important in the pre-start-up phase and continue to be so throughout the rest of the cycle, although the type and nature of the entrepreneur's required skills and know-how will change over time.

(i) Awareness phase

In the awareness phase, the policy objective is to raise the level of interest people have in considering the entrepreneurship option, perhaps even providing opportunities for them to recognise their entrepreneurial qualities and behaviours. It has to do with developing the entrepreneurial "mind-set" so Motivation measures are very important. A number of possible actions could be adopted to create more awareness of entrepreneurship within the population, motivate students and very young people to become interested in entrepreneurial behaviour, and promote role models, as examples. Opportunity measures are not of significant importance in this phase, although information about potential business opportunities and the available support for new entrepreneurs could have a positive impact on the general publics' perceptions of the opportunities available. Skills-oriented measures in this phase will be of a general nature, for example, those that can be learned in schools or through extracurricular activities. SME policy does not play a significant role in this phase. Neither is there a lot of ongoing research concerning the effects of different policy measures in this phase. However, it seems to be an area of increasing research interest as more efforts are being made to measure the attitudes of different groups of the population towards entrepreneurship, measure the effects of entrepreneurially-oriented learning methods in schools, and isolate the effects of early role models.

ii) Pre-start-up (nascent) phase

In the nascent phase, policy is concerned with developing individuals' intentions and actions towards starting a business, supporting nascent entrepreneurs, and perhaps promoting the pursuit of certain types of opportunities (e.g., innovation-related). Different groups of the population could be targeted with information and advice regarding the possibility of starting a business; support could be offered to university spin-offs and incubators; seed financing made available; and self-employment training programmes offered to the unemployed, to give some examples. There is a role for entrepreneurship education in secondary and vocational parts of the school system and in universities. Enterprise centers and business support organisations will play a big role in this phase, working to help people through the process of exploring ideas, gaining knowledge and skills, preparing business plans, and mobilising resources. SME policy plays a marginal role. Motivation measures are still of great importance. Opportunity measures increase in importance, particularly, in the areas of access to counseling assistance, entrepreneurial networks, and community support; and Skills-oriented measures become very important. There is a considerable amount of recent research seeking to identify the barriers and challenges in the nascent phase of the entrepreneurial process, such as the lack of seed financing; to evaluate the results of measures taken to encourage unemployed people to start firms; and to explore the nature of academic entrepreneurship, to name a few.

iii) Start-up phase

In the start-up phase, individuals actually start their businesses. There is a decreasing emphasis on Motivation-oriented measures (although there is an ongoing role for promotion of entrepreneurship and positive role models) and an increasing emphasis on Skills and Opportunity-based measures. Measures to reduce regulatory and procedural barriers to entry are of importance, as are measures to provide counseling and information, start-up financing, market plan assistance, and training opportunities. Measures promoting growth possibilities may also be introduced. This is a phase where many service providers are working and where there is great research interest. It could be research concerning the structure of start-ups, the characteristics of entrepreneurs, the type of business ideas and opportunities, team-building companies, the conversion of nascent entrepreneurs, and the number of jobs generated from start-ups, to give some examples. Again, it is an area mainly for measures taken in the entrepreneurship policy domain, but it is in the grey area of the two policy wedges, so there are overlaps with SME policy measures.

iv) Early post-start-up phase

In the early post-start-up phase, policy interest will shift to early success and failure, the potential of growth companies, seed financing possibilities, market development, administrative and regulatory burdens, networking, information and counseling, and technology transfer issues, just to mention a few. This is also a phase where many service providers target their support and where policymakers implement many measures. It is an area of great research interest regarding job generation, growing companies, failures, regional dimensions, and the characteristics of different types of entrepreneurs. It is mainly an area for entrepreneurship policy, but again falls in the overlapping grey area with SME policy.

v) Maintenance and expansion phase

In the maintenance and expansion phase, policy deals with sustainability, productivity and growth issues. Policy measures are concerned with problems of administrative and tax burdens, labour regulations and rules, technology adoption, growth financing, internationalisation, and bankruptcy issues. Research interest focuses on the effects on technology transfer, success and failure issues, the importance of ease of exit, the competition aspects of new entrants, fast-growth firms ("gazelles"), and evaluation of the effectiveness and efficiency of different policy measures. It is a diminishing phase for Motivation-oriented measures, still a phase for Skills-oriented measures and an increasingly important phase for all types of Opportunity and administrative-based measures. SME policy plays a large role, while the role of entrepreneurship policy decreases.

When we examine the evolution of government SME policy, which began as early as the 1950s and 60s in countries like Canada, the US, Sweden and Taiwan, we see that the initial policy emphasis was on Opportunity measures affecting existing firms. The primary aim was to address perceived or actual market failures, such as information asymmetries and the failure of capital markets to make financing available to small firms. Policy next moved to addressing the lack of SME management skills, believed to be a barrier to the performance of small enterprises and a major contributing factor to the lack of growth of most small firms and their lower productivity and competitiveness levels. As knowledge about barriers to development of the SME sector advanced, governments shifted their attention to administrative and regulatory burdens, especially those perpetuated by government failures. Research on the time spent by small and large firms on regulatory and administrative compliance revealed a disproportionate burden on the smaller firms. The United States Office of Advocacy was one of the first, in 1980, to take actions in this area,[9] followed more than a decade later by Canada and countries in Europe. Interest in reducing regulatory barriers to entry started in the early 2000s, propelled largely by a 75-nation study on barriers to entry (Djankov et al., 2000) and the EU benchmarking study on the administration of start-ups (European Commission, 2002c). As interest in entrepreneurship emerges in different countries, governments are moving into new areas of policy development, seeking more to address systemic failures in the cultural, institutional and socio-political environment for entrepreneurship, as well as failure of the education system to provide knowledge about the entrepreneurial process. Thus, we see more initiatives in the areas affecting Motivation and Skills.

The majority of existing government policy actions still emphasise Opportunity measures, the area of traditional SME policy focus (i.e., access to resources and information; reducing administrative and regulatory burden). We propose that to build an entrepreneurial economy more attention has to be paid to Motivation and Skills-oriented measures. Government practices in our 13 countries offer some insight on how governments are moving in this direction. Since the mid-1990s, governments in all of these countries have adopted policies and programmes designed to improve the environment for new entrepreneurs. While the specific and practical aspects of doing this vary across countries, we were able to identify certain patterns from an analysis of their collective actions that allowed us to configure a framework of entrepreneurship policy measures.

THE ENTREPRENEURSHIP POLICY FRAMEWORK

In the 13 countries we studied, we found a fairly consistent set of SME policy priorities, although governments differed in how broad policy goals are achieved and in their approach to SME interventions. Policies fell into five general areas: (1) creating a favourable business environment; (2) reducing administrative burden; (3) enhancing SME performance; (4) improving the quality of business support; and (5) increasing SME access to procurement opportunities.

However, in our 2000-01 study we were primarily interested in national policies meeting the parameters of our definition of entrepreneurship policy. What we found were an array of policies and initiatives that we were able to categorise into six areas of a policy framework (Stevenson and Lundström, 2001):

1. entrepreneurship promotion;
2. entrepreneurship education;
3. the environment for start-ups;
4. start-up and seed capital financing;
5. business support measures for start-ups; and
6. target group strategies.

Figure 2-4 models this framework of entrepreneurship policy measures.

The broad collective objectives for policies and measures in these areas included: to build an entrepreneurship culture; to prepare the next generation of entrepreneurs; to reduce specific barriers to entry; to fill gaps in start-up and early-stage financing; to enhance business support for start-ups; and to increase the start-up rates of under-represented groups.

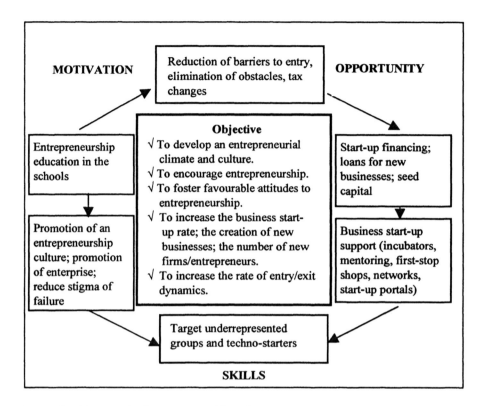

Figure 2.4. Framework of entrepreneurship policy measures

When we applied the framework to a 2004 update of government policy actions, we found diversity in the extent to which individual governments were undertaking policy initiatives in each area of the framework, although most had stated policy objectives for each area. See Table 2-3. All central/national governments have as an objective to fill gaps in the area of start-up and seed financing; over 90 percent have a stated objective to reduce barriers to entry and to improve access to start-up support; 85 percent stress the importance of increasing awareness of entrepreneurship within society to strengthen their entrepreneurial culture; 85 percent have a stated objective to increase the business ownership rates of defined segments of the population; and over 75 percent have the stated objective to integrate entrepreneurship within all levels of the education system.

But we find gaps between these stated objectives and the extent to which different governments are implementing supporting policy initiatives in each framework area. To make this assessment, we compiled a checklist of policy measures relevant to each of the six framework areas, allotted 0 to 1 points to each item in the list, depending on whether there was evidence that actions were being taken by each government individually, and then totalled the scores for each item, noting the percentage of countries with relevant actions. We added measures for three additional areas: (i) general policy approach/ commitment to entrepreneurship policy; (ii) policy structure for entrepreneurship; and (iii) performance tracking, and scored these as well. We refer to the resulting scale as the "entrepreneurship policy comprehensiveness scale". More information about how we developed this instrument is included in the methodology description in the Appendix.

Table 2-3. Percentage of governments with stated objectives in E-policy framework areas

Entrepreneurship Policy Framework Objectives	% of governments
1. Promotion of entrepreneurship: objective to increase awareness of entrepreneurship; foster an entrepreneurial culture	85%
2. Entrepreneurship in the education system: objective to increase emphasis on entrepreneurship in the education system	77%
3. Easing entry, early-stage survival/growth and exit: objective to ease entry, early-stage survival and growth, and exit by reducing administrative and regulatory burdens	92%
4. Access to start-up, seed, and early-stage financing: objective to increase the supply of financing to new entrepreneurs and early-stage firms	100%
5. Business support for start-up and early-stage growth: objective to increase the amount and quality of business support to nascent and new entrepreneurs	92%
6. Policy for target groups: objective to increase the start-up rates of under-represented groups in the society or to increase the number of innovative entrepreneurs	85%

The total scores for each country in each policy-related area are presented in Table 2-4. We will refer to this table again in Chapter 3.

In the next six sections of this chapter, we discuss each of the framework areas. For each, we present our findings regarding government actions, a framework map of the collective policy measures/options, some illustrative examples from government practices, and a comparison across countries of the extent of their policy activity.

Table 2.4. Scoring of entrepreneurship policy comprehensiveness by country (in percentages)

Entrepreneurship Policy Lines and Measures	AU	CA	DK	FI	IS	IE	NL	NO	ES	SE	TW	UK	US	Avg
1. Promotion of entrepreneurship	62.5	43.8	56.3	68.8	12.5	37.5	37.5	12.5	50.0	75.0	87.5	100.0	87.5	56.3
2. Entrepreneurship in the education system	81.6	28.9	76.3	89.5	13.2	47.4	84.2	71.1	52.6	42.1	15.8	76.3	28.9	54.5
3. Easing entry, early-stage survival/growth, and exit (removing barriers)	77.3	65.9	93.2	65.9	34.1	70.5	79.5	61.4	79.5	65.9	47.7	93.2	100.0	72.0
4. Access to start-up, seed, and early-stage financing	60.0	90.0	80.0	86.7	76.7	83.3	90.0	66.7	93.3	80.0	90.0	90.0	100.0	83.6
5. Start-up and early-stage growth - business support	84.4	53.1	53.1	68.8	34.4	81.3	68.8	34.4	75.0	87.5	93.8	100.0	81.3	70.4
6. Policy for target groups	65.0	95.0	35.0	60.0	40.0	35.0	75.0	40.0	70.0	90.0	40.0	100.0	70.0	62.7
7. General policy approach/commitment	41.7	8.3	83.3	83.3	33.3	58.3	83.3	66.7	66.7	83.3	66.7	83.3	66.7	63.5
8. Policy structure for entrepreneurship	60.0	40.0	100.0	100.0	50.0	70.0	60.0	60.0	100.0	80.0	100.0	100.0	80.0	76.9
9. Performance tracking	58.3	50.0	91.7	83.3	16.7	25.0	100.0	16.7	58.3	100.0	58.3	100.0	83.3	64.7
Overall score: E-policy comprehensiveness (1-9)	70.6	56.5	73.8	76.6	35.0	60.7	77.1	51.9	72.0	73.4	61.2	92.0	77.1	67.5
Country ranking on policy comprehensiveness (1-9)	8	11	5	4	13	10	2	12	7	6	9	1	2	

1. Entrepreneurship Promotion

"Promotion" is an area of entrepreneurship policy worthy of further development because of the critical role it plays in fostering a culture supportive of entrepreneurship, changing "mind-sets", and influencing the Motivation component of the policy framework. Vesalainen and Pihkala (1999) indicate that the first stage of the individual entrepreneurial process begins with awareness that the option exists. This is followed by the formation of attitudes and beliefs, personal identification with the "entrepreneurial role", formation of the intent to start a business, the search for an idea, the business planning and preparation phases and, finally, the start-up. These researchers determined that a person's motivation to explore entrepreneurship is initially heavily influenced by external factors, like entrepreneurship culture or the existence of entrepreneurial "heroes", which bear an influence on each person's occupational entrepreneurial identity. The importance of role models in influencing higher entrepreneurial activity levels is consistently reinforced in GEM country reports. Both the level of respect for those who start a business and the prevalence of stories in the media about successful entrepreneurs are suggested by GEM researchers as indicators of an entrepreneurial culture. However, weak entrepreneurial cultures and a lack of role models continue to be reported deficiencies in Australia, Ireland, the UK and the Netherlands (Hindle and Rushworth, 2003; Fitzsimons and O'Gorman, 2003; Harding, 2003; Bosma and Wennekers, 2004), as well as in other GEM countries.

In spite of its importance in fostering a stronger entrepreneurial culture, entrepreneurship promotion is the least well-articulated area of entrepreneurship policy.[10] In government policy statements, references to entrepreneurship promotion seem to be a generic caption for "any and all" activities geared to stimulate entrepreneurial activity, including education in the schools, eliminating barriers to new business entry, and increasing the visibility of government programmes and services in support of start-ups. While these are all necessary pieces of the entrepreneurship policy framework, what we mean by "entrepreneurship promotion" is activity intended to create widespread awareness of the role of entrepreneurship and small business in the economy, to increase the visibility and profile of entrepreneurship, to generate more favourable attitudes towards it in society, and to reward and recognise entrepreneurs as role models.

Our original mapping of the policy measures and initiatives to achieve these promotional objectives, as collectively employed by the ten governments in our 2000-01 study, included five types: (1) sponsorship of television programmes and advertising campaigns; (2) entrepreneurship awards programmes; (3) promotion of entrepreneur role models through print publications; (4) sponsorship of national entrepreneurship-related conferences and regional events; and (5) use of radio, print media and webcasting to profile entrepreneurship issues. The framework map of these entrepreneurship promotion options is illustrated in Figure 2-5.

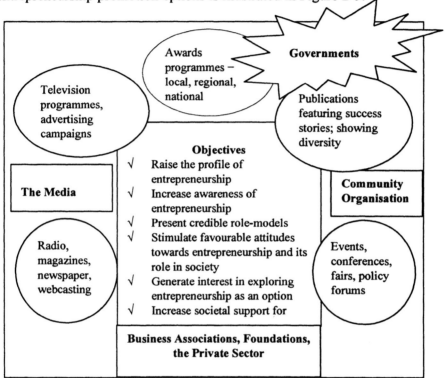

Figure 2.5. Framework map of entrepreneurship promotion options

Table 2-5 indicates overall percentages for country activity on each item in the entrepreneurship promotion policy scale. We found evidence in 85 percent of the countries that the national government has a stated objective to create more awareness of entrepreneurship or to promote a culture of entrepreneurship. This objective is articulated in terms of promoting more favourable attitudes towards entrepreneurship (e.g., Sweden, the UK); promoting entrepreneurship as a career alternative (e.g., Australia, Finland); promoting positive attitudes towards enterprise in the schools (e.g., Ireland and the UK); and promoting a stronger entrepreneurship culture (e.g., Denmark, the Netherlands, the UK). In only 38 percent of the cases is it evident that a specific budget has been allocated for awareness campaigns or specific promotional programmes. Promotional strategies often target youth, for example, the Australian government's National Awareness and

Innovation Strategy (NAIS) and the UK government's Enterprise Insight campaign, "Make Your Mark: Start Talking Ideas", aimed at the 14-25-year old age group. In fact, it is quite common for governments to tie their promotional objectives to specific awareness creating activities for school-aged youth and young people.

Table 2-5. Prevalence of entrepreneurship promotion policy measures in 13 countries

Promotion of entrepreneurship	% of countries
Is there a stated policy objective to increase broad-based awareness of entrepreneurship and to promote an entrepreneurial culture?	85%
Does the government sponsor events that profile entrepreneurship and provide start-up information?	85%
Does the government alone, or in partnership with private sector organisations, recognise entrepreneurs through national, high profile award programmes?	77%
Do these awards recognise diversity in entrepreneurship (e.g. women, ethnic minorities, youth, etc.) and success at different stages of business development, including start-ups, young and growing firms?	62%
Does the government engage with the mass media in the promotion of entrepreneurship?	54%
Does the government engage in activities to nurture the media to be more involved in covering the entrepreneurship story (e.g., seminars with reporters, frequent press releases and press conferences, story-feeds, etc.)?	38%
Is a portion of the central government's budget allocated for entrepreneurship promotion activities?	38%
Are efforts in place to track attitudes of the population towards entrepreneurship, awareness levels and levels of intent to start a business?	38%

Governments in almost all of the countries sponsor national events and activities to profile entrepreneurship. The Canadian, US, and Australian governments have been hosting an annual Small Business Week for several years; the US government hosts an annual Minority Enterprise Development Week; the Swedish government sponsors an annual Entrepreneurship Week in partnership with NUTEK and the Swedish Foundation for Small Business Research; the Finnish government hosts regular regional entrepreneurship forums; the Spanish government holds periodic "salons d'emprende"; the UK government has recently proclaimed an annual Enterprise Week to debut in the fall of 2004; and the Danish government has implemented a series of "road shows" in schools to raise awareness of entrepreneurship among senior secondary students.

Over three-quarters of the governments support national level entrepreneurship awards programmes. Examples are the President's Small Business Person of the Year Awards (the US), the Queen's Awards for Enterprise (the UK), the Golden Key Awards (Finland), the National

Enterprise Awards (Ireland), and the Danish Entrepreneur Award. Although not as pervasive across countries, these awards programmes will often recognise certain types of entrepreneurs (e.g., Canadian Woman Entrepreneur of the Year) or businesses at different stages of development (e.g., Australia's Micro-Business Award; Student Enterprise Award in Ireland; Taiwan's Rising Star Award; Spain's Young Entrepreneur Award).

Just over half of the governments appear to use the mass media to promote entrepreneurship, specifically television and radio, but only 38 percent take steps to nurture the media by providing entrepreneurship-related features and success story profiles. Mass media initiatives to promote entrepreneurship are most evident in Taiwan, the UK, the US, Canada and to some extent Finland. Activity of the Small and Medium Enterprise Administration (SMEA) in Taiwan illustrates the most ardent example of promotion as a sustained government policy priority and offers a good example of the use of radio and television.[11] The US is also an excellent example. There we find evidence of lots of nationally-driven efforts to promote entrepreneurship – celebratory events, awards programmes, regional seminars and conferences, and sponsorship of radio and television programmes – which are often carried out in partnerships with the private sector. Governments in Taiwan, the US and Finland seek to develop positive relationships with members of the media to encourage broader coverage of the entrepreneurship story. The US Small Business Administration Office of Advocacy, for one, routinely sends profiles of award winners to the media, as well as statistical information on the small business sector. Other countries have plans to be more active in this area. For example, according to their 2003 action plan for entrepreneurship, the Danish government will sponsor a national media campaign to thank its entrepreneurs (Ministry of Economy and Business Affairs, 2003).

It is common to find governments acting in partnership with the private sector to promote entrepreneurship. In the UK's Enterprise Insight campaign, the Department of Trade and Industry partners with the Confederation of British Industries, the Federation of Small Businesses, the British Chambers of Commerce, the Institute of Directors, the Prince's Youth Business Trust and Shell Livewire. In the implementation of its NAIS, the Australian Department of Industry, Tourism and Resources partners with the Young Entrepreneurs' Association, and in its Small Business Awards programme with Telstra. In Canada and the US, where there is pervasive media promotion of entrepreneurship, much of the activity is actually driven by the private sector, e.g., banks, large management consulting firms, telecommunications companies, and entrepreneur associations.

The policy comprehensiveness of entrepreneurship promotion measures varies considerably across governments (see Table 2-6). In most individual governments, the range of applied policy initiatives to promote entrepreneurship does not reflect the diversity demonstrated by the collective set of policy options in the framework map. Governments in the UK, the US and Taiwan employ the broadest number of possible options. The least number are evident in the government policies and practices of Norway, the Netherlands, Ireland and Iceland.

Table 2-6. Policy comprehensiveness ratings for entrepreneurship promotion items by country

UK	100.0%	AU	62.5%	ES	50.0%
TW	87.5%	DK	56.3%	CA	43.8%
US	87.5%			NL	37.5%
SE	75.0%			IE	37.5%
FI	68.8%			NO	12.5%
				IS	12.5%
Average score = 56.3%					

National GEM research teams have projects in all of our case countries. This means data is collected on attitudes towards entrepreneurship and nascent entrepreneur activity levels, but it does not appear that this information is always used by their respective governments as policy input. The UK government demonstrates the strongest example of efforts to track and measure changing attitudes of the population towards entrepreneurship. In a regular Household Survey of Entrepreneurship, the UK Small Business Service (SBS) monitors progress towards the Government's Public Service Agreement target of "increasing the number of people considering going into business" (Small Business Service, 2004d). The Survey measures peoples' attitudes, key influences and levels of enterprise activity; the main motivations and barriers to starting a business; and variations both between regions and demographic groups. It further provides evidence to support the development of the Small Business Services' core strategies of: (i) building an enterprise culture; (ii) encouraging a dynamic start-up market; and (iii) encouraging more enterprise within disadvantaged communities and under-represented groups.

An interesting type of entrepreneurship promotion activity is emerging in the US – the concept of promoting entrepreneurship among federal and state politicians and government officials. This private-sector driven effort began in 2000 with the establishment of the National Commission on Entrepreneurship (NCOE), funded for three years by the Kauffman Foundation. The NCOE ended in 2002 but its advocacy mandate was assumed by the Public Forum Institute which now coordinates the National Dialogue on Entrepreneurship.[12] The "dialogue" involves regular briefings of members of Congress and other officials on Capital Hill in Washington on the role of entrepreneurship in local communities and how federal policy issues can have a direct impact on entrepreneurs who assume the risk of starting a business, including reducing regulatory burdens, protecting intellectual property and effective technology transfer. The main thrust of this advocacy effort is to call attention to the policy challenge of stimulating higher levels of innovative, growth-oriented entrepreneurship, a topic we will discuss in more detail later in this chapter.

Before leaving this discussion, we make two final observations about promotion as an area of entrepreneurship policy. The first observation is that, although governments in most of our countries stress the importance of promoting an entrepreneurship culture, the countries where promotional activity is most pervasive are the ones with already strong entrepreneurship cultures and high SME density, business ownership levels, or nascent entrepreneur activity levels (e.g., Taiwan, Canada and the United States). The second observation is that high levels of awareness and positive public attitudes towards entrepreneurship do not necessarily lead to higher start-up rates. This observation is made in the Dutch and British GEM country reports (Bosma and Wennekers, 2004; Harding, 2003) and in the Routamaa (2003) report on Finland. So promotion of entrepreneurship needs to be supported by other policy initiatives.

We look next at the entrepreneurship education component of the Entrepreneurship Policy Measures framework.

2. Entrepreneurship Education

Fostering entrepreneurship education is an area of government policy worthy of considerably more strategic attention given the role of the education system in fostering cultural attitudes and preparing young people for future careers. It is a major component of both the Motivation and Skills areas of the entrepreneurship policy foundations.

When attempting to integrate entrepreneurship in the education system, the types of questions that have to be resolved are similar across countries. How is entrepreneurship education defined? What does entrepreneurship education entail? What should be taught at what level? How should it be taught? Who should teach it and what preparation do they need? What materials and resources need to be developed? How can these be shared? What extracurricular activities should be included? What partnerships are needed with the business community? How will outcomes be measured?

How much will it all cost? What is the role of a government's ministry of economic affairs or industry versus the role of its education ministry?

The framework map of collective measures employed by governments to implement entrepreneurship education initiatives at the elementary and secondary school level is presented in Figure 2-6.

When we completed our review of entrepreneurship policy in the first set of ten countries in 2000-01, seven governments had the stated objective to integrate entrepreneurship education in the school system. Only four had concrete national policy initiatives in place to achieve this objective: Australia, Finland, the Netherlands and the United Kingdom.

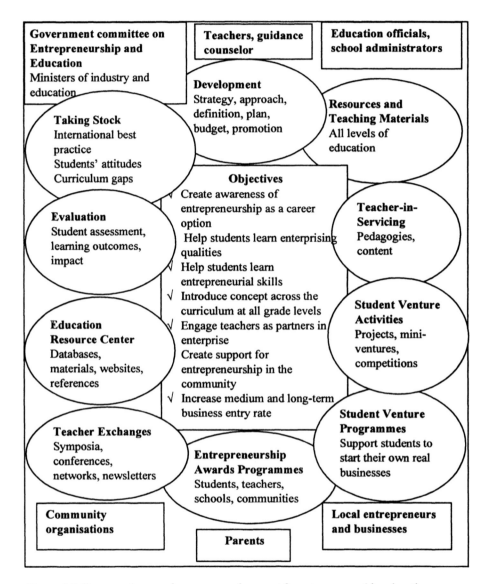

Figure 2.6. Framework map of measures and support for entrepreneurship education

National ministries of economic affairs or industry in these countries had decided to push the entrepreneurship education agenda forward for several reasons: to address high youth unemployment rates (Finland);˙to prepare the next generation for the probability of having self-employment as part of their career biography (the Netherlands); to influence longer-term increases in business entry and survival rates (Australia); or to build the base of an emerging "entrepreneurial economy" (the UK). Ministries responsible for economic affairs or industry had entered into discussions with ministries of education regarding the potential for including entrepreneurship-related outcomes in the national curriculum guidelines and had for the most part succeeded. Curricula and resource materials were being developed for all grade levels (from Kindergarten to upper secondary levels) and funding had been designated for pilot projects to introduce this material into classroom-based environments and for the training of teachers on how to introduce entrepreneurship concepts across the curriculum.

Lessons learned from the experiences of these four countries reveal a relatively consistent and shared view that entrepreneurship education includes both elements of enterprising behaviours and entrepreneurship skills, is appropriate for all grade levels, should employ a cross-disciplinary approach and be taught through many subject areas.[13] Furthermore, the successful implementation of a comprehensive entrepreneurship education programme requires:

- Inclusion of enterprise/entrepreneurship as a component in National Curriculum Guidelines;
- Development of curriculum, teaching resources, and teaching methods that emphasise student-centered learning and "hands-on" project-oriented activities;
- Professional development of teachers;
- Building of resource centers and networks for the exchange of best practice;
- Support of school administrators and education officials;
- Business-education partnerships and community support;
- Opportunities for students to experiment with venture projects and activities, including student venture programmes;
- Significant budget allocations; and
- Commitment from both the ministries of industry or economic affairs and education.

In our recent review of the situation in 13 countries, we found ten governments with national objectives for entrepreneurship education in either their entrepreneurship or innovation policies and seven with substantial national initiatives: Australia, Denmark, Finland, the Netherlands, Norway, Spain, and the UK. Table 2-7 identifies the major entrepreneurship education programmes in these seven countries. In all of these cases, implementation of the programme is a collaborative effort of two or more ministries, an important structural component to achieve a coordinated and comprehensive policy in the area.

Table 2-8 presents a tally of the percentages of countries with actions in the critical education areas. Although entrepreneurship education is a national policy objective in ten countries (77 percent), only 62 percent have a plan or strategy for making this happen; just more than half have undertaken a content analysis (taken stock) of the existing curriculum; less than half have managed to have entrepreneurship outcomes adopted as part of their National Curriculum Guidelines; less than a third deliver training programmes to prepare teachers in the instruction of entrepreneurship (or enterprise) curriculum; and only 15 percent appear to have a national action plan for the in-servicing of teachers.

Table 2-7. Entrepreneurship education programmes in selected countries

Country	Programme	Start Date	Collaborating Ministries
Australia	Enterprise Education in the Schools Programme	1996	Council of Ministers of Education, Employment, Training and Youth Affairs
Denmark	Action Plan to promote entrepreneurship in schools (element in the 2002 Better Education Action Plan)	2002 (2-year project)	Ministry of Education; Ministry of Science, Knowledge and Innovation
Finland	Entrepreneurship Spearhead Project (continuation of programme started in 2000)	2002	Ministry of Trade and Industry; Ministry of Education plus others
The Netherlands	National Entrepreneurship Education Programme	2000	Ministry of the Economy; Ministry of Education
Norway	National Strategy Plan for Entrepreneurship in Education	2002	Ministry of Trade and Industry; Ministry of Education and Research; Ministry of Local Government and Regional Development
Spain	Royal Decrees on entrepreneurship in the schools (compulsory inclusion at all levels)	2003	Ministry of Education, Culture and Sport; Ministry of Economy
The UK	Enterprise Education Programme	2004	Small Business Service; Department of Education and Skills

We do, however, see evidence that curriculum is being developed in over 75 percent of the countries and courses and material are being taught to students at the elementary, secondary and vocational/technical school levels in certain regions and schools. Even if the training of teachers is not systematic, some governments have developed teaching packages for schools and guidelines for teachers (e.g., Spain, Norway, Australia, and the UK) and plans are underway in countries such as Norway, Finland and Denmark to introduce entrepreneurship as a course in teacher training colleges and as part of teacher continuing education programmes. Governments in all of the countries promote and support the activities of international organisations such as Junior Achievement or Young Enterprise, providing funding so more students can be exposed to these practical programmes in more classrooms and schools. The Mini-Enterprises in the Schools project is also very popular in the European countries.

Table 2-8. Prevalence of actions to integrate entrepreneurship education in the school system in 13 countries

Entrepreneurship in the education system	% of countries
Is there a policy objective to integrate entrepreneurship into all levels of the education system?	77%
Has there been a study (stock-taking) of the extent to which entrepreneurship is included in education at the school level?	54%
Is entrepreneurship included as an element/outcome in National Education Curriculum Guidelines?	46%
Is there a Steering Group/Committee on Entrepreneurship and Education with representatives from the ministries of Industry and Education, and the private sector to oversee integration of entrepreneurship in the school?	46%
Is there a plan/strategy to integrate elements of entrepreneurship into all levels of the educational system in a cross-disciplinary fashion?	62%
Elementary level?	54%
Secondary level?	77%
Vocational/technical level?	69%
Is there a plan to promote the teaching of entrepreneurship in the elementary, secondary and vocational/technical education system?	62%
Is there an Action Plan for the in-servicing of teachers?	15%
Are training programmes being delivered regionally to introduce educators to the strategies of teaching courses/modules on entrepreneurship/enterprise?	31%
Have curriculum and learning materials being developed for each level of the education system?	77%
Do mechanisms exist for the national sharing of information and experience (e.g., educators' conferences, seminars, databases of resource materials)?	62%
Is there public funding support for extra-curricular entrepreneurial activities (e.g., JA, Young Enterprise) to support student venturing?	100%
Are entrepreneurship courses widely offered to college and university students?	100%
To engineering, science and other students?	92%
Does the government provide incentives for universities to broaden these programmes?	46%
Does the government, alone or with private sector partners sponsor national student business plan competitions?	62%
Is there a national budget allocation for development and implementation of entrepreneurship/enterprise education initiatives and programmes?	54%

Entrepreneurship courses are being taught at a number of universities in each of the countries and efforts are in place to include entrepreneurship in vocational/technical schools and programmes. At the post-secondary level, governments are funding business plan competitions, campus-based incubators, entrepreneurship learning programmes for new graduates, and seed capital programmes.

The overall policy comprehensiveness scores for the 13 countries in this area of the entrepreneurship policy framework are presented in Table 2-9.

Table 2-9. Policy comprehensive ratings for entrepreneurship education items by country

FI	89.5%	ES	52.6%	SE	42.1%
NL	84.2%	IE	47.4%	CA	28.9%
AU	81.6%			US	28.9%
UK	76.3%			TW	15.8%
DK	76.3%			IS	13.2%
NO	71.1%				
Average score = 54.5%					

Countries with low scores are likely worth commenting on. In Ireland, many school-aged youth are exposed to an excellent entrepreneurship education initiative offered in schools through the Young Entrepreneurs Association, but the government has not launched a national action plan to formally integrate entrepreneurship in the curriculum. There are some excellent initiatives to imbed entrepreneurship education in the primary and secondary school systems in certain regions of Canada, Sweden and the US, but national policy plans have not been adopted by their national governments, entrepreneurship is not included in National Curriculum Guidelines, there are no coherent strategies to train teachers and so on. The Taiwan government has the stated objective to compile entrepreneurship-related curricula and teaching materials but primarily at the post-secondary level and efforts have not really gotten started yet. The Icelandic government has introduced entrepreneurial activities as an elective module in the General School Curriculum and implemented it into about a third of the system but does not have a comprehensive national initiative.

Recent developments in elementary and secondary school level entrepreneurship education

Since our studies in 2000-2002, major developments have occurred in the entrepreneurship education area. Entrepreneurship education is a component of the EU Multiannual Programme on Entrepreneurship and SMEs (2001-05) and since mid-2001 member States are required to report on their activity and to participate in the BEST Procedure programme on entrepreneurship education and training. Fostering an entrepreneurial mindset (entrepreneurial attitudes and skills) among young people is one of the five priorities in the European Action Agenda for Entrepreneurship (European Commission, 2004a) and the Commission is calling upon Member States to integrate entrepreneurship education into all schools' curricula and to provide schools with the proper support to allow them to put in place effective and high quality education schemes. Expert informants in almost every GEM country stress the importance of integrating entrepreneurship throughout the education system, as do official government policy documents in most countries. But many gaps remain unaddressed.

In 2004, the EU published an overview of activities in European countries to promote entrepreneurial attitudes and skills through primary and secondary education (European Commission, 2004c). In a chapter on building a policy for entrepreneurship education, the report commented on the newness of this area for Europe, stating that little is being done at the moment. Entrepreneurship is neither required nor promoted in the curriculum, there are few efforts to revise the curriculum to look for opportunities to offer entrepreneurship as a subject or a cross-curricular theme, and planned new initiatives were not viewed as being sufficient to make entrepreneurship education widespread in the school system and generally available to students. The review concluded that most students do not have the possibility to take part in entrepreneurship courses and programmes. Lack of teacher training materials and provision, limited exchange and dissemination of good practices, inadequate efforts to integrate extra-curricular programmes into the education stream, and lack of a coherent framework for entrepreneurship education were among the major barriers cited. According to the findings of the report, major incentives are needed to motivate teachers, schools and departments of education. Additionally, the report noted the need for development of performance indicators to measure the success of efforts to integrate entrepreneurship education and suggested several possibilities.

The challenges seem to be well-defined. Now the task is to engage central/national governments in development and implementation of strategic actions. With adoption of the EU Action Agenda for Entrepreneurship we can expect these developments to accelerate. In the meantime, we noted that several European governments in our studies, including the UK, Denmark, Finland, Norway and Spain, now include entrepreneurship or enterprise-related outcomes in their National Curriculum Guidelines. The UK government has recently announced a new £60 million Enterprise Education entitlement that will provide all Key Stage 4 pupils with the equivalent of five days of enterprise learning (Small Business Service, 2004a). Enterprise Advisors will also work with teachers in 1,000 secondary schools to encourage enterprise practice among teachers and pupils in the most disadvantaged regions.

Although there are many challenges to the process of integrating entrepreneurship in the school system, the examples offered by Australia, Finland, the Netherlands, and the UK demonstrate that initial barriers can be overcome. Communities, schools, education officials, and even parents may, at first, resist efforts to teach entrepreneurship-related curriculum. Finnish officials overcame this initial resistance by producing a series of local newspaper articles on the importance of entrepreneurship to the Finnish economy. These served to "ready" the community for entrepreneurship in the schools. In the Netherlands, the Dutch Ministry of Economic Affairs launched an €8 million subsidy programme to provide incentives to members of the education community to pilot entrepreneurship projects. From 2000-03, 130 projects were developed in the various educational sectors, including curriculum and resource materials for different grade levels and entrepreneurship activities in the schools. A database of existing "best-practice" projects is now being promoted for adoption and replication throughout the education system. An "entrepreneurship road show in education" is currently being planned to promote the teaching of entrepreneurship in schools. One of the objectives of this initiative is to involve entrepreneurs in school visits so students can learn lessons about the opportunities provided by independent entrepreneurship. These examples also demonstrate that it is possible to overcome perceived difficulties in developing collaborative partnerships between ministries of economic affairs or industry and education to integrate entrepreneurship in the curriculum.

Entrepreneurship education challenges at the post-secondary level

Universities in all of the countries offer at least some courses in entrepreneurship and there are indications that these courses are available to engineering, science and other non-business students in some universities in almost all of the countries, although to varying degrees. There was evidence in only seven of the countries that the ministry responsible for small business, entrepreneurship or innovation provides incentives to universities for the broadening of these programmes: Denmark, Finland, Ireland, the Netherlands, Norway, Sweden and the UK. The Danish government has earmarked DKK 40 million to establish an Entrepreneurship Academy to offer credit courses in entrepreneurship to tertiary students (tender issued May 2004); the Finnish government is funding a trial to offer a polytechnic post-graduate degree in small business and entrepreneurship know-how; the Irish government provides funding to all universities and Institutes of Technology for the establishment of campus incubators and delivery of the

Graduate Enterprise Platform to students and researchers who want to start high-potential enterprises;[14] the Dutch government has funded several universities to implement activities in favour of entrepreneurship; the Norwegian government supports the Norwegian School of Entrepreneurship (a collaboration of five universities) and five ministries are cooperating in the Dynamic Local School and Entrepreneurship project, which among other things, will develop university-level courses emphasising entrepreneurship and business formation; the Swedish government has funded a three-year project to establish municipal colleges of entrepreneurship and technology where women as well as men can be encouraged to engage in technology-based entrepreneurship; and the UK government is very much involved in advancing entrepreneurship course developments within the university environment as part of both its small business and innovation agendas. Entrepreneurship education was given a high priority in the government's 2001 *White Paper on Enterprise, Skills and Innovation*[15] and the Department of Education and Skills has funded a number of pilots at post-secondary institutions to assess the extent of and potential for self-employment as a career objective for graduates, the start-up patterns and experiences of graduates, and the characteristics of successful graduate start-ups (Graduate Start-up Scheme). Thirteen Science Enterprise Centers have been funded to partner with university Business and Management Schools to develop curriculum materials and case studies to aid in teaching the management of high-tech, fast-growth enterprises as well as to provide entrepreneurship skills to science and engineering graduates. In line with the UK government's objective to increase the number of students and recent graduates who give serious thought to entrepreneurship as a career, the Department of Trade and Industry is now launching a Council for Graduate Entrepreneurship to encourage universities and other post-secondary institutions to incorporate training in business start-up skills in the curricula and to investigate gaps in the provision of information, support, and advice and financial barriers that may impede graduates from starting a business (Small Business Service, 2004a). Efforts to introduce all students to entrepreneurship-related courses are expected to accelerate.

There is surprisingly little systematic and rigorous research on the propensity of university students to become entrepreneurs following graduation. A notable exception is Finnie et al. (2002) who conducted a longitudinal study of the entry of Canadian university graduates into self-employment. They found that five years after graduation self-employment rates were 9.9 percent to 11.1 percent for male graduates (depending on the programme of study and degree level) and 5.3 percent to 6.7 percent for female graduates. The self-employment status was generally associated with enhanced labour market outcomes and greater worker satisfaction than paid employment. The incidence of self-employment among Canadian university graduates has been rising since 1995. There is also relatively little research on the actual impact of university-based entrepreneurship education (Gillen et al., 1996). What limited research does exist suggests that the propensity to be self-employed is positively correlated with the number of entrepreneurship/ small business courses a student takes and that the greater the number of courses taken the greater the likelihood of self-employment. One of the most systematic studies by Charney and Libecap (2000) found that, compared to other business graduates, entrepreneurship graduates among the almost 2,500 alumni of the Berger Entrepreneurship Program at the University of Arizona were three times more likely to start new businesses, were three times more likely to be self-employed, had annual incomes that were 27 percent higher, owned 62 percent more assets, and were more satisfied with their jobs. Entrepreneurship education increased the probability of being instrumentally involved in a new business venture by 25 percent and increased the annual income of graduates by US$12,000. The entrepreneurship graduates were more likely to start or work for high-technology companies and to be involved in new product development and R&D activities. The study also found that small firms employing entrepreneurship graduates had greater sales and employment growth than those that employed non-entrepreneurship graduates. The findings of this research underscore the advantages of entrepreneurship education – for both graduates and the companies they might work for.

Unfortunately the majority of university students do not have the opportunity to take entrepreneurship courses. Even in the US, which is considered the world leader in university entrepreneurship education,[16] courses are mostly restricted to business students, of which only 16 percent nationally are enrolled in such courses. Graduates who start businesses without the benefit of having taken any entrepreneurship-related courses are less likely to have the know-how and knowledge to fully develop their businesses and thus economic development opportunities are lost. There is general agreement that emphasis on opportunity recognition, business planning, marketing and financial skills would be an advantageous complement to the technical skill and knowledge base of college and university students, but there are many challenges in the process of infusing entrepreneurship across disciplines.

Governments have a growing interest in the role of universities in economic development and, thus, in entrepreneurship. The main reason for this interest is linked directly to realising the aims of their innovation agendas. Studies examining the current state of affairs in universities have been conducted in the United States and the United Kingdom.[17] Both the US-based National Governors' Association and the National Commission on

Entrepreneurship have produced studies on the university-industry technology transfer interface, including an assessment of the extent to which universities invest in entrepreneurial support activities.[18] If innovation drives productivity and economic growth; if new, knowledge-based firms are drivers of innovation; if knowledge-based firms germinate from knowledge environments; and if governments want to realise more gains from their investments in university research, then it makes sense to target universities for gains in innovation performance. The Kauffman Foundation notes that investors seeking out start-up ideas are increasingly targeting universities and that a host of new investment organisations specialising in campus start-ups are springing up in the United States.

Several governments are engaged in spearheading initiatives to stimulate more commercialisation of university-based research, foster more spin-off firms and encourage both faculty and students to become entrepreneurs. Many of these efforts are targeted at science, technology, and engineering faculties. The UK government is particularly aggressive in this regard. Since 1999, almost £45 million has been allocated to university funding under the Science Enterprise Challenge to establish world-class centers for the commercialisation of research, foster scientific entrepreneurialism and incorporate enterprise teaching into the higher education science and engineering curricula (Small Business Service, 2001). Governments in Ireland, Taiwan, Finland, the UK, the Netherlands, Australia and other countries have funded programmes for the development of university-based incubators so students, faculty members and staff will have access to start-up space, business advice, mentoring and a rich circle of researchers, technologists, venture capitalists, business consultants, advisers and experienced mentor entrepreneurs. In some cases, funds have been allocated for University Innovation Centers, as well as for the establishment of technology transfer and university-industry liaison offices. Impact studies of university spin-off activity offer a rich area for future research.

In addition to the funding of incubation infrastructure, governments are also involved in creating entrepreneurship awareness among students and providing other academic spin-off supports (i.e., seed capital funds, mentoring, intellectual property advice, and assistance with prototype development). In the category of awareness, the most common form of support is for business plan competitions. Governments in Sweden and Finland provide sponsorship support for Venture Cup, a national annual business plan in which thousands of university students participate. The Dutch Ministry of Economic Affairs funds a New Venture Business Plan competition that is open to all post-secondary students and Enterprise Ireland sponsors a similar competition for the best business plans developed by university and college students. As part of the Australian government's 2001

Innovation Strategy, *Backing Australia's Ability*, a budget allocation was made for a Business Plan Competition Support Programme to help tertiary educational institutions implement student business plan competitions.[19] This is intended to raise the profile of entrepreneurship and facilitate the establishment of new start-ups.

Moving Forward with University Entrepreneurship Programmes

The Kauffman Foundation (2001) has identified a number of opportunities and gaps vis-à-vis further adoption of entrepreneurship education in American universities. This list is not unique to the United States, many points of which are reinforced by experts in other of our case study countries and articulated in various country GEM reports during the past four years. First of all, scholars and industry observers expect continued growth in overall interest in entrepreneurship, including a growing demand from students for entrepreneurship content in their courses. However, there is a particular untapped opportunity for integrating entrepreneurship in non-business core programmes, like engineering, science, and the arts (Kauffman Foundation, 2001, p. 17). Some American leaders in entrepreneurship education believe it is time for Entrepreneurship Studies to be set up as a discipline within the universities separate from the Business Schools where is it currently located. This would allow students from a wide range of disciplines to access entrepreneurship programmes and enable these "Entrepreneurship Schools" greater flexibility in offering services to all faculties within the university. This concept is the early stages of being realised by eight US universities with the aid of matched-funding grants (totalling US$25 million) from the Kauffman Foundation. These eight campuses have committed themselves to make entrepreneurship education available across-campus enabling any student in every field to study entrepreneurship and have access to entrepreneurial training. Entrepreneurship will be offered as a minor to all undergraduate students, more professors will be trained to teach entrepreneurship and students will be encouraged to run businesses on campus (the concept of "dorm enterprises"). The creation of these new interdisciplinary programmes is expected to transform the way universities prepare students for entrepreneurship. As Carl Schramm, president and CEO of the Kauffman Foundation states, "If roughly one in ten Americans is trying to start a business at any given time, shouldn't we be preparing them to succeed?"[20] This US initiative is being driven by a private sector foundation, as opposed to government, but we felt it was worthy of noting because of its innovativeness.

Many barriers still exist to the infusion of entrepreneurship courses across disciplines. Primary among these are the lack of resource and support materials and training for non-business instructors. At the college level, instructors also complain about lack of time to fit an entrepreneurship module in already crammed technical programme areas. Among the main barriers to the broad-based inclusion of entrepreneurship in US-based university education, Kuratko (2003) emphasises the following:

- The ongoing "waging war" for complete respectability and leadership of the entrepreneurship area (entrepreneurship may be legitimised but is not fully respected as an academic discipline);
- The shortage of entrepreneurship faculty at every academic rank;
- The need for more business schools to develop sound PhD programmes in entrepreneurship;
- Slow adoption of innovative instructional technologies to deliver entrepreneurship courses to students (e.g., video conferencing, web-streaming of video case studies, online coaching of students); and
- The push for leading-edge entrepreneurship researchers to publish in mainstream management journals.

According to the Kauffman Foundation, the field of entrepreneurship research must advance further if it is to fully build legitimacy as a discipline. This means developing more theories and becoming more quantitative and scientific. Awards for excellent research in entrepreneurship and recognition of entrepreneurship scholarship are needed to enhance the dignity of the field. The FSF-NUTEK International Award for Entrepreneurship and Small Business Research is an excellent initiative in this regard.[21] Since 1996, eleven internationally renowned researchers have received the award including David Birch, Arnold Cooper, David Storey, Ian MacMillan, Howard Aldrich, David Audretsch and Zoltan Acs, Giacomo Becattini and Charles Sabel, William Baumol, and Paul Reynolds.

In terms of future challenges, more opportunities must be identified to meet the growing demand for entrepreneurship researchers and professors. This includes expanding PhD programmes in Entrepreneurship and supporting and encouraging young faculty in the field. More efforts are needed to educate and in-service the growing number of regular and adjunct professors in the teaching of entrepreneurship. Professors need more pedagogical tools if they are to adopt more experiential learning approaches, build venturing into graduation requirements for students who really want to become entrepreneurs and use new technologies to deliver entrepreneurship education programmes. Opportunities also exist to develop new course offerings "about" entrepreneurship for public administration and economics students (i.e., emphasise policy issues) and other students who may enter careers in the entrepreneurial support environment (e.g., small business counseling, community enterprise, micro-lending, or angel investment). Good practices in some of these areas are profiled in Stevenson and Lundström (2002).

Exposing students to entrepreneurship in the education system is considered to be a very important factor in improving the overall entrepreneurial culture and capacity of a nation, but to achieve medium and long term increases in the rate of entrepreneurial activity, other adjustments in the support environment will inevitably have to be made. Is it relatively easy to start a business? Is there a clear pathway into self-employment? Are there adequate sources of financing for new businesses? Are existing business support organisations predisposed to providing assistance to nascent entrepreneurs? Is this assistance readily accessible? Are there special initiatives to address the challenges and barriers faced by young entrepreneurs (e.g., lack of credibility, experience, collateral)? Are there hidden disincentives to the self-employment option in the taxation and social security systems? These aspects of the entrepreneurship policy framework must also be addressed. We next look at the regulatory and business environment affecting the entry of new firms.

3. Reducing Barriers to Entry, Early-Stage Growth and Exit

Much of the focus on barriers to entry is being driven by the policy research, discussion and other efforts of the OECD and the EU (OECD, 1998, 1999; European Commission, 1998b, 2002c). Both organisations have been advocating in favour of actions to reduce or modify regulations that directly or indirectly discourage the creation and expansion of smaller enterprises or that create obstacles to the formation of new and innovative enterprises. The European Union continues to call for the adoption of proactive initiatives to facilitate the creation of new enterprises (i.e., single locations for registration purposes, single registration documents, single business identification numbers, and sharing of data between public authorities involved in business registration).

There are a number of possible areas where a national/central government can make adjustments in its administrative, regulatory and legislative systems to facilitate entrepreneurial activity. Certain actions can be taken to reduce the time and cost of registering businesses, while others will improve the opportunities entrepreneurs have to start and grow businesses (e.g., more open competition policies, tax breaks). Policy options in these areas could influence people's motivation to start a business as well as create better opportunity conditions. In some countries, mostly European, governments are examining labour market, social security, taxation, and bankruptcy regulations for the "quiet disincentives" which act to inadvertently discourage individuals from moving into self-employment from employment or unemployment. The major objective here is to adjust the features of these systems that negatively influence the risk-reward assessment of entrepreneurship as an occupational choice. The majority of existing governments' efforts, however, relate to Opportunity rather than Motivation measures.

Based on the collective practices of governments in our first study of 10 countries, we identified four broad categories of possible policy actions:

A. Ease of starting a business: simplifying start-up procedures and processes;

B. Legislation affecting entry and exit: adjusting laws related to competition, the formation of limited liability companies, bankruptcy procedures, inheritance laws, and the filing of patents and intellectual property protection;

C. Labour issues: creating more flexibility in labour market regulations and requirements; and

D. Taxation: improving the taxation regime.

The framework map of entrepreneurship policy responses in these areas is modelled in Figure 2-7.

Almost all of the governments have initiatives to review and reduce administrative burdens on SMEs. These efforts are driven by ongoing evidence that administrative burdens bear proportionately heavier on smaller firms and contribute to the lower productivity of SMEs compared to large firms. Over two-thirds of the governments have established better regulation units to monitor the impact of new legislation and regulations on small firms and most use some form of business impact assessment test to measure the direct and indirect costs of proposed new legislation and regulations on SMEs. But since this book is about entrepreneurship policy rather than SME policy, we do not go into an elaborate discussion of government actions to reduce SME burdens, choosing instead to zero-in on those policy measures identified as part of government strategies to create dynamic start-up markets.

Most of the 13 governments have a stated objective to reduce barriers to entry and exit, although the policy actions of some are clearly more intense than others, and governments, of course, differ considerably in their approaches. In Finland, the government's objective is to eliminate obstacles to entrepreneurship, to take measures to make it easier for enterprises to enter the market and to remove barriers to their operation; in the Netherlands, it is to eliminate barriers to entry and ease administrative burden for new entrepreneurs; in the UK, it is to reduce all barriers to entrepreneurship and to set out a legislative framework supportive of enterprise and the encouragement of risk-taking; and in Spain, it is to stimulate the creation of new businesses through simplification of start-up procedures.

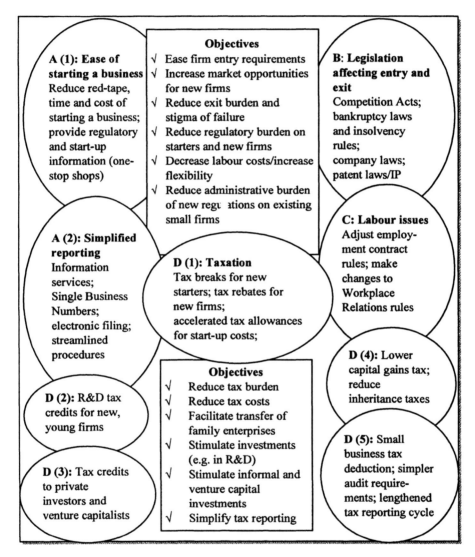

Figure 2.7. Framework map of policy options to ease entry, growth and exit

The policy comprehensiveness ratings for each item in this area of entrepreneurship policy are presented in Table 2-10 and discussed in more detail in the next section.

Table 2-10. Prevalence of measures to ease entry, growth and exit of firms in 13 countries

Easing entry, early-stage survival/growth, and exit (removing barriers)	% of countries
Is there a stated policy objective to ease the process of starting a business or to remove disincentives to the start-up decision?	92%
Has the government reviewed the time and cost of starting a new business?	85%
Do efforts exist to examine barriers to entry and exit with a view to eliminating unnecessary barriers?	77%
Have business registration procedures been streamlined for new firms?	100%
Does the government use a Single Business Number for new company registrations and ongoing dealings with government departments/ agencies?	85%
Is there a single point of entry where new entrepreneurs can access information about government regulations and obtain advice?	100%
Does the government have initiatives to reduce/relax administrative burden for newly-started enterprises (e.g., exemptions from certain regulatory obligations in the start-up phase)?	54%
Has Company Law been reviewed to reduce the time and cost of incorporation (e.g., simpler filing/reporting processes; lower paid-in capital requirements; lower cost)?	85%
Has the government reviewed its Competition Policy to ensure open competition for the entry of new firms in all sectors? To protect small firms from unfair competition vis-à-vis large firms? Public sector enterprises?	92%
Have bankruptcy laws been adjusted to reduce the penalties of "failure" and increase an entrepreneur's opportunity to restart (e.g., more time to restructure; shortened discharge periods)?	69%
Has the government reviewed barriers to the transfer of businesses?	77%
Has the government undertaken actions to simplify patent processes and strengthen intellectual property and protection policies?	77%
Has there been a review of any biases in labour market policies that favour paid versus self-employment? Is there provision for flexible employment contracts to allow people freedom to move into and out of self-employment?	62%
Has there been a review of non-wage costs and administrative burdens that prevent new firms from hiring their first employee?	38%
Does the central government offer concessional or favourable tax rates to newly-started firms (e.g., VAT exemptions; income tax rebates; reduced corporate tax; accelerated capital cost allowances)?	77%
Do special tax credits exist to encourage R&D activity by new/small firms?	77%
Are tax incentives used to encourage informal investment in new and growth-oriented firms?	62%
Are tax incentives used to encourage venture capital investments in early-stage ventures (e.g., tax concessions; pooled capital funds)?	62%
Has the government lowered its Capital Gains Tax to encourage private investment?	69%
Has the government acted to reduce SME administrative burden?	92%
Has the government set up a "better regulation unit" to monitor the impact of all new legislation and regulations on new and small firms?	69%
Are business impact assessment tests used to measure the costs of proposed new legislations/regulations, and affects on barriers to entry and growth?	77%

A: Ease of starting a business

All of the governments have taken actions to streamline their business registration procedures. They have moved to one-stop shops or "single entry points" to facilitate the business registration process and to provide more readily accessible information about government regulations. Efforts are underway to reduce both the time and cost of starting a new business by simplifying regulatory and administrative processes, particularly in countries where these barriers are highest. In countries where it is not difficult or costly to start a business, governments are, of course, not focusing as greatly on this area of policy (e.g., Australia, the US and Canada), but, like in the others, taking steps to examine and reduce any undue administrative, red-tape and paper work burden for existing SMEs.

Governments in most countries have adopted single business numbers and electronic processes for dealings with the business community on registration and regulatory issues, including payment of tax obligations. Just over half of the governments have put measures into place to reduce or relax the administrative burden on new firms by exempting them from certain regulatory obligations during the start-up phase, but these relate mostly to reducing reporting requirements.

B: Legislation affecting entry and exit

Several of the governments are reviewing (or have already done so) the range of legislative areas affecting new business entry: competition policy; company law; bankruptcy legislation; and patent law.

Almost all governments are doing work in the area of Competition policy. The objective is to enable new firms to enter the market in all sectors of economic activity and for small firms to be able to compete on a fair basis with large private sector firms and public sector enterprises. The Dutch government formed an Inter-ministerial Commission on Market Regulation in 2003 and a Bill has been drafted to improve efficiencies in the Competition Act. The goal is to achieve more liberalisation in certain sectors, open up previously closed sectors (e.g., healthcare, public housing, professional services) and remove restrictive ground rules and other barriers to competition. In the UK, major provisions were made in 1998 to guard against anti-competition agreements and abuses of dominance. The Danish government is examining the effects of State aid on market distortions and implementing a range of initiatives to open up new markets and increase competition in service areas historically provided for by public enterprises.

Governments in Australia, Iceland and Canada monitor unfair trading practices and the Icelandic government is seeking to reduce state ownership in certain sectors. The Irish government did a major review of its Competition Law in 2000 and continues to work on the regulation of markets. Even the US has an ongoing government process to reduce barriers to entry through more open competition.

Updating their laws regarding the formation of limited liability companies is also a priority of almost all of the governments. These efforts are most pronounced in the UK, Ireland, and Spain, although governments in Denmark, Taiwan, and Finland have also simplified the company incorporation process by reducing the number of required shareholders and complexities in filing procedures and reporting and auditing requirements. The Danish government has recently drafted a new Company Act that is under review. In most cases, incorporation procedures were initially constructed with large firms in mind. Many of these requirements were inappropriate in the small firm context; changes will reduce the complexity and cost of incorporation so more new and small firms can become limited liability companies.

It should be noted, however, that the costs associated with business incorporation vary widely across countries. These costs are nominal in the UK, Ireland, the US, Canada and Australia, but the paid-in capital requirements in certain countries will still present barriers for many new entrepreneurs. In Denmark, for example, it costs approximately US$18,000 to capitalise a limited company (capital to be held on deposit); in Sweden the paid-in capital requirement is about US$10,000.

Another legislative area affecting business dynamics pertains to bankruptcy procedures. Protecting entrepreneurs and their firms as well as company creditors is seen as a major policy issue by governments in the UK, the Netherlands, Spain and Sweden. Several governments have taken actions to reform their insolvency procedures so troubled firms have more of an opportunity to restructure rather than going into bankruptcy. Even in cases where the business cannot be "saved", bankruptcy measures should not be so stringent as to prevent the "failed" entrepreneurs from having the chance to start another business, so governments are also taking steps to reduce discharge periods to three years or less. The UK's 2002 Enterprise Act is a case in point. This new bankruptcy regime allows a "swifter fresh start" for entrepreneurs who fail through "no fault of their own". The fear of punitive bankruptcy laws is believed to be a factor in the decision of many potential entrepreneurs NOT to start a business (Boston Consulting Group, 2002). Many governments, like that in the UK, are keen to reduce this "stigma of failure" because it is a deterrent to new business entry.

The next area of legislation is that affecting the transfer of family businesses to the next generation. This is seen as a particularly important entrepreneurship policy issue because of the large number of business owners in many countries who will reach retirement age within the next 10 years. Over 40 percent of Sweden's business owners are over 51 years of age. This corresponds to about 200,000 companies whose owners will have reached retirement age by around 2015.[22] The Dutch government estimates that 18,000 business transfers every year can be expected in the Netherlands and that a successful transfer retains an average of five jobs (while starters create an average of two jobs).[23] The European Commission estimates that 10 percent of the business transfers in Europe lead to the unnecessary winding up of a business because of inadequate preparation for succession, inability to sell the business, or punitive inheritance taxes (European Commission, 2002d). Consequently we found evidence of concrete policy actions in this area in 9 of the 13 countries.

The most common action was to make modifications to the taxation of intergenerational business transfers. The US government was planning to permanently repeal the "death tax", which would allow family-owned businesses to be passed from one generation to the next without having to sell assets to pay punitive taxes (2004 proposal), saving family-owned businesses an estimated US$104 billion in 10 years. Governments in Sweden, Spain, Finland, Ireland, Iceland and Australia were also implementing various actions (or had already done so) to effect a reduction in the amount of Gift, Inheritance, or Capital Gains Tax due when a family business changes hands or when the owner passes into retirement; this issue was under review in the UK and the Netherlands.

The most comprehensive set of policy actions to ease the transfer of family-owned businesses is found in the Netherlands and Spain. Simplifying the business transfer process is one of the three action priorities in the Dutch government's entrepreneurship policy platform (Ministry of Economic Affairs, 2003a). Initiatives to overcome the barriers identified as being the most problematic include an awareness campaign to prompt entrepreneurs over the age of 50 to start thinking about succession planning; the offering of free advice through the Chambers of Commerce on succession issues; streamlining of fiscal policies related to the procedures for the valuation of companies after the owner's death; and matchmaking events to bring sellers and potential buyers of businesses together. The government's goal is to reach at least 10 percent of the potential market with these policy measures.

In Spain, a working group of experts from the Ministry of the Economy and the Ministry of Justice was created in 2001 to study all issues affecting family-owned enterprises. Legislative reform was approved in March 2003, Inheritance and Gift Tax reductions were put into place and the Ministry of the Economy published a Guide for family-owned SMEs that provides relevant information on the forms of establishment of this type of business, family agreements, succession issues and the settlement of disputes (Ministry of the Economy, 2003).

In light of growing demands for the commercialisation of research and innovative technologies, many of these governments have also started to examine intellectual property policies and patent laws and the extent to which these favour the formation and early-stage development of new innovative, technology-oriented businesses.

C: Labour issues

Governments in eight of the countries were examining biases in their labour market and employment policies that might inadvertently favour paid versus self-employment, but only five appeared to be reviewing possible barriers faced by new firms in hiring their first employees (e.g., non-wage costs, the level of administrative complexity). For example, in Finland, 75 percent of SMEs employ no more than two employees yet they must conform to collective agreements and are bound by law regarding use of fixed-term employment contracts. This presents little flexibility in hiring practices and discourages small firms from hiring employees because it is expensive to downsize. One of the big issues in European countries is the fact that self-employed people lose social security benefits. This poses a large disincentive for people considering entrepreneurship, but most European governments have not been able to arrive at a policy solution.

In terms of existing practices, the Dutch government is evaluating the Working Conditions Act (2004) with a view to simplification and deregulation and considering a tax facility so small businesses can deduct employee dismissal costs. The Swedish government has identified areas where entrepreneurs need to be put on an equal footing with employed people and are reviewing ways to encourage more labour force mobility. The Australian government has amended its Workplace Relations Act to allow more flexible work arrangements. The Norwegian government has made changes to social security protection that permits self-employed women the same maternity benefits as employed women (all other labour market policies are under review as part of the Innovation Policy).

In countries, such as Canada, the US, Taiwan and Denmark, there are already relatively flexible labour market rules with few barriers to the hiring of new employees.

D: Taxation

Governments use the taxation system to facilitate the entry and growth of new firms in three different ways. About three-quarters of the governments offer concessional or favourable tax rates to newly-started firms. The UK government has introduced a zero rate of corporation tax on the income of new firms and implemented a 50 percent capital cost allowance for first-year start-up plant and equipment costs to improve the cash flow of new firms. The Irish government rebates taxes paid by individuals starting businesses through a Seed Capital Scheme. The Swedish government allows new enterprises a three month respite on the preliminary payment of taxes. The Spanish government has reduced the tax rate for businesses with revenues of less than €5 million, allows a deferment of company tax for the first two tax periods of a new business to encourage business investment and exempts new businesses from paying business tax in the first year. The Dutch government has introduced the Self-Employed Person's Allowance that gives starters a higher allowance to make reserves for expansion and other investments. Australian, Finnish, Canadian, Danish and UK governments have implemented minimum income thresholds below which new and small firms do not have to collect and remit Value-Added (VAT) or Goods and Service (GST) Tax. Swedish, Dutch, and Norwegian governments are reviewing the tax treatment of an entrepreneurs' income from self-employment versus that of an incorporated company to remove inequities.[24]

Almost two-thirds offer tax credits to both informal "angel" investors and venture capital firms to direct a larger flow of capital into new and early-stage companies with high-growth potential (sometimes on a geographic basis). We noted that the use of tax incentives is less likely to be a policy choice in the Nordic countries (with the exception of Denmark). In Australia, the government offers tax credits to individuals so they will invest money as part of the Pooled Investment Funds Programme and also provides tax concessions to angels. In Canada, the federal government gives tax concessions to investors in Qualified Limited Partnerships and to individuals investing in Labour Sponsored Venture Capital Companies (LSVCCs). The Irish government gives tax relief to investors for investments of up to £250,000 in any one year and in certain sectors. The Dutch programme allows private individuals who invest in start-up companies to deduct any losses from their taxable income. In Spain, the government offers tax exemptions and deductions to encourage new venture capital providers. The UK has various schemes. The Enterprise Investment Scheme encourages business angel investment; the Community Development Tax Relief Scheme provides incentives for individuals and organisations lending to or investing in Community Development Financial Institutions (CDFIs) and tax incentives are offered to investors in Venture Capital Trusts.

Almost 70 percent of the governments have lowered the rate of tax on reinvested Capital Gains with the goal of increasing the level of private sector reinvestment of capital.[25] The capital gains tax issue is under review in Finland, and Iceland has a plan to lower its wealth tax.

Over three-quarters of the governments offer tax credits to private companies as a mechanism for leveraging R&D investments in the early-stage development of new technologies or products. These programmes are normally available to any company whose project qualifies under its rules, but not specifically targeted to start-up or early-stage companies. In fact, new and small firms may even find it difficult to take advantage of these incentives because of complexities in the application and approval processes. One notable exception is a Dutch scheme which offers an R&D Allowance for the newly self-employed whereby they can write off up to €5,500 of R&D expenses against taxation income (up to €11,000 for the existing self-employed).

Different governments employ different combinations of strategies and measures to create better conditions for the start-up, growth and exit of enterprises in this part of the entrepreneurship policy framework. In Table 2-11, we present the policy comprehensiveness scores for each country. This reveals that the US, the UK and Denmark have policy measures in more of the areas.

Table 2-11. Policy comprehensiveness for measures to ease firm entry, growth and exit

US	100.0%	IE	70.5%	NO	61.4%
UK	93.2%	SE	65.9%	TW	47.7%
DK	93.2%	FI	65.9%	IS	34.1%
NL	79.5%	CA	65.9%		
ES	79.5%				
AU	77.3%				
Average score = 71.9%					

4. Start-up and Seed Capital Financing

Lack of access to financing is viewed as one of the most significant barriers to the start-up and growth of small businesses. With a history of at least half a century,[26] it is one of the oldest SME policy issues. Because of the lack of access to financing, entrepreneurs are impeded in their efforts to start, expand, modernise and grow their businesses. This stunted growth prevents small firms from increasing employment and productivity and diminishes their capacity to contribute fully to overall economic growth in the economy. In today's economy, capital markets are much more developed. Traditional lenders are increasingly targeting the small business sector as a profitable growth market. However, financing gaps still appear to exist in segments of the market, defined either in terms of stage of business development, target group, sector or geographic region. It is also the case that capital market systems are not equally developed in all countries.

As noted in Stevenson and Lundström (2001) and Lundström (ed.), (2003), central/national governments in each of our study countries have policies related to improving access to SME financing, although they differ in the length of time they have focused on the issue, the diversity and multiplicity of their policy measures, the extent of direct government financing, the emphasis on debt versus equity programmes, and the extent to which they attempt to address information asymmetries affecting entrepreneurs and financiers. Having said that, the policy comprehensiveness score for financing-related items is the highest for any of the entrepreneurship policy framework areas (84 percent). This means it is the policy area where governments are overall the most active.

Governments focus on the SME financing issue because they are trying to fill "gaps". The task is then one of determining what the gaps are and how best to fill them. There appear to be five major reasons for making interventions in the SME financing arena, all based on "market failure" arguments:

- loans to small firms pose higher transaction costs for traditional lenders and thus reduce the competitive ability of new and small firms to secure debt financing.
- small firms pose a higher lending risk because of perceived higher failure rates.
- new and young firms are less likely to meet the collateral security requirements of traditional lenders and less able to demonstrate through a proven track record that their businesses will generate sufficient profits to repay the loan and service the debt.
- new technology-oriented and early-stage firms pose a high risk because of the uncertainty of their commercial viability, making it difficult for them to attract financing.
- entrepreneurs are subject to information asymmetries and thus disadvantaged in terms of access to information about sources of financing and financing options compared to large firms.

Government intervention seeks to address these failures by introducing measures to: (1) reduce the transaction costs of lending to small businesses (simplifying loan approval processes, using online loan applications); (2) reduce the risk banks take in lending to small businesses (guarantees, loan loss reserves); (3) improve access to financing in cases where innovative entrepreneurs are unable to attract traditional financing (risk-sharing measures); (4) increase the flow of equity capital (incentives for informal investors and venture capitalists); and (5) reduce the asymmetry of information for SMEs (initiatives to bridge the communication gap between financiers and entrepreneurs and to improve the flow of information about financing options/sources).

Individual governments make use of different mechanisms and instruments to achieve these goals, but most national-level governments are actively involved in a multiplicity of measures. These include the creation of small business banks (Canada and Taiwan); government small business loan guarantee programmes; the delivery of micro-loan funds and growth loan funds; R&D seed capital programmes; venture capital programmes; investment tax credits; support for angel investor networks; financing databases; and investment match-making programmes.

Loan guarantee programmes are used to either reduce bank risk in small business lending or to increase the level of understanding banks have about the small business market and client. Micro-loan funds are often targeted to specific groups, such as women, young people and ethnic minorities, or to economically disadvantaged regions. R&D grants and loans and venture capital funds are most often directed at early-stage high-potential firms that have difficulty attracting risk financing. Governments support the development of venture capital funds to address regional imbalances, fill a gap for start-up or mezzanine financing or even to focus on a particular demographic group (e.g., the US SBA-funded venture capital corporation for women-owned firms). In Ireland, Australia, the Netherlands and the UK, governments seek to overcome the "innovation progression gap" by funding university-based seed funds which are intended to stimulate the commercialisation of R&D. Investment tax credit schemes are a strategy to encourage higher levels of private sector equity investment in SMEs, but not all governments choose to use the tax system for this purpose. Governments in many countries support the development of business angel networks, databases and other matching-making forums to improve the flow of information between individuals with money to invest and new entrepreneurs who need it. The framework map of the collective policy options and measures for dealing with SME financing gaps is presented in Figure 2-8.

A government's approach to addressing the small business financing gap will depend greatly on its assessment of the "availability" versus "access" problem, its priorities for economic development, the state of its private sector capital markets and its views on the interventionist role of government in the marketplace. For example, in some countries (e.g., Spain, Denmark and Finland) capital markets are not viewed by their governments as well developed. Therefore, these governments have had to take steps to create a more market-driven capital system, in the meantime using government funds to make more capital available to SMEs at every stage of the cycle from pre-seed to start-up to Initial Public Offering (IPO). Some governments are very actively engaged in direct SME financing programmes, such as in Canada, Taiwan, and the UK, while others play only a minimal direct role. The Dutch and Australian governments, for example, do not generally offer direct SME financial assistance programmes except to support innovation activity. Both offer concessions or loans to new firms undertaking R&D or to existing firms developing new products, technologies or services with technical risk.

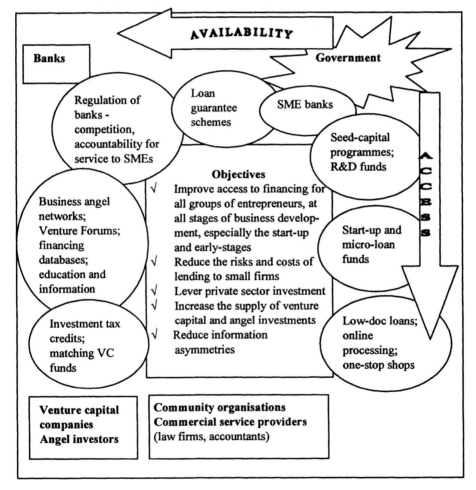

Figure 2.8. Framework map of the range of financing instruments, measures and partners

Since our 2000-01 study, we see a number of trends in government SME financing schemes. First of all, it appears that individual governments are seeking to offer a broader range of product offerings (from micro-loans to pooled investment funds), delivering them in more diverse ways (e.g., partnerships with banks, third-party agencies), and employing more diverse policy instruments (e.g., tax credits, direct loans, loan guarantees, investment matching services). We also note several other trends and developments: (1) fewer grants and subsidies and more repayable loan and equity programmes; (2) more efforts to segment the SME market by size of firm (e.g., micro-loans for micro-enterprises), stage of firm development (e.g., pre-seed funds for early-stage firms), sector (e.g., biotechnology firms), target group (e.g., loans directed towards women or techno-starters) and geographic region (e.g., venture funds in disadvantaged regions); (3) a growing emphasis on equity financing programmes; (4) a significant shift in policy attention to the financing needs of new firms, including measures that will increase the supply of informal and formal equity investment directed to start-up companies; and (5) an increasing emphasis on efforts to bridge the gap between informal private investors (business "angels") and entrepreneurs in need of equity. While a large amount of government resources is being allocated to address SME financing gaps, not much is often known about the actual impact of these efforts or the extent to which it is solving the problem. Neither is it clear how much the problem is one of lack of availability versus lack of access; in other words, financing may be available, but small firm owners may lack the know-how and ability to secure it.

Because we were primarily interested in policies and measures to stimulate an increase in business start-up and early-stage growth activity, we paid particular attention in our case studies to the trends in start-up and seed financing. When governments shift their focus to entrepreneurship policy, in fact, one of the first questions they have to ask is: how much of the available SME financing is finding its way into start-up firms? Not very much data exists about this.

Most governments have undertaken recent reviews of the current situation regarding financing gaps for new firms. The Finnish government determined that financing is not a problem for existing SMEs but that gaps exist for new start-ups and growth firms that do not have a history of accounts and established market positions. As a result of these findings the Finnish Industrial Investment Fund has refocused its investment activities on special funds for seed and start-up businesses. A recent study of the financing gaps in Taiwan concluded that more funds needed to be directed to start-ups, especially in technology areas (CHIER, 2002). Studies in Sweden conclude there is a lack of capital for certain phases of business development and that new starters experience more problems attracting capital because they do not have a track record and are difficult to assess (Ministry of Industry, Employment and Communications, 2003a). The Dutch government is examining where the problem lies for small business in accessing commercial loans (results expected in 2004), but has already identified a gap between the supply and demand for venture capital at the lower end of the capital market - for investments up to €1 million (Ministry of Economic Affairs, 2004). In Australia, the majority of private venture capital goes to larger, more established enterprises or to management buy-outs (Department of Industry, Tourism and Resources, 2003a). This is true even in the United States – in 2002, only 1.4 percent of US venture capital was invested in start-up firms and another 19.2 percent in early-stage companies (Minniti and Bygrave, 2004). These percentages have been diminishing steadily since 1997. Findings from the UK government's Small Business Investment Task Force, which examined the problems faced by start-up and early-stage firms, found that access to financing is difficult for certain regions and groups and that there are market imperfections in the provision of small amounts of equity-based risk capital to smaller firms. Only two percent of total private equity is invested in start-up businesses and only four percent in early stage companies (Small Business Service, 2004b). Indications are that less than 30 percent of commercial bank loans are small business loans, only a small percentage of which goes to new firms.[27] Reynolds et al. (2000) estimate that the size of the informal investment market is significantly larger than the formal venture capital market and that over 80 percent of informal angel investment is directed to new firms. This evidence reinforces the conventional wisdom that not enough outside formal debt and equity capital is finding its way into new and early-stage firms.

The next section places primary emphasis on our findings regarding the types of start-up and seed capital financing actions and measures we found in our 13 cases countries. Policy comprehensiveness ratings for items in the financing area are presented in Table 2-12.

Each of the 13 governments has a stated policy objective to increase the amount of funding available for new and early-stage companies. Measures implemented to address this goal have two primary aims: (1) to fill the start-up financing gap for people who do not meet the "track record" and collateral security criterion of traditional financiers; and (2) to fill the seed capital and mezzanine financing gap for technology-oriented and high-growth potential firms.

Table 2-12. Prevalence of start-up and seed financing measures in 13 countries

Access to start-up, seed, and early-stage financing	% of countries
Is there a concrete policy objective to increase the amount of financing available to new and early-stage companies?	100%
Has the government undertaken a review of financing gaps for new entrepreneurs, including an assessment of the proportion of existing equity and debt financing going to new and early stage versus mature enterprises?	92%
Have efforts been made to redirect more of the available supply of capital to new firms?	77%
Is there a government-supported micro-financing programme to enable more people to start new businesses?	85%
Do micro-loan programmes exist for under-represented groups who may have more difficulty accessing conventional financing (e.g., women; ethnic minorities; young people)?	54%
Does the government fund special seed programmes to support the start-up and early stage development of innovative, techno-starts?	100%
Is there a government-backed credit guarantee scheme to reduce the lending risk of new, small, and early-stage enterprises?	77%
Are pre-commercialisation funds made available to promising new technology firms (for prototype development, etc.)?	92%
Does the government deliver its own loan or equity programmes for new and early stage enterprises?	92%
Does the government partner with banks and lending institutions to improve the financing prospects of new and growth-oriented firms (e.g., mandate banks to report on lending activity to new/small firms, to allocate a certain loan amount to small firms or open "SME windows")?	62%
Has the government facilitated the development of databases on the types and sources of available venture funding to better inform new entrepreneurs?	85%
Has the government implemented initiatives to bridge information gaps between private investors and early-stage entrepreneurs (e.g., sponsor venture fairs, "investor-readiness" seminars)?	85%
Does the government support the development of angel networks or databases to bridge gaps between entrepreneurs and informal investors?	92%
Does government stimulate the availability of venture capital funds for early-stage, high-tech and regional firms (e.g., use public funds to leverage private investment)?	100%
Has the government relaxed regulations for 2nd tier stock markets?	92%

All of the governments have established special seed programmes for the funding of new innovative technology firms; all but one has a pre-commercialisation fund; and all of them support the development of venture capital funds and activity with programmes or initiatives that either use the investment of public funds to leverage private venture capital investment or offer tax incentives for private sector investment in pooled investment funds. All except one either supports the development of business angel networks or delivers government loan and equity programmes in favour of new and early-stage companies. In Finland, Iceland, Denmark, Spain, Norway and Taiwan there are government programmes aimed specifically at the funding needs of pre-start-up or start-up firms. The Finnish Industrial Development Fund supports a special fund for start-up and seed businesses; the Norwegian government's programme, Etablerer stipend, makes seed capital available for nascent entrepreneurs to help them establish their businesses; the Icelandic government's Entrepreneurial Grant helps cover costs during the pre-venture stage; the Danish government's Entrepreneurship Fund assists new companies in the pre-venture stage; the Taiwan government implemented a micro-loan programme for starters in January 2003; and the Spanish Mutual Guarantee Scheme focuses on new or recently created businesses. The Dutch government feels it is urgent to stimulate business angels to bridge the gap in risk financing for starting companies, the UK government is seeking ways to make it easier for small firms to obtain financing from angels, and support for the development of business angel networks (BANs) is very popular among European governments. All of these types of programmes are relatively new with major developments occurring since the year 2000.

Eight-five percent of the governments see a role for themselves in reducing information asymmetries by supporting actions to network private investors and entrepreneurs (e.g., venture fairs, financing seminars, web-based matchmaking services), offering training and educational programmes to increase the "investor-readiness" of both entrepreneurs and investors, and/or facilitating the development of financing databases that include information on the sources and types of available financing. In most cases, this information is accessible on a government website.

On the debt side, eighty-five percent of these governments fund micro-loan programmes, almost two-thirds of which designate a portion of these funds for selected target groups, such as women, ethnic minorities, and young entrepreneurs.   This practice tends to be more predominant in countries were the government focuses on provision of tailored services to meet the needs of groups that are under-represented in business ownership.

Just over three-quarters of the governments offers a small business loan guarantee programme, although it is not clear what percentage of guaranteed loans go to new businesses or the overall reach of these programmes compared to the potential market. Over 60 percent of the governments partner in other ways with the banking system to improve the financing prospects of small firms, and in some cases, to channel more funds to start-ups. These partnerships or relationships may be more pronounced in the US, Canada, Taiwan, and Ireland. In Ireland, for example, Enterprise Loan Funds have been put into place by all of the main Irish banks to assist starting and early-stage companies.

The overall approaches adopted by governments aim either to make financing more broadly available to all small firms and at each phase of the business development cycle or focus more selectively on making financing available to higher risk, innovative, technology-based start-ups and early-stage companies. The multiplicity of instruments and programmes characteristic of governments in the first group of countries is reflected in higher policy comprehensiveness ratings (see Table 2.13). This includes the US, Spain, the UK, Taiwan, Canada and the Netherlands, all of which have very high scores. Countries with average or low ratings are more reflective of the second approach where governments tend to focus on those market failures affecting innovative entrepreneurs and firms and, thus, have fewer policy measures.

Table 2-13. Policy comprehensiveness scores for access to start-up financing items

US	100.0%	FI	86.7%	IS	76.7%
ES	93.3%	IE	83.3%	NO	66.7%
UK	90.0%	SE	80.0%	AU	60.0%
TW	90.0%	DK	80.0%		
CA	90.0%				
NL	90.0%				
Average score = 83.6%					

The diversity of government financing incentives and mechanisms in a country will depend on a number of factors: (i) the prevailing economic situation; (ii) the competitiveness of its banking system and capital markets; (iii) the financing behaviour of its small businesses; (iv) the level of availability of private sector financing; (v) the attitude of the government about the extent to which it should intervene in the workings of the market place; (vi) the research knowledge-base of the financing barriers of different target groups; and (vii) the degree to which the lack of financing is believed to be an impediment to SME start-up and growth. In good practice countries, governments have lots of research data on the behaviour of firms and financing gaps, target multiple types and sources of financing, implement measures to address both availability and access barriers and pay attention to the question of financing the needs of new entrepreneurs and their early-stage ventures. In entrepreneurial regions, start-up and early-stage firms have access to multiple types and sources of financing, there are competitive banking systems and local communities have a culture of angel investing.

However, access to financing is not the only challenge to be overcome by new entrepreneurs. They also have a need for "know-how". Access to information, advice, technical expertise, counseling and mentoring services, and informed networks is also incredibly important. We now move to a discussion of government practices in addressing these knowledge needs of new entrepreneurs.

5. Start-Up Business Support

According to the European Commission, business support services aim to assist enterprises or entrepreneurs to successfully develop their business activity and to respond effectively to the challenges of their business, social and physical environment (European Commission, 2001, p. 6). The Commission further explains that these services would typically be available to any actual or potential entrepreneur that wanted to make use of them and would involve the provision of information, advice or forms of training that stop short of formal programmes, as well as facilitate financing. Under its Multiannual Programme for Enterprise and Entrepreneurship, 2001-2005, the Commission set up a Best Procedure Project on Business Support Services to identify the central issues and corresponding best practices in the area[28] and in October 2001, launched the Support Measures and Initiatives for Enterprises (SMIE) database of good practice measures and initiatives across Europe. EU Member States are also required to report on their "top class business support" actions on an annual basis (one of the objectives of the European Charter for Small Enterprises).

When we looked at business support practices in our first examination of entrepreneurship policy in 10 countries, most governments were at the beginning stages of thinking about how best to address the needs of new and potential entrepreneurs. One of the major trends at the time was to set up "single entry points", or "one-stop shops", to make it easier for entrepreneurs to access information and to deal with government departments and agencies on start-up matters. Governments were also moving to online and electronic mechanisms to impart information and services to entrepreneurs and SMEs.

The second major trend was use of segmentation strategies in the design and delivery of business support structures and services. Governments were starting to set up different organisational structures to meet clients' needs on the basis of type and size of businesses, stage of business development and growth, or phase of the entrepreneurial process. For example, in Ireland, the mandate of the network of City and County Enterprise Boards (CEBs) was to deal with start-ups and small firms with less than 10 employees, while Enterprise Island specialised in services to growth-potential firms with 10 to 50 employees. This trend towards segmentation and specialisation by stage of business development or firm size was evident in several countries. The usual system of support organisations included networks of government-operated or funded business service centers and enterprise centers that provided advice, counseling and technical and management assistance. In some cases, the government was the predominant provider of these services; in others, it was a partnership between the central government and the Chambers of Commerce; in others, it was the private sector; or in some cases, a combination of these. For example, in Taiwan, the Ministry of Economic Affairs operates a network of SME Guidance Service Centers, but this is supplemented by services offered by the National Association of Small and Medium Enterprises (NASME) and the China Youth Career Development Association (CYCDA). The Chambers of Commerce are important delivery partners for governments in Spain and the Netherlands.

Consistent with this trend towards segmentation, special support structures for target groups of entrepreneurs were also becoming more of a phenomenon. These took the form of dedicated enterprise centers for groups such as women and youth or new technology-oriented firms (discussed in the next section). Structures to support innovative entrepreneurship, such as national incubator strategies, were being implemented in the UK, the Netherlands, Australia and Taiwan, although various forms of incubators (Business Innovation Centers, Science and Technology Parks, etc.) could be found in all countries.

In terms of providing access to learning supports for new entrepreneurs, national mentoring programmes were an emerging trend. Governments in the UK, Ireland, Finland, Taiwan and the US had developed and funded specific policy measures to make formal mentoring services available to new and growth-oriented entrepreneurs. Other governments were experimenting with mentoring approaches on a smaller scale.

We also noted a trend towards use of more standardised tools and products in the delivery of entrepreneurship and self-employment training programmes, such as the Pro-Start and Post-Start training products offered through the Finnish Employment and Economic Development Centers. The FastTrac Entrepreneurial Training Program, developed in the US, was a leading example of a standardised programme for entrepreneurial training offered throughout the majority of US States and licensed for use in Australia and Sweden, among other countries. Some governments were targeting high-growth potential firms with customised packages of business development services. In Australia (AusIndustry), Ireland (Enterprise-Ireland), Sweden (ALMI), and the UK (Business Links), business development officers were delivering "holistic" business consultancy approaches, a change from their traditional "programme-delivery" roles. A case in point was Enterprise Ireland's Business Development Model for

Growth Firms, a systematic client intervention approach geared to enhancing the management skills and growth capacity of existing entrepreneurs.

The final trend was the movement of some governments to improve the overall quality of service to small business owners by setting professional standards for the delivery of business advice. Professional development programmes leading to certification against occupational standards were being offered by institutes in the UK, Ireland, Australia and parts of Canada and the US. The UK was clearly the leader in this area, but other governments were beginning to focus on the need for training of government and private sector providers of information and advisory services to entrepreneurs.

The framework map of these collective options and business support approaches is configured in Figure 2-9.

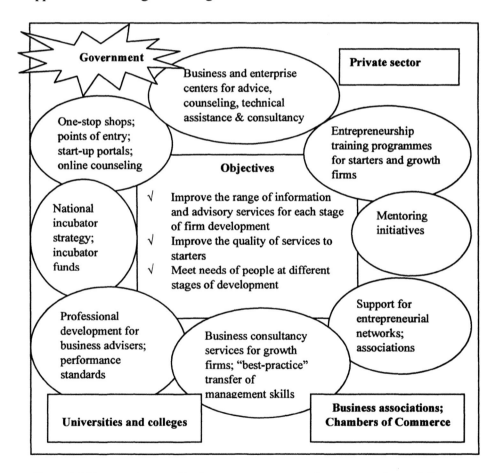

Figure 2.9. Framework map of business support measures for start-up and growth firms

Current trends and developments

The provision of quality business support to entrepreneurs in nascent and start-up phases is becoming a very important policy issue as governments seek ways to create more dynamic start-up markets. It constitutes part of the entrepreneur's "opportunity structure" in the framework of entrepreneurship policy measures. The overall rationale for paying attention to this is that individuals who, alone or in teams, are trying to start a business often lack know-how regarding the steps to take. They will often seek advice from people in their personal networks who may or may not be better informed than they are. Although it appears that the majority of new starters do not avail themselves of government assistance, some governments are keen to increase the take-up rate of advisory services because of the impact professional advice can have on both start-up and survival rates. According to a recent UK study, about 50 percent of start-up entrepreneurs seek professional external advice, but the ones who do build sales faster and are 20 percent more likely to survive than those who do not (Barclays, 2002). Improving access to professional advisory services can potentially increase the entry rate of nascent entrepreneurs and lead to higher quality start-ups with greater chances of survivability, growth and job creation.

Our 2004 analysis of current government practices in the 13 case countries reveals that significant developments are taking place in the re-orientation of business support structures and services in favour of nascent and start-up entrepreneurs. The policy comprehensiveness scores for items in the business support scale are presented in Table 2-14.

Almost all of the governments have a stated policy objective to increase the level of pre-start-up, start-up and early-stage growth support. Several have commissioned recent evaluations or studies of how well existing support systems are meeting the needs of micro-enterprises and starters (notably in Ireland, the Netherlands, Australia, the UK, Finland and Taiwan).

All of the governments have start-up information on their websites. Almost all operate a "one-stop shop" to provide start-up information and referral services, support a network of enterprises centers mandated to assist new entrepreneurs (as well as existing small firms), and provide some level of support for the start-up of R&D-based spin-offs. Just over three-quarters support national mentor programmes for new entrepreneurs or growth firms, provide for the delivery of entrepreneurship training programmes, and fund national incubator strategies for new enterprises. Less than two-thirds are actively involved in supporting different kinds of entrepreneurial networking activities and just over a third emphasise professional development opportunities for their business advisers. There is evidence in most countries that some measures are in place to evaluate the take-up, impact, and quality of business support services but the extent of this varies considerably across countries.

Table 2-14. Prevalence of start-up business support measures in 13 countries

Start-up and early-stage growth - business support	% of countries
Is there a stated policy objective to increase the level of support for nascent, new and early-stage entrepreneurs?	92%
Does the government make provisions to ensure that the needs of nascent and early stage entrepreneurs are met through existing SME service delivery networks?	92%
Are there "first" or "one stop shops" in place to provide new entrepreneurs with business start-up information, assistance and advice?	92%
Is there a government-sponsored web portal that provides start-up and other information to nascent and new entrepreneurs?	100%
Is there a network of business enterprise centers in all regions of the country with the mandate to assist new entrepreneurs?	85%
Does the government facilitate the development of mentor programmes for new entrepreneurs and growth firms?	77%
Does the government partner with private sector organisations and NGOs to delivery entrepreneurship training programmes? Are subsidies available to support the training of new entrepreneurs?	77%
Is there a national incubator strategy with government funding to subsidise the initial funding of incubators in key regions?	77%
Does the government provide support to encourage spin-off companies from university and publicly-funded R&D (e.g., cluster networks)?	92%
Does the government support the professional development of business advisers and economic development agents?	38%
Are performance standards in place?	23%
Are measures in place to evaluate the take-up, impact, and quality of business support services to new and early-stage entrepreneurs?	92%
Does the government convene forums for the exchange of best practices among service delivery agents?	62%
Does the government support the development of entrepreneur associations for peer mentoring and self-help?	62%
Are these associations consulted about the needs of new entrepreneurs?	62%
Are there forums and horizontal networks for all actors (e.g., educators, regulators, advisers, policymakers, researchers, and entrepreneurs?	62%

The most substantial structural changes taking place at the moment are in Denmark, the UK, Finland, Norway, Spain and Taiwan. In each of these countries, the government is restructuring the current business support system and/or establishing new institutional arrangements to focus on the needs of start-up and early-stage entrepreneurs. The UK Department of Trade and Industry is in the process of reducing its portfolio of 183 schemes into 10 new products and developing options for a single delivery plan that brings together all government funds for small business into a coherent integrated system. In April 2004, the department launched a "core offer for start-ups" that defines all the services a start-up can expect from the Business Links network. This new service is being aggressively promoted to potential entrepreneurs. Business Links development advisers are being trained on the range of new products and services, including a tool-kit on supporting women entrepreneurs and a learning programme on how to deliver a newly-developed package of products/services for innovative firms (e.g., training on technology strategies, patent office training). The objective is to be more efficient and effective in providing support to new businesses.

The Danish government has integrated its local and regional advisory services into a new "Entrepreneurial Nodal Points" structure that will serve as the contact point for entrepreneurship in each county. The Finnish government has integrated the services of several government agencies and organisations into a Regional Service Centers system that includes "New Business Centers" as a central component. The objective is to improve the quality of business advisory services for start-ups and small businesses. In Iceland, Service Centers for Entrepreneurs and SMEs (IMPRA) have been in place since 2000. These centers help entrepreneurs evaluate business ideas, make connections with sources of financing and so on.

As of January 2004, the Norwegian government has reorganised its public support system by combining the services of four existing institutions into a new enterprise for innovation and internationalisation. Its aim is to better serve entrepreneurs, young enterprises and start-ups to enhance innovation in Norway through guidance, competency enhancement and network building measures applicable to entrepreneurs. The Spanish government has created an Information Centre and Business Creation Network (CIRCE) to serve as a one stop shop to help establish new businesses. Beginning in 2003, partnerships were created with Chambers of Commerce to set up these one-stop shops in their offices throughout the country. The "Business Promotion Plan for the Self-Employed" is a new policy action of the Spanish government aimed to help self-employed people develop growth plans. In Taiwan, the government has established a Start-up Guidance Service Center to cater to the needs of start-ups and is planning to establish a Start-up and Innovation College. So we can see that entrepreneurship support is assuming a priority position in government policy, no longer an "add-on" to established SME support measures and programmes.

These new structures are often complemented by parallel institutional arrangements and institutions to foster innovation activity and spin-off firms. It is increasingly common for governments to fund business incubator programmes, business/technology innovation service centers, science parks, and university technology transfer offices to help new technology-based start-ups gain access to high-quality expert advice, know-how and financing. This is emerging as a priority in each country with interesting recent developments in Finland, Taiwan, Denmark, Ireland, Iceland, Norway, Sweden, Australia and the UK.

Finally, although there is evidence of networking activity in the majority of these countries, it is not often a main priority of government policy. In countries such as the United States, Canada and Taiwan there is lots of support for the networking activity of entrepreneurs as well as for exchange of experiences among business support agencies and organisations, but this is not the case in all countries. Certainly as the demand for entrepreneurship support services continues to grow, there will be a need for competence building and experience exchanges among policymakers, researchers, regional service providers and business advisers. One of the innovative approaches we noted was a project in Sweden. NUTEK, the Swedish Business Development Agency, which prepares the entrepreneurship policy positions for the Ministry of Industry, Employment and Communications, has formed a national network of regional contact points for entrepreneurship. NUTEK uses this network to stimulate discussion about entrepreneurship and to gain insight into the work being carried out at the regional level. The ultimate goal is to work together in the creation of projects that support a consistent and long-term structure to promote entrepreneurship in the Regions. Initiatives such as this are very important because many national-level policies for entrepreneurship can only be delivered at the regional level and insufficient attention is often paid to ensuring regional service providers have the building blocks they need to help achieve national priorities. Organising a network of entrepreneurship support organisations should be a top priority for regional or national economies that are just developing their focus on entrepreneurship.

Governments have a number of options at their disposal for removing barriers and providing assistance at each stage of a firm's development through business support measures. Although there is quite a bit of consistency in the mechanisms used by individual governments to provide business support services to entrepreneurs, some are more advanced than others in terms of focusing specifically on the start-up market. Thus we see a range of policy comprehensiveness scores across countries (see Table 2-15).

Table 2-15. Policy comprehensiveness ratings for start-up support measures

UK	100.0%	ES	75.0%	DK	53.1%
TW	93.8%	FI	68.8%	CA	53.1%
SE	87.5%	NL	68.8%	IS	34.4%
AU	84.4%			NO	34.4%
US	81.3%				
IE	81.3%				
Average score = 70.4%					

With the exception of Canada, countries with lower policy comprehensiveness ratings do not have yet have the diversity of policy measures evident in the UK, Taiwan and Sweden, as examples. This could be because they have only recently adopted an entrepreneurship policy approach or because their prime goal is to serve start-ups through generic SME or innovation support structures. In the case of Canada, the SME support system is well established but national incubator strategies, mentoring programmes and entrepreneurship-focused horizontal networking initiatives do not exist.

As governments make the shift towards entrepreneurship policy the question inevitably becomes how to more effectively meet the needs of potential and early-stage entrepreneurs. Focusing resources on the pre-start-up and start-up stages of business development can have the impact of accelerating the number of new firms, as well as their survival and growth rate. Instead of focusing on the issue of whether to target scarce government resources on new versus existing SMEs, governments are starting to adopt more of process perspective – providing support at each stage of development.

For countries with a longer history of SME support, the trend among governments is to apply new technologies to service delivery (e.g., online services, entry points and one-stop shops) and to adopt measures such as mentoring services and technology incubators. As governments strive to ensure a greater coherence in support service provision and to better meet the needs of new and early-stage entrepreneurs, a substantial restructuring of existing services may be required. This could include clarifying the roles of small business support agencies, rationalising and streamlining the structure to reduce duplication and overlap, improving the quality of advisory services and start-up advice, setting up regional entrepreneurship centers, addressing the needs of target groups (like minorities), and developing better public-private sector relationships with Chambers of Commerce, banks, professional services companies, trade associations, etc.

One of the big needs in the area of start-up business support is for the training and orientation of new actors in the field – small business regulators, counselors and advisers, incubator managers, entrepreneurship trainers, and mentors, to name a few implicated by this discussion. An additional need is for systematic evaluation of the effectiveness of different approaches. The work of the European Union to document best practices and to benchmark various approaches based on evaluation results is an excellent first step.

In the next section, we elaborate on the final area of the entrepreneurship policy framework – target group policies and strategies.

6. Supporting Target Groups

In this area of the entrepreneurship policy framework, the government's emphasis is very much on what can be done to increase business ownership rates and entrepreneurial activity levels among specifically targeted groups of the population that are under-represented in a country's self-employment and business ownership statistics. The decision to implement target group policies is usually based on statistics confirming differences in business ownership rates among demographic segments of society. Further research on the reasons for lower than average business ownership or start-up rates is often done to identify any market failures or systemic barriers which prevent these groups from having equal access to the opportunities and resources necessary to start firms.

Over 85 percent of the governments have stated objectives related to increasing the business ownership rates of particular target groups. These objectives might be stated in terms of supporting youth entrepreneurship (Australia, Canada, Finland, Ireland, Spain, the Netherlands, Sweden, Taiwan, and the UK); abolishing barriers to female entrepreneurship (e.g., Finland, Sweden, the UK); increasing the number of new businesses among under-represented ethnic minorities (e.g., Sweden, the UK, the US); increasing Aboriginal entrepreneurship (e.g., Canada, Australia); encouraging the unemployed to become self-employed (most countries) ; or stimulating technology entrepreneurs (e.g., Australia, Denmark, Ireland, the Netherlands, Norway, and the UK).

A total of ten different targets group were identified, although individual governments differed in their target group selections. This choice depended on the demographic make-up of their populations, what problems they were trying to address (e.g., diversity, social inclusion, unemployment, labour force integration) and whether they wanted to increase start-up rates among under-represented groups or in the area of innovative entrepreneurship. Policy measures include setting up special development agencies, enterprise centers, or incubators for the target group; providing dedicated advisory services, entrepreneurship training programmes and web portals;

establishing special loan funds or income support programmes; supporting entrepreneurship award programmes and promoting role-models reflective of the target group demographic; encouraging the formation of peer-group networks and associations; and establishing procurement set-asides so members of the target group can have a better competitive opportunity to secure government procurement contracts. The collective framework map of target groups, policy options and measures is presented in Figure 2-10.

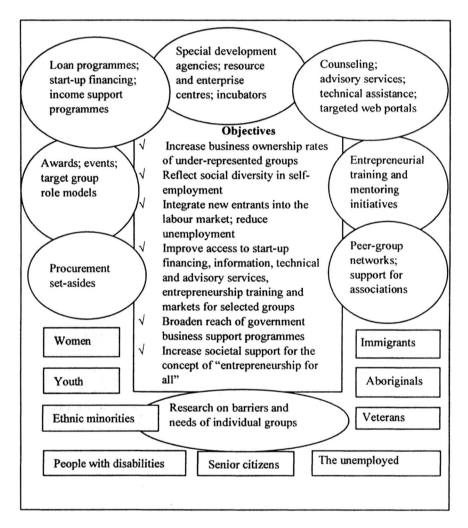

Figure 2.10. Collective framework map of options for target groups and policy measures

All but one of the governments have special programmes to encourage entrepreneurship among women; over three quarters have initiatives in support of young entrepreneurs; over 60 percent target ethnic minority or aboriginal groups; over 60 percent have programmes to encourage unemployed people to become self-employed; 46 percent target groups such as war veterans (the US), people with disabilities (Canada, the US, and Spain) or senior citizens (the Netherlands); 31 percent have programmes to attract immigrant entrepreneurs; and 100 percent have some policy initiatives intended to encourage graduates, researchers or technologists to start enterprises based on innovative technologies with commercialisation potential (see Table 2-16).

Table 2-16. Prevalence of actions in support of target groups in 13 countries

Target group policies	% of countries
Is there a stated policy objective to increase entrepreneurial activity levels of certain segments of the population?	85%
Does the government conduct research on the entrepreneurial activity rates of demographic groups within the population and track the start-up, survival and growth rates for each demographic group of entrepreneurs?	69%
Has the government examined the specific barriers and challenges faced by different demographic groups, including their take-up rate of existing business support services and programmes?	69%
Does the government target initiatives for:	
Women	92%
Young people	77%
Ethnic minorities/Aboriginal groups	62%
The unemployed	62%
Veterans, senior citizens, people with disabilities	46%
Immigrants/expatriates	31%
Are there policy initiatives in favour of innovative entrepreneurs and spin-offs from government-funded and university R&D (e.g., promotion of entrepreneurship among new graduates, university researchers, and technologists support for commercialisation efforts; seed funds; R&D tax breaks; university incubators)?	100%

Not all governments support target groups to the same degree. Governments in the US and Canada target the largest number of different target groups and do it with more intensity. In both cases, these governments provide special programme support for seven different groups, while in Denmark, Norway and Ireland, for example, only three target groups receive special support.

To illustrate the concept of intensity, we will use the example of women entrepreneurs. In Canada and the US, with the most intense efforts, the development of women entrepreneurs is supported by national networks of government-funded women's enterprise centers, micro-loan programmes for women, award programmes, dedicated web-portals, peer-group network and mentoring programmes, and in the US with a five percent federal procurement allocation for women-owned firms. In other countries, there are diminishing levels of support intensity.

Finland's support for women entrepreneurs has advanced over the past three years, now consisting of a micro-loan programme, expert advice, mentoring, a new training programme for women entrepreneurs (leading to a vocational diploma) and a Women's Enterprise Agency. The Icelandic government provides a Women's Loan Guarantee Fund, a Women's Start-up Fund, an online resource center (www.online.wbc.org), and start-up courses for women. Other countries supporting women entrepreneurs, such as Sweden, Australia and Spain have fewer policy measures. The Swedish government funded a Business Advisors for Women project; the Australian government funds mentoring programmes, a web-based resource center for women business owners, and entrepreneurship certification training; and the Spanish government funds a micro-credit programme for women and offers technical assistance and management training to women through a women's desk in offices of each regional government.

Countries with the least intensity of support are the Netherlands, Denmark and Ireland. In the Netherlands, women are mentioned as a target group but the position of the Dutch government is that women are not subject to any particular market failures so support for women's entrepreneurship is more on the promotions side – sponsoring exhibitions and trade missions for them. The Danish government produced a report on the needs of women entrepreneurs in 2002 but few policy actions have ensued. Women are not currently a nationally supported target group in Ireland, a country with the lowest percentage of women entrepreneurs in this group of 13 countries (15.7 percent based on 2001 OECD labour force statistics).[29]

One of the major observations regarding women entrepreneurs is that the countries with the most intense government support appear to have the highest rates of female entrepreneurship, although in all of these countries, employed women are much less likely than employed men to be self-employed and more likely to have smaller businesses with fewer employees and lower growth rates.

Canada and Taiwan have the most extensive set of policy measures for young entrepreneurs. These include youth enterprise centers, micro-loan programmes, awards programmes, and promotion of peer-group entrepreneurial role models. Governments in Australia, the UK and Spain promote entrepreneurship among young people and offer mentoring and funding programmes, in the first two cases, through programmes like Shell Livewire and the Prince's Youth Business Trust.

Support for ethnic minorities varies as well. The US Small Business Administration provides a comprehensive package of services to Hispanics, African-Americans and other ethnic populations; the UK government has set up an Ethnic Minority Business Forum to provide advice on support for ethnic entrepreneurship; the Dutch government supports ethnic entrepreneurship by financing networks, coaches and some credit schemes; the Swedish government provides funding for offices of the Swedish Association of Ethnic Entrepreneurs; the Finnish government has translated its business start-up brochure into several languages; and the Danish government has recently launched an initiative to promote entrepreneurship among ethnic minority groups where there are high unemployment rates.

Governments with self-employment programmes for the unemployed tend to have similar approaches – income support for several months while the business is getting started, perhaps supported with entrepreneurial training and mentoring services. Governments in Spain, Canada and the US have funded national initiatives to encourage and support people with disabilities to explore entrepreneurship.

Governments in Canada, the UK, Ireland and Taiwan have programmes to attract immigrants who will enter the country and start businesses. In Taiwan and Ireland, the major target is expatriated nationals who are provided with incentives to return for the purpose of starting high potential ventures.

All of the governments are seeking to increase the number of start-ups based on the commercialisation of innovative technologies being developed in R&D environments. Some have more comprehensive strategies in place to encourage and support this than others. In Norway, the government targets managers, employees, students and researchers at universities, colleges and research institutes to help them develop business ideas; the UK, Irish, Dutch, Swedish and Australian governments target university researchers and graduates; and the Danish government targets researchers and people with technical expertise and knowledge. These identified target groups are provided with access to various supports and resources including opportunity identification and idea development training, technical and management expertise, pre-commercialisation and seed funds, incubation services, mentoring and so on, all with the purpose of motivating them to start high-growth potential enterprises. This is not the case in all countries. Support for the development of innovative enterprises exists in Canada, the US, Spain, Taiwan, Finland and Iceland, but government strategies (e.g., innovation centers, seed funds, incubators, technical assistance services) are not directed to precisely specified target groups of potential entrepreneurs.

So while they support innovation, they do not necessarily support the development of innovative entrepreneurs. We will discuss this further in Chapter 3.

We present the target group policy comprehensiveness ratings for each of the countries in Table 2-17. These ratings reflect a combination of multiplicity in the number of groups targeted and the range of services offered to support each target group.

Table 2-17. Government policy comprehensiveness scores for target group approaches

UK	100%	AU	65%	TW	40%
CA	95%	FI	60%	IS	40%
SE	90%			NO	40%
NL	75%			DK	35%
ES	70%			IE	35%
US	70%				
Average score = 62.7%					

As this indicates, governments vary considerably in the level of their policy comprehensiveness. Since target group policy ended up being one of the typologies we introduce in the next chapter, we will provide a more detailed discussion of specific government approaches later.

In this chapter, we have defined the entrepreneurship policy framework and described each of the six framework areas, including illustrations of policy measures in each of the areas based on examples from current government practices. However, not all governments place the same degree of priority on each of these areas when developing their policy positions. In the next chapter, we move to a discussion of how different governments combine the various policy measures into an overall entrepreneurship policy. We will elaborate on the different types of entrepreneurship policy based on these patterns of configuration.

---

[1] It is noted that the UK government refers to its policy in favour of increasing the number of entrepreneurs as "enterprise" policy and it does this within the context of its policy for small business (Small Business Service, 2004a).

[2] Stevenson (1996), p. 11.

[3] See Gartner and Carter (2003), p. 195.

[4] See Carree and Thurik (2003), p. 441.

[5] See McGrath, 2003, pp. 516-517.

[6] The continuous supply of new entrepreneurs is needed to start new businesses to replace the stock of firms lost due to exits. The start-up and growth of new firms is also needed to create new employment and to replace jobs lost due to exiting and downsizing firms of all sizes.

[7] For example, see the *European Observatory for SMEs, Third Annual Report* (1995) produced by the European Network for Small Business Research (ESRN).

[8] This material was first presented in Lundström and Stevenson (2001), pp. 37-44.

[9] The US Congress passed the Regulatory Flexibility Act in 1980 requiring federal agencies to produce small business impact statements on any new major proposed regulations.

[10] The European Charter for Small Enterprises, for example, states that strategic efforts to promote entrepreneurship as a valuable and productive life skill and to foster entrepreneurship are essential to make Europe more entrepreneurial and innovative, yet the EU's enterprise policy benchmarking exercise does not, per se, require member States to report on their specific activities in the area of entrepreneurship promotion.

[11] More detailed descriptions of these government-led activities in Taiwan are presented in Chapter 10 of Stevenson and Lundström (2001) and Chapter 9 of Stevenson and Lundström (2002).

[12] See www.publicforuminstitute.org.

[13] A number of critical barriers and success factors in the implementation of entrepreneurship education programmes is discussed in Chapter 10 of Stevenson and Lundström (2002).

[14] The Graduate Enterprise Platform is a one-year rapid incubation activity that offers training, business facilities, mentoring and financing to college and university graduates who want to start a business. These graduates are able to start their enterprises in a campus incubator, funded under Enterprise-Ireland's Campus Incubator Programme, an important component of the government's high-potential start-up strategy. As well, enterprising grads are able to access start-up seed capital from the CampusCompanies Venture Capital Fund along with its strategic advice, network of business contacts and management development assistance.

[15] See Department of Trade and Industry (2001). *White Paper on Enterprise, Skills and Innovation*. London. February.

[16] According to Kuratko (2003), entrepreneurship education in the US has exploded to more than 2,200 courses at over 1,600 universities, 277 endowed chairs in entrepreneurship and over 100 established and funded entrepreneurship centers.

[17] See National Association of State Universities and Land-Grant Colleges, *Shaping the Future: The Economic Impact of Public Universities*, Office of Public Affairs, Washington, DC, August 2001; "Universities and Economic Development," Higher Education: Quality & Employability, DfEE, United Kingdom, June 1998.

[18] See for example, Tornatsky, Louis, *Building State Economies by Promoting University-Industry Technology Transfer*, National Governors' Association, Washington, DC. http://www.nba.org

[19] "Promoting Young Entrepreneurs: Business Plan Competition Support," Industry, Science and Resources, Australia. http://www.isr.gov.au/innovation

[20] From "$25 million in Kauffman Grants to Transform Culture of Entrepreneurship on Eight Campuses." Accessed from http://www.Kauffman.org/pages/396.cfm September 5, 2004.

[21] See www.fsf.se or www.nutek.se for additional information about this international awards programme.

[22] See NUTEK (2003), p. 28.

[23] See discussion in *Action for Entrepreneurs!*, Ministry of Economic Affairs (2003a), p. 43.

[24] Since the majority of start-ups are sole proprietorships, income earned from the business is taxed at the higher personal income rates. This puts new starters at a disadvantage versus those who incorporate their businesses from the beginning.

[25] It should be noted that Capital Gains Tax rates vary across countries.

[26] The US government passed the US Small Business Act of 1953 which provided loan assistance to small firms; the Canadian government passed the Canada Small Business Loans Act in 1961 which was the beginning of its government-backed small business loan guarantee programme delivered through the banking system.

[27] Based on research in the US, Canada and Taiwan where governments require banks to report annually on their small business lending practices.

[28] European Commission, "Creating Top-Class Business Support Services," Commission Staff Working Paper, Brussels, 28.11.2001 SEC (2001) 1937, p. 7.

[29] See *OECD Small and Medium Outlook 2002*, p. 246, for a comparison of female self-employment rates in OECD countries.

Chapter 3

ENTREPRENEURSHIP POLICY TYPOLOGIES

In Chapter 2, it is apparent that individual governments place different weightings of emphasis on areas of the entrepreneurship policy framework and on specific measures within each of those areas. They also differ in the extent to which they have committed to entrepreneurship policy objectives at the national level. Governments adopting an integrated approach to entrepreneurship policy have only started strategically doing so since the year 2000.

In our original study of 10 countries, we identified four major configurations of entrepreneurship policy approaches. This formed the basis for our entrepreneurship policy typology description in Stevenson and Lundström (2001), which we briefly review in this chapter and then apply to the patterns we see in the current practices of the 13 governments. We also bring together the entrepreneurship policy comprehensiveness ratings for each of the governments and explain some of the patterns of similarity and difference. This adds more insight to our understanding of the nature of entrepreneurship policy and its evolution over time.

Before proceeding, we want to stress the point that the configuration of a government's entrepreneurship policy approach appears to depend on a number of contextual factors. These include, among other things, the country's economic structure and level of development; its economic, political and social priorities; the size and role of its government; the views held by government about where growth comes from and what factors lead to it; its levels of unemployment, self-employment and business ownership; the rate of its entrepreneurial dynamism (i.e., entry and exit rate of businesses); and the depth of its existing SME support infrastructure. We will deal in more detail with the potential link between these contextual factors and a government's entrepreneurship policy approach in Chapter 4.

THE TYPOLOGY DESCRIPTION

In our first study of entrepreneurship policy, we found only a few cases where individual governments had introduced measures in all of the framework areas. Others, irrespective of their social, economic, political or cultural contexts, had introduced some aspects of entrepreneurship policy, often tending to favour one combination or another of possible measures from the policy palette. We were able to cluster the different approaches into four broad policy types. We refer to these as: (1) "E-extension" policy (as in an add-on to SME policy); (2) "new firm creation" (or business start-up) policy; (3) "niche" entrepreneurship policy (target group approach); and (4) "holistic" entrepreneurship policy. See Figure 3-1.

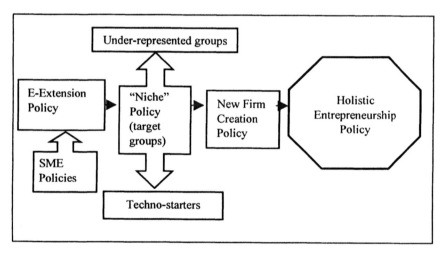

Figure 3.1. Entrepreneurship policy types
Source: Stevenson and Lundström (2002), p. 55.

Using the typology as a framework, we grouped countries according to the patterns we saw in their dominant entrepreneurship policy approach. As might be expected, an individual government's approach did not fall exclusively within only one category of the typology. However, individual governments did tend towards one dominant approach that was often supplemented by a secondary approach. The dominant policy type in the US, Australia, Canada, Sweden and Taiwan was E-extension; in Spain, New

Firm Creation policy; in Ireland, "Niche" entrepreneurship policy (with a focus on innovative entrepreneurs); and in Finland, the Netherlands and the UK, "Holistic" entrepreneurship policy. Regardless of their dominant approach, governments in each of the countries favoured "niche" policy as a secondary approach, except of course, in Ireland.

The E-extension policy approach describes the situation where a government introduces entrepreneurship-oriented measures within their SME policy framework. The general thrust of this approach is to assist "ready entrepreneurs" through the business planning and early-stage start-up process with advice, information, counseling and, perhaps, financing. These services are "added-on" to the business support offerings already delivered through an existing institutional SME support system. In New Firm Creation policy, the focus is on removing barriers to, and facilitating, the actual business creation process. "Niche" entrepreneurship policy includes measures to address the specific needs of particular target groups of the population where potential exists for increased start-up or business ownership rates. "Holistic" entrepreneurship policy is a complex of the other three types and has the broader objective of creating an entrepreneurial society, strengthening both the culture of, and climate for, entrepreneurship. It will include the integration of entrepreneurship education in schools and promotion of entrepreneurship. This latter policy type addresses the short-term and long-term development of an entrepreneurial population. We next briefly describe each of the four types of entrepreneurship policy and then apply the typology to current policy practice in the 13 countries.

E-Extension Policies
Policies to Improve Access to Start-up Support Services and Financing

A government with an E-extension approach is one that does not have a specified entrepreneurship policy. Some accommodation is made to respond to local or regional demand for indigenous start-up activity by extending services already provided through existing national SME programmes and services – that is, by "adding-on" entrepreneurship-oriented "bits" in more of a piece-meal fashion. Such entrepreneurship-oriented measures might include the provision of start-up information, business planning assistance, or self-employment training initiatives. However, the primary policy focus of these governments is geared towards addressing market failures and "levelling the playing field" for existing SMEs. Entrepreneurship-oriented measures tend to be a marginalised priority and weakly resourced compared to SME policy measures.

This was most likely to be the dominant approach in countries where the government has long-standing SME policies and well-established SME support networks in place (e.g., Australia, Canada, Sweden, Taiwan and the US). These are countries with few regulatory or administrative barriers to the business start-up process and where it is not generally difficult, time consuming, or costly to start a business. They also tend to be countries with a well-developed culture of entrepreneurship, which is certainly the case in Canada, Taiwan and the US, although less so in Sweden and Australia (self-reportedly due to a lack of role models).

To a great extent, the E-extension approach can be described as a reactive response to growing demand from nascent and new entrepreneurs for start-up information, advice, and financing or as a strategy for generating employment, especially in high unemployment regions. Policy measures in this typification are likely to focus on improving "access" to resources – elements of the "Opportunity" circle of the Entrepreneurship Policy Foundations framework. For example, services offered through existing SME support delivery networks might be extended by offering start-up seminars. The government may make use of its existing SME website to provide tailored information for business starters, thus making it easier for people to access information on starting a business. The network of local government SME offices may work at the community level to promote entrepreneurship as a job creation strategy. The secondary policy approach in these countries is largely aimed at addressing the specific start-up needs of groups of the population under-represented in business ownership, i.e., the adoption of "niche" policies. These policy measures might include the provision of special micro-loan or counseling programmes to specific target groups, such as women or youth, or the setting up of local enterprise centers and mentoring initiatives.

Countries with E-extension approaches, with the exception of Sweden, were ones with high levels of self-employment, high start-up rates, and/or high nascent entrepreneur prevalence rates. Because of these high levels of entrepreneurial dynamism, their governments perhaps do not see any immediate compelling reason to make major adjustments in their policy positions to further influence an "entrepreneurial climate". This might explain why there were few national policy directives in these countries to foster an entrepreneurial culture, to examine specific barriers to entry or to integrate entrepreneurship in the education system. With the exception of Australia, none of these countries has a national programme to integrate "enterprise" in the K-12 education system. As we will describe later in this chapter, policy shifts can be seen in some of these countries over the past three years.

New Firm Creation Policy
Policy in Favour of Reducing Barriers to Entry and Exit

New Firm Creation policy (sometimes referred to as Business Start-up policy) is concerned with simplifying the start-up process and eliminating government-induced administrative and regulatory barriers to business entry and exit. Again, emphasis is on aspects within the "Opportunity" circle, except in this case moreso on the regulatory and administrative aspects (i.e., adjusting for government failure). One of the big administrative/regulatory issues affecting entrepreneurial activity levels has to do with the time and cost of starting a business – the number of days it takes to obtain approvals, the number of required procedures, the number of regulations that have to satisfied, and the cost of business registration and regulatory compliance. The objective of New Firm Creation policy is to reduce this time and cost to a minimum so more people will be able to start and formalise their businesses. A number of other government policies and structures also tend to be reviewed, including regulations and policies related to competition, social security, employment, taxation, bankruptcy and insolvency, and company law. This is a huge job because a vast number of government ministries and departments are implicated, as we described in the previous chapter, and several ministries, departments and regulatory agencies have to be engaged in the review process.

This approach to entrepreneurship policy was the dominant one of the Spanish government, an appropriate choice for Spain, given the many structural and regulatory barriers to the business creation process that existed in 2000-01. The level of self-employment in Spain is high (over 17 percent[1]), but over 95 percent of Spanish firms have fewer than five employees; micro-enterprises with limited access to the capital and resources needed to grow. Lack of formalisation exacerbates this problem. The unemployment rate is also high (almost 12 percent in 2003[2]) so entrepreneurship and new firm creation is seen by the government as a necessary vehicle for generating employment.

Spain's experience with SME policy is very recent, with most of the significant developments taking place since 1996. In response to its policy challenge, the Spanish government has set up One-Stop Shops for Enterprises to simplify the process of setting up companies (fewer forms, fewer permits and fewer steps) and significantly reformed Company Law so informal economy businesses and micro-firms can more readily become part of the formal economy. The goal of the Directorate General of SME Policy since 2001 has been to encourage the creation of small enterprises through the government's New Enterprise Project.[3] A number of initiatives have been implemented to help women, young people, and the unemployed to become self-employed and to promote entrepreneurship in the education system, particularly at the vocational level. More aggressive efforts to promote entrepreneurship in the culture were only getting started in 2001 and advancements have occurred since then.

Governments in the UK, the Netherlands, Sweden and Finland were also diligently reviewing barriers to entry and exit, undertaking extensive reforms to Company Law, Bankruptcy Law and insolvency rules, reviewing competition policies and seeking to create more transparency for new entrepreneurs and existing SMEs.

"Niche" Entrepreneurship Policy
Policy Tailored to Increasing Entrepreneurial Activity amongst Specific Groups of the Population

"Niche" entrepreneurship policy focuses on stimulating higher start-up rates among particular segments of the population. The rationale for target group policies could be job creation, social inclusion, gender equity, labour market integration, or wealth creation. The overall target of this approach is either to improve the business ownership levels of under-represented groups, for example, women, young people, ethnic minorities, and the unemployed (Type 1), or to accelerate the take-up of high-tech, innovative entrepreneurship from amongst post-secondary graduates and scientifically, technologically-oriented researchers and experts (Type 2). In either case, governments justify their interventions on the basis of social, systemic or market failures. Under-represented groups may face social or economic barriers to the entrepreneurial process and techno-starters may face market failures due to the uncertainty and high risk associated with high-technology businesses. "Niche" policy is likely to include Motivation and Skills-oriented measures as well as Opportunity measures.

Ireland was the only country in our first study where "niche" entrepreneurship policy appeared to be the dominant type, in their case, Type 2. The Irish government has introduced a comprehensive package of incentives and assistance aimed at producing more entrepreneurs and spin-off firms from within university and technology institute environments. The target group is people with post-secondary educations, especially researchers with commercially-promising technologies, and new graduates. Policy measures include funding for campus incubators, pre-seed funding for commercialisable R&D, campus venture capital programmes, enterprise platforms (entrepreneurial skills development, mentoring and management assistance) and national business plan competitions. Such techno-starter policies are also in place in the Netherlands, Australia, Taiwan, Norway, Denmark and the UK, countries where governments have linked entrepreneurship to the innovation agenda. "Innovation" was only beginning to emerge as a policy area in 2000-2001, but there have been major developments in the overlap between entrepreneurship and innovation policy since then, a theme we shall discuss shortly.

We found examples of Type 1 "niche" entrepreneurship policy in each of the first 10 case countries where governments were targeting one or more underrepresented groups for tailored entrepreneurship support. The most intense adoption of this policy approach was by the US government. The US Small Business Administration delivers comprehensive entrepreneurial development programmes for women entrepreneurs, African-Americans, American-Indians, Hispanics, other ethnic minorities and veterans. These measures include support for national networks of dedicated enterprise centers, micro-loan funds, awards programmes, training, counseling and mentoring services and web-based information portals. Governments in other countries were targeting fewer demographic groups with fewer measures, although there has been growing interest in target group initiatives over the past three years, especially those directed towards women and ethnic minorities.

"Niche" entrepreneurship policy is often complementary to a government's dominant E-policy approach. This policy type may be more effective in countries where the overall entrepreneurship culture is strong, but where special efforts are needed to help certain groups of the population overcome adverse effects. As a stand-alone policy it might have some limitations. If the overall culture of entrepreneurship is weak, if there are general barriers to business entry, or if opportunities to gain entrepreneurial knowledge and skills are deficient, target groups could still face difficulties in their entrepreneurial endeavours. Thus a "niche" policy approach might make more sense in the context of a broader set of entrepreneurship-oriented policies. It is also interesting to note the differences in policy actions, depending on whether the target group is Type 1 or Type 2 (see Table 3-1).

Table 3-1. Comparison of Type 1 and Type 2 "niche" E-policies

Policy features	Type 1 – Under-represented groups	Type 2 – Techno-starters; innovative entrepreneurs
Rationale for policy	Job creation, social inclusion, diversity; gender equity	Wealth creation; innovation; creation of value from R&D
Basis of demographic selection	Groups with lower than national average self-employment or business ownership rates	People with post-secondary educations; working in post-secondary educational environments (graduates, researchers, technologists)
Objectives	Develop entrepreneurial potential; increase start-up rates	Stimulate innovative start-ups; foster development of high-growth potential firms
Dominant policy areas		
Financing	Micro loan programmes; loan guarantee schemes	Equity financing schemes (pre-seed funds, angels, venture capital)
Support Infrastructure	Dedicated enterprise centers/agencies	Technology incubators/ innovation centers
Business support measures	Advice and counseling	Technical assistance and consulting
Regulatory issues	Government procurement set-asides	Review of intellectual property rules; simplification of patenting laws and procedures
Networks	Support for formation of entrepreneur associations	Support for cluster networks; networks of high-growth firms
Skills development	Self-employment training	Entrepreneurial skills, business development support

"Holistic" Entrepreneurship Policy
Policy to Strengthen Entrepreneurial Culture, Climate and Capacity

"Holistic" entrepreneurship policy is the most comprehensive type. It incorporates the policy measures of the other three types – reducing barriers to business entry; ensuring the small business support system is able to respond to the needs of nascent and new entrepreneurs (from all walks of life); and making financing available for start-up businesses – but, in addition, focuses on integrating entrepreneurship within the education system, promoting an entrepreneurial culture and creating a positive climate for entrepreneurship. It responds to all three of the Entrepreneurship Policy Foundations through a combination of Motivation, Opportunity and Skills-oriented measures. Governments in the Netherlands, Finland and the UK best illustrated this as a dominant policy approach in 2001. Through this more comprehensive and integrated approach, these governments were attempting to address a range of "failures" – systemic failures, social failures, education failures, information asymmetries, market failures and externalities. Their national government policy objectives include promoting an entrepreneurship culture, reducing barriers to entry and exit, imbedding entrepreneurship education in schools, improving access to start-up financing, information and assistance, and addressing the start-up needs of target groups. The main impetus for the "holistic" approach is to achieve higher levels of dynamism, innovation, productivity and growth through robust entrepreneurial activity – to become more entrepreneurial societies.

In Table 3-2, we draw some comparisons between the objectives, policy areas, measures, policy structures, and limitations of the four entrepreneurship policy types. What this illustrates is that the prevailing policy mix and policy structure will differ according to the dominant entrepreneurship policy approach. Each typology has its own set of weaknesses, challenges and limitations.

E-POLICY COMPREHENSIVENESS AND POLICY TYPE

In Chapter 2, we talked about our entrepreneurship policy comprehensiveness measure, the explanation of which we describe in the Appendix. As a reminder, the comprehensiveness rating is a measure of the number of actions taken in a policy area, given the possible range of options, in other words, the scope of government policy. The checklist of policy actions and measures was based on our compilation of the collective actions being taken by the different governments in 2000-01 and updated in 2004 to reflect policy advancements.

Table 3-2. A comparison of entrepreneurship policy typologies

Features	E-Extension Policies	New Firm Creation Policies	"Niche" Target Group Policies	Holistic E-Policy
Objectives	Improve access to start-up supports through existing SME support structures; better service to starters.	Reduce barriers to business entry and exit; simplify start-up procedures and requirements; increase the start-up rate.	Increase the start-up rate among groups under-represented as business owners or potential starters of innovative firms.	Strengthen entrepreneurial culture, enhance entrepreneurship as a career option, create dynamic start-up market/ better growth conditions.
Policy Rationale	Market failures; information asymmetries.	Government failures; market failures.	Systemic failures; social equity; market failures.	Government failures; education failures; market failures; information asymmetries.
Policy Areas	Business information; advisory, planning, and training services; regional and community economic development programmes.	Competition; bankruptcy; company law, business registration procedures; social security regulations; employment rules and taxation.	Immigration policies; business support policies; financing; incubation; innovation policies; gender policies.	Entrepreneurship awareness; entrepreneurship in national education curricula; start-up support, information, financing; infrastructure; regional policy.
Measures	Micro-loans; business advisory services; web-portals; self-employment training programmes; local services.	Flexible labour markets; open competition; less stringent bankruptcy laws, fewer business registration steps, lower cost, faster approvals; simplified incorporation processes; one-stop shops; reduced tax burden.	Tailored supports for each identified target group - enterprise centers; promotion and awards programmes; start-up loan funds; web portals; networks and mentoring programmes; incubation units; role-models.	Promotion and awards programmes; role-models; entrepreneurship in the schools; one-stop shops; enterprise centers; incubators; mentoring and peer networking programmes; start-up advice and web portals; seed capital and micro-loans.

Table 3.2. A comparison of entrepreneurship policy typologies (*cont.*)

Features	E-Extension Policies	New Firm Creation Policies	"Niche" Target Group Policies	Holistic E-Policy
Most likely policy structure	Vertical; limited interaction with ministries of education or regulatory departments.	More horizontal – many government departments implicated.	Vertical; limited interaction with ministries of education or regulatory departments; could be links with S&T ministry.	Horizontal, inter-ministerial structure. Recognise that many areas of government impact on business start-up and growth.
Limitations	Start-up initiatives are "added-on" to existing local SME support structures on a piecemeal basis; limited focus on entrepreneurship in the education system; and removing barriers to entry.	Primary focus on changes to the "business environment", simplifying the business start-up phase; less emphasis on longer term strategy of promoting enterprise culture and integrating entrepreneurship in schools.	Focus on target groups may lead to overlooking the growth potential of non-targeted groups or low-tech sectors; may have limited focus on regulatory changes or fail to address overall weaknesses in the culture for entrepreneurship.	Difficulty in managing policy inter-dependencies across departments and levels of government.

Source: Stevenson and Lundström (2002), p. 60.

We presented country scores for each area of the policy framework in Table 2-4. The total comprehensive scores ranged from a high of 92 percent for the UK to a low of 35 percent for Iceland and, of course, scores within each of the six policy framework areas also varied widely. Figure 3-2 is a graphic representation of how the patterns of entrepreneurship policy configuration differ among countries.

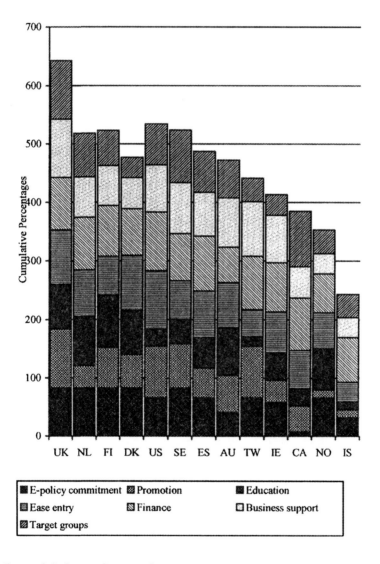

Figure 3-2. Scores for commitment to E-policy and the six framework areas by country
Note: The vertical axis presents the cumulative of percentage scores in each of the six policy framework areas, plus a measure for entrepreneurship policy commitment (explained below) for a total of 700 percentage points.

This shows more clearly that governments place different levels of emphasis on the policy framework areas. One example would be the difference in policy scope of national-level entrepreneurship education measures in the UK, the Netherlands, Finland and Australia compared to the US, Taiwan, Canada and Iceland.

One will note in Figure 3-2 that in countries with the highest policy comprehensive scores, governments tend to have a higher level of entrepreneurship policy commitment. The items we used to measure policy commitment are listed in Table 3-3. How easy or difficult it was to find evidence of these items for scoring was often the first clue. In countries without this clear commitment, the policy evidence is more difficult to piece together even if certain support programmes and initiatives might be in place. That said, in most of the countries we could find central government policy documents stating the importance of entrepreneurship to the economy.

Table 3-3. Overall country percentages for policy commitment items for the 13 countries

General policy approach/commitment		% of countries
Are there policy statements regarding the importance of entrepreneurship to the economy in the central governments national development plan?		92%
Is there a clear set of specific policies and plans to identify and remove obstacles to entrepreneurial activity, improve the wider environment and foster new enterprises?		85%
Has the central government adopted a "concrete" policy framework for entrepreneurship (specific document with policy lines of action)?		31%
Are policy objectives for entrepreneurship embedded as a line of action in another policy framework?		54%
In SME policy?	46%	
In Innovation Policy?	31%	
Have targets been set for increasing the start-up rate, the level of entrepreneurial activity, or the number of new entrepreneurs/new businesses?		62%
Is there a central government budget allocation for entrepreneurship policy measures?		77%

Many of the governments had a clear set of policies and plans to identify and remove obstacles to entrepreneurship or to improve the business environment for new business entries. However, governments in only four countries (Denmark, Finland, the Netherlands and the UK) had a concrete policy framework for entrepreneurship that was laid out in a specific document with identified policy actions. In seven additional cases, entrepreneurship was embedded as a line of policy action in another of the government's policy frameworks, either the SME policy framework or the

Innovation policy framework. For example, in Iceland, Spain, Sweden, Taiwan, and the US, entrepreneurship objectives are embedded in the government's SME policy. In Australia and Norway, it is a policy line of action in the government's national innovation policy where the government focuses mainly on stimulating certain kinds of entrepreneurial activity, predominantly business start-ups in high-technology areas with high growth potential. Four of the 13 governments included entrepreneurship in more than one other policy framework. Almost two-thirds of the governments had set targets for increasing the start-up rate, the level of entrepreneurial activity or the number of new entrepreneurs/businesses, some of these targets being more quantifiable and measurable than others. Just over three-quarters had allocated an identifiable budget for implementation of entrepreneurship policy measures, but the amount of this varied substantially.

Ratings for policy commitment in each country appear in Table 3-4. The first four of the five countries with high ratings are ones where we found a "holistic" entrepreneurship policy approach. As policy commitment scores decrease, so generally do overall entrepreneurship policy comprehensiveness scores. However, this is bit confounded because, in some countries, governments with low overall entrepreneurship policy comprehensiveness ratings score higher on a measure for innovative entrepreneurship policy, as we shall demonstrate later.

Table 3-4. E-policy comprehensiveness ratings for policy commitment by country

UK	83.3%	NO	66.7%	IE	58.3%
NL	83.3%	ES	66.7%	AU	41.7%
FL	83.3%	TW	66.7%	IS	33.5%
DK	83.3%	US	66.7%	CA	8.3%
SE	83.3%				
Average = 63.5%					

Next, before moving to a discussion of recent trends and developments in the evolution of entrepreneurship policy, we present our categorisation of entrepreneurship policy approaches for national-level governments in the 13 countries, showing both their dominant and secondary policy approaches (Table 3-5). We present more discussion of these policy approaches in the next section.

Table 3-5. Grouping of governments by dominant and secondary E-policy type

E-Policy Type	I S	C A	A U	T W	U S	S E	I E	N O	E S	D K	F I	N L	U K
E-extension	**	*	**	**	**	**	*	*	*				
Hybrid		*											
New Firm Creation					*			**					
Niche	*¹	*¹	*²	*²	**¹	*¹	**²	**²	*¹	*²	*¹	*²	*¹&²
Holistic										**	**	**	**

** = Dominant E-policy type; * = Secondary E-policy type
Note: Superscripts for "niche" policy designate Type 1 or Type 2 target group priority.

CURRENT TRENDS IN POLICY DIRECTIONS

In our 2004 review of their policy directions, we identified a number of significant developments in the practices of the 13 governments. First of all, we see a greater movement of more governments towards "holistic" entrepreneurship policy. Governments in the UK, the Netherlands, Finland, Denmark, and Sweden all issued new policy documents in 2003 or 2004. These documents set out a series of policies and initiatives to address all areas of the entrepreneurship policy framework and each stage of the entrepreneurial process. The overall objectives in these policy documents are more deliberately and strongly stated in terms of increasing the entrepreneurial dynamic, encouraging more entrants, easing exits, and facilitating good start-up conditions.

As we saw in Chapter 2, more governments are becoming increasingly active in promoting an entrepreneurship culture; setting up new structures to streamline and improve the delivery of support services to new entrepreneurs; undertaking efforts to include entrepreneurship in the school system; redirecting more of the flow of capital to new start-ups and early-stage growth firms; and implementing target group strategies, with particular advancements in support for women entrepreneurs, ethnic minorities and innovative entrepreneurs.

As we also pointed out earlier, there is considerable variance in e-policy comprehensiveness scores across governments. Some are more actively engaged than others in implementing the range of possible policy measures. Governments with more holistic approaches have higher scores. Governments with lower scores tend to be delivering entrepreneurship initiatives as a policy line of action under the rubric of their SME policy, for example, Canada, Taiwan and Spain, or have embedded them within recently developed Innovation Policy, such as in the case of Norway and Australia. Some of the governments could even be said to now have hybrid approaches where entrepreneurship development plays a more highly prioritised role in their SME and Innovation Policy frameworks.

We also see governments in transition – moving from one entrepreneurship policy type to another along a continuum. Although the main policy of the Swedish Ministry of Industry, Employment and Communications is still SME-oriented, the government has been slowly gaining momentum with an entrepreneurship policy agenda. The stated goal of the government's 2003 Budget Bill is the creation of 150,000 new businesses between years 2003-06; equivalent to 37,500 new businesses per year (NUTEK, 2003). The government estimates that the number of start-ups would need to increase to over 45,000 businesses per year until 2010 in order to compensate for the loss of job opportunities caused by the structural rationalisation of large firms. A National Entrepreneurship Programme was launched in 2002 with three-year funding of SEK 12 million for implementation of actions to: (1) improve legislative rules concerning entrepreneurs; (2) integrate entrepreneurship in education and other forms of training; (3) make it easier for women, immigrants and the unemployed to start a business; and (4) improve the supply of capital to growth companies. This is not a significant amount of budget compared to investments in entrepreneurship policy measures in Denmark and the UK, but the commitment to entrepreneurship policy has been growing over the past few years.

The Irish government's priority focus on Foreign Direct Investment, the competitiveness of existing SMEs, and the sustainability and encouragement of high-growth innovative enterprises, is starting to shift more in favour of indigenous micro-enterprise development. This shift is a response to a changing economic environment. Growth from Foreign Direct Investment activity is declining and GEM data reveals that the Total Entrepreneurial Activity (TEA) rate has dropped by 30 percent between 2002 and 2003 (Fitzsimons and O'Gorman, 2003). In July 2003, the government established an Enterprise Strategy Group to advise on policy options to generate future economic growth and employment. More attention is being considered for broader promotion of an entrepreneurship culture, stronger support for indigenous start-ups in any sector, and ensuring finance is available to entrepreneurs and start-up companies (Forfas, 2004).

In Taiwan, the government is working on a more integrated set of policies to foster innovative entrepreneurship, a response to their changing competitive position in the global marketplace (SMEA, 2003). This includes strengthening the provision of education for entrepreneurial activity, formulating new regulations concerning financing to newly-started companies, setting up a SME Innovation and Start-up College, working with universities to change policies with respect to allowing commercial enterprises to operate from university-based incubators, and achieving better mechanisms for the operation of business incubators.

The Spanish government has been gradually building more support for entrepreneurship, making considerable strides regarding entrepreneurship in education, promotion of entrepreneurship, and establishing business support infrastructure for all start-ups, as well as for innovative entrepreneurs.

HOLISTIC ENTREPRENEURSHIP POLICY IN PRACTICE

Governments with holistic entrepreneurship policy approaches in 2001 (Finland, the Netherlands and the UK), which they had each initiated in 2000, continue to renew their commitment by advancing the policy agenda. Their recent entrepreneurship policy documents adopt an entrepreneurial process perspective with measures to address each stage of the development cycle of an entrepreneur (Ministry of Trade and Industry, 2004; Ministry of Economic Affairs, 2003a; Small Business Service, 2004a).

The major impetus for the governments in these three countries to initially adopt entrepreneurship policy as a priority was low entry/exit dynamics or low growth in the stock of firms. The Netherlands and Finland, in the late 1990s, had relatively low numbers of business owners per 1,000 inhabitants[4], low start-up rates and low self-employment rates. The Netherlands and Finland had relatively low shares of total employment in SMEs[5] and the UK had had no net growth in the number of enterprises since 1995. In fact, the number of self-employed persons in the UK had decreased by 10 percent since 1990. In all three cases, the governments had a desire to be more competitive in the global economy and believed that increasing the level of entrepreneurial activity would lead to higher levels of innovation, productivity, and economic growth. However, the entrepreneurship policy course may be a long one.

Entrepreneurship Policy in Finland

Finland's unemployment rate continues to be high[6], it has a rapidly aging population, and, according to EnterpriseFinland (2003), the total number of businesses has significantly decreased in recent years. The Government Institute for Economic Research (VATT) predicts that Finland needs a minimum of four percent economic growth by 2010. Growth in the SME sector is seen as critical to achieving the employment share of that overall economic growth. One of the main objectives of the government's Entrepreneurship Policy Programme (Ministry of Trade and Industry, 2004) is to contribute to the priority targets of the National Government Programme to create 100,000 new jobs, raise the employment rate to 75 percent in the long-term, safeguard economic growth, balance regional development and improve the competitiveness of enterprises (as reported in Ministry of Trade and Industry, 2003). The government's stated challenge is to secure a net annual increase of 5,000 new businesses and to emphasise the creation of a positive atmosphere that will produce the 5,000 or more new entrepreneurs needed to start them. The platform laid out in the Entrepreneurship Policy Programme consists of five sub-areas:

- Entrepreneurship education and training and counseling;
- Business start-ups, growth and globalisation of enterprises (e.g., start-up financing; support for growth companies; transfer of family businesses; development of women as entrepreneurs);
- Taxes and payments affecting entrepreneurial activity;
- Entrepreneurship in regions; and
- Legislation affecting enterprises and the functioning of the market (including lowering the threshold of becoming an entrepreneur, developing social security for entrepreneurs and reforming insolvency legislation).

This Programme builds on the previous two-year Entrepreneurship Project (2000-2002) and elevates entrepreneurship policy as a government priority.

Entrepreneurship Policy in the Netherlands

Despite all of the government's efforts to stimulate entrepreneurship in the Netherlands over the past two decades, the number of start-ups is still quite low when compared internationally (Bosma and Wennekers, 2004). Since 2003 the Dutch economy has been performing poorly[7] and public appreciation of entrepreneurship has been diminishing. Dutch people attach positive values to entrepreneurship, many claim to possess the skills required to start a business, but few appear willing to do it in an environment with strong working conditions and social security. Although the number of entrepreneurs is not trailing that of neighbouring countries, there is a downward trend in the number of business starts and in the performance of existing companies and a rise in company failures (Ministry of Economic Affairs, 2003a). The number of annual start-ups dropped by 20 percent between 2000 and 2003, from a high of 55,000 down to 44,000.

What remains curious about the Dutch government's efforts to become more entrepreneurial as a nation is that the 2004 policy framework is at least the fifth policy or discussion document on entrepreneurship that has been released and acted upon over the last fifteen years (Ministry of Economic Affairs, 1987, 1995, 1998, and 2000a). Some of the best entrepreneurship research in the world is being done on the state of Dutch entrepreneurship. Why are they not getting more consistent positive results is a compelling question? Bosma and Wennekers (2004), in their analysis of the 2003 GEM results for the Netherlands, suggest that there may be structural weaknesses in the framework conditions for entrepreneurship in the Netherlands (e.g., areas of taxation and social security) and that one of the most important things to do is to reduce the "opportunity costs", or risk-reward ratio, associated with starting a business versus being employed or unemployed.

The current priority of the Dutch government is to strengthen the economic dynamic in order to restore the country's level of competitiveness. Entrepreneurship is an essential component of meeting that imperative by creating employment, increasing productivity and innovation, and fostering sustainable economic growth. The government's policy rationale also states the positive effect of entrepreneurship on social-cultural development, such as individual development, the emancipation of women and the integration of ethnic minorities. The new government's *Action for Entrepreneurs!* is based on three policy streams: Action Plan Start, Action Plan Growth, and Action Plan Business Transfer and Winding Up. The three priorities of Action Plan Start are:

- Making the Dutch culture more entrepreneurial by devoting more attention to enterprise in education;
- Improving the starting position of new businesses by making it easier to raise start-up capital and addressing the needs of target groups (e.g., women, ethnic minorities, and techno-starters); and
- Improving the quality of legislation and public service provision for new businesses, making it easier to deal with administrative procedures and apply for subsidies.

Policies measures under the remaining two policy streams include improving capital access for growth enterprises, simplifying company law for limited liability companies, simplifying business transfer processes for family-owned enterprises, and creating more flexible labour markets, among others.

Entrepreneurship Policy in the UK

The UK Department of Trade and Industry has identified enterprise as one of the five drivers of productivity. Enterprise development is seen as a critical part of the solution to the country's productivity gap with major competing countries such as France, Germany and the United States, behind which it is trailing by about 20 percent (Small Business Service, 2004b). Although enterprising small businesses are recognised as being important to the process of creative destruction and for the role they play in innovation, research evidence suggests that market failures still act to constrain new business in the UK. Rates of entrepreneurial activity remain only moderate by international standards and significantly lower than in the US and Canada (Harding, 2002). Female self-employment rates are considered low by European standards, there are significant regional differences in entrepreneurial activity levels, and, until recently, growth in the stock of firms has been slow.

Current government policy reinforces the importance of increasing entrepreneurial activity levels if the UK is to realise its vision of becoming the best place in the world to start and grow a business.[8] The government's 2004 Action Plan for Small Business is based around seven themes:

- Building an enterprise culture.
- Encouraging a more dynamic start-up market.
- Building the capacity for small business growth.
- Improving access to finance for small business.
- Encouraging more enterprise in disadvantaged communities and under-represented groups.
- Improving small businesses' experience of government services.
- Developing better regulation and policy.

A comprehensive set of policy measures has been materialised to significantly impact on the level of entrepreneurship and the number of people considering entrepreneurship as an option. There are national initiatives to promote entrepreneurship; expose all secondary students to entrepreneurship in the classroom; offer a "core" service to start-ups; fill gaps in start-up financing; reduce regulatory obstacles to start-up and growth; offer tax relief to new businesses; support incubating environments for innovative start-ups; and decrease the gap in start-up rates among women, ethnic minorities, and people in the most disadvantaged regions of the country.

Entrepreneurship Policy in Denmark

The remaining country with holistic entrepreneurship policy is Denmark. The Danish government's ambition is for Denmark to be an entrepreneurial nation but they needed a strategy to realise this. Denmark ranked 13th of 40 countries on the TEA rate in the 2003 GEM study and comparisons with OECD countries reveal that Denmark lies a few points lower than many European countries on the growth rate of newly started companies. The government estimates that a rise in the number of company start-ups per annum of 2,000 (the current number of start-ups per year is roughly 18,640) would result in GDP growth of over DKK 100 million annually (Ministry of Economy and Business Affairs, 2003). The government estimates that 60,000 new jobs are needed by 2010 to support planned development in taxation and public expenditure growth (Ministeriet Beskæftigelses, 2003). To realise this growth in GDP and employment and to "release Danish dynamism", the government set about to create better conditions for entrepreneurs.

The Danish government launched its plan of action for promoting entrepreneurship in August 2003 with a budget allocation of DKK 435 million over four-years (Ministry of Economy and Business Affairs, 2003). The goal of the plan is to create good conditions for the growth dynamics of the future, that is, entrepreneurs. The objective is to increase the number of people choosing to establish their own companies and to quickly position them for growth. The five lines of action are to:

- Create a stronger entrepreneurship spirit and culture;
- Relax administrative burdens to ease the starting of a company;
- Provide professional advisory services at the local level;
- Ensure a competitive financial market and taxation system; and
- Foster the commercialisation of research.

There are initiatives to integrate entrepreneurship education in the schools; implement a "minimum scheme" of regulatory requirements for new firms for the first three years; make amendments to bankruptcy legislation to reduce the penalties of failure; streamline the business support delivery system and offer more private sector mentorship for new entrepreneurs; establish an Entrepreneur Fund to improve access to seed capital; launch a national incubator programme; and implement an incentive programme to promote the transfer of technology from public sector research results. As we shall see later, Denmark is also very strong on the subset of policies for innovative entrepreneurship, as is the UK.

UNDERSTANDING ENTREPRENEURSHIP POLICY POSITIONS

Now that we have described the general nature of a holistic entrepreneurship policy, we will take another look at the overall policy positions of the 13 governments, trying to make sense of why they have adopted the orientations they have. We will discuss this question, in all of its complexity, more fully in Chapter 4; our proposition being that a large number of variables come together in order to make a determination of the appropriate entrepreneurship policy approach in differing contexts. However, here, we take three indicators – GDP per capita, the business ownership rate, and the TEA rate – and sort countries into "above" or "below" average categories. We chose these particular indicators because, logically, entrepreneurship policy is a response either to a lack of, or a need for, more entrepreneurs (density) and/or entrepreneurial activity (dynamic), the premise being that increases will lead to economic growth. These are both driving objectives in governments' entrepreneurship policy documents. The 13 countries fall into four groupings, which we then examine in relationship to policy comprehensive ratings. The four groupings are presented in Table 3-6.

Countries in the first group (Group 1) have both above average business ownership and TEA rates. Governments in these countries tend to score lower than average on entrepreneurship policy comprehensiveness, but as we shall discuss later, also tend to score higher on innovative entrepreneurship. The fact that they already have high levels of entrepreneurial activity may be the reason why entrepreneurship policy per se is not as high a priority as in the set of Group 2 countries.

Table 3-6. Grouping of countries by GDP per capita, BO rate and TEA rate

BO rate and TEA rate	Above average GDP	Below average GDP
Group 1 Above average BO rate Above average TEA rate (Low E-PC)	Iceland (35%)	Ireland (61%) Canada (56%) Australia (71%)
Group 2 Below average BO rate Below average TEA rate (High E-PC)	Denmark (74%)	The Netherlands (77%) The UK (92%) Finland (77%) Sweden (73%)
Group 3 Below average BO rate Above average TEA (High or low E-PC)	The US (77%) Norway (52%)	
Group 4 Above average BO rate Below average TEA rate (Just above or below average E-PC)		Taiwan (61%) Spain (72%)

Note: The average business ownership (BO) rate for these countries is 13.0 percent; the average TEA rate (2003) is 7.4; the average GDP per capita is US$30,046 (PPP). E-policy comprehensiveness scores for each country are noted in brackets (rounded-off figures). The average entrepreneurship policy comprehensive score is 67.5 percent.

Group 2 countries have below average business ownership and TEA rates. Governments in these countries are the ones with the strongest commitment to entrepreneurship policy, score among the highest on entrepreneurship policy comprehensiveness, include the four countries with holistic entrepreneurship policy, and are concerned with increasing their entrepreneurial activity levels. What sets these countries apart from the others is the following:

- There is a clear statement in policy documents about the importance of "business dynamics" to economic renewal and growth and the contribution of new firm entries to productivity improvements and overall competitiveness of the economy.
- The government's plan for accelerating entrepreneurial activity levels is presented in one policy framework document, together with rationale, objectives, explicit targets, identified policy lines for action and a set of stated policy and programme priorities and measures. This policy framework is likely reinforced in the policy documents of other ministries or government departments.[9]
- The policy includes specific targets to either increase the number of people considering entrepreneurship as an option, the start-up rate, the number of entrepreneurs, or the level of dynamism.
- A budget has been included to fund implementation of the entrepreneurship initiatives (not just for a few measures that might fit within the framework).
- There is clear responsibility in one of the main ministries for implementation of the entrepreneurship policy framework across ministries (and perhaps levels of government) and in a broad number of areas affecting the environment for entrepreneurial activity.
- Performance indicators outlining measures for improved entrepreneurial climate and culture conditions or improved conditions for actual start-ups are included in the policy framework document.

Group 3 countries have below average business ownership rates, but high TEA rates. Both also have higher than average GDP per capita, in fact the highest among the countries in this study. The US has an above average entrepreneurship policy comprehensive rating and Norway a below average rating. Norway, however, scores 24 percentage points higher for innovative entrepreneurship policy. The US also scores higher for innovative entrepreneurship but the spread is not as great as that for Norway.

The Group 4 countries, which include Spain and Taiwan, have high business ownership rates, but below average TEA rates. SME policy is dominant in these countries, but their governments are very concerned about improving the conditions for new business creation and stimulating new technology firms. They are also the lowest GDP per capita countries in this study.

We realise that we do not have enough cases to draw broad generalisations from this categorisation, but it would be interesting to explore the relationships between entrepreneurship policy comprehensiveness, business ownership rates and TEA rates in a larger set of countries with different levels of GDP per capita. We also realise that country groupings might change if we selected a different set of criteria, but these are the ones which entrepreneurship policy is attempting to directly influence.

To further explore patterns between policy comprehensiveness ratings and business ownership and TEA rates, we reduced the policy comprehensiveness score by a factor of ten and graphed it against these rates for each country. The results appear in Figures 3-3 and 3-4. It appears that as country business ownership rates and TEA rates get higher, policy comprehensiveness ratings go down. Policy comprehensiveness scores are higher in countries with lower than average business ownership and TEA rates. Intuitively, this makes sense. Governments in higher business ownership and TEA rate countries are less concerned about raising the level of entrepreneurial activity.

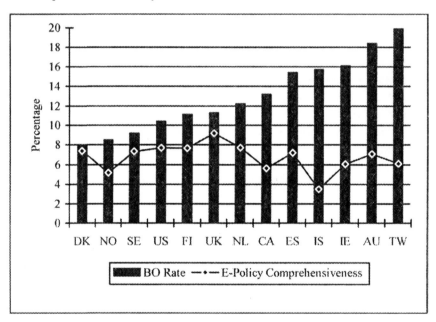

Figure 3-3. Business ownership rates (2002) and e-policy comprehensiveness scores

Source: Business ownership rates were obtained from COMPENDIA data (2002).
Taiwan data was derived from the *2003 White Paper on SMEs in Taiwan (SMEA)*.

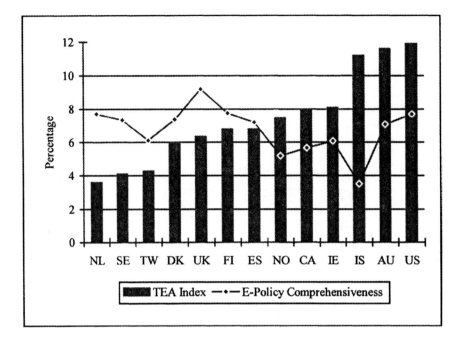

Figure 3-4. TEA Index (2003) and e-policy comprehensiveness scores
Source: GEM data. Taiwan TEA rate is for 2002.

Countries with higher entrepreneurship policy comprehensiveness scores tend to be ones with business ownership rates of less than 12 percent and TEA rates of less than 7. Again, this is a very simplistic analysis but one worthy of further exploration.

The Divergence of "Holistic" and "Innovative Entrepreneurship" policy

We found evidence in all countries of policy efforts to stimulate more entrepreneurial activity in areas related to R&D and technology innovations, some more aggressive and targeted than others. We were curious whether there were differences among governments in their overall approaches to entrepreneurship policy, particularly with respect to having a broad, comprehensive policy versus a narrower focus on policy for innovative entrepreneurship. We selected 17 items from the entrepreneurship policy comprehensive scale; actions associated with government policy to stimulate technology-based start-up activity, and compared the scores for these items across countries. These included actions such as: offering tax incentives to stimulate venture capital investments; reducing the capital gains tax; taking actions to simplify patent processes; providing pre-commercialisation funding; funding national incubator strategies; and offering entrepreneurship education to science and engineering students. We found, indeed, that a group of governments scored quite differently on this set of items than they did overall (see Table 3-7).

Table 3-7. Country ratings and rankings for e-policy and innovative-e-policy

	E-policy comprehensiveness rating	Rank	Innovative E-policy rating	Rank
UK	92.0%	1	97.1%	1
NL	77.1%	2	76.5%	6
US	77.1%	2	85.3%	4
FI	76.6%	4	67.6%	10
DK	73.8%	5	94.1%	2
SE	73.4%	6	67.6%	10
ES	72.0%	7	64.7%	12
AU	70.6%	8	85.3%	4
TW	61.2%	9	73.5%	8
IE	60.7%	10	88.2%	3
CA	56.5%	11	73.5%	8
NO	51.9%	12	76.5%	6
IS	35.0%	13	47.1%	13
Average	67.5%		76.7%	

Note: Scores for innovative e-policy were compiled from a subset of 17 entrepreneurship policy comprehensiveness items.

In fact, as overall e-policy comprehensiveness scores went down, innovative entrepreneurship policy comprehensiveness scores went up (see Figure 3-5). This was particularly evident in Denmark, Australia, Taiwan, Ireland and Norway, and to a lesser degree in the US and Iceland. With the exception of Denmark, these are all countries with above average business ownership rates or above average TEA rates or both. They include all of the above average GDP per capita countries as well. Governments with holistic entrepreneurship policy and high policy commitment tend to score well on both measures. They incorporate parallel measures to stimulate development of this target group activity within their comprehensive entrepreneurship policy frameworks. Governments in the other countries seem to make more of a policy choice.

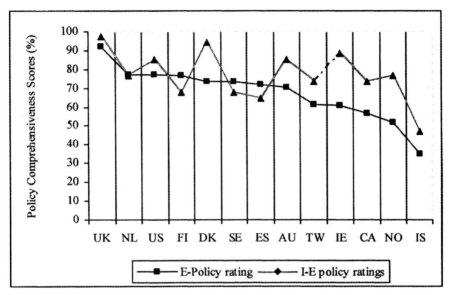

Figure 3-5. Countries with lower overall E-policy scores rate higher on I-E-policy

The trend towards development of comprehensive innovation policy frameworks did not emerge in most countries until after 2001. When we completed our first two studies in 2000-2002, we saw only the early emergence of policy targeted towards promoting "innovative entrepreneurship" – the examples of Ireland, Australia, the Netherlands, and the UK being the most prominent cases. Since then, Canada, Norway, and Denmark have released innovation policy documents and Sweden is in the process of developing a comprehensive innovation strategy. The impetus behind the development of more comprehensive innovation policy frameworks is, at least to some extent, due to the fact that countries are not experiencing demonstrable economic gains from their science and technology or R&D policies and programmes. Too much R&D is thought to be "sitting on the shelf" in university or government laboratories. To realise more economic and social gains from leading edge research, governments have started to place greater emphasis on the commercialisation of promising R&D and technology, a process requiring appropriate intellectual property ownership and protection rules; patenting filing and approval processes; high-risk development capital; incubation facilities; "receptor" capacity; and a supply of more sophisticated entrepreneurs.

Innovative entrepreneurship policies aim primarily to increase the number of technology-oriented start-ups (including spin-offs from R&D activity) and to stimulate the growth path of higher-growth potential firms. The primary focus of policy orientation and funding support is tertiary level universities, colleges and Institutes of Technology, and research institutions, places where new knowledge is being created and new technologies spawned. Essential to the spinning-off of innovative new firms is a supply of able entrepreneurs. The pool of potential innovative entrepreneurs is likely highly educated, found in these centers of knowledge-creation, and its members as equally unaware of their own entrepreneurial potential as they are of the market potential of their scientific or technological discoveries. They could be graduate students, researcher-professors, scientific researchers or technologists. The questions for governments are how to approach the task of motivating and developing the competence of this pool of future entrepreneurs so they can successfully pursue spin-off opportunities from university and public-funded R&D activities, as well as how to create the enabling environment needed for this to happen.

Based on an examination of government practices in a number of countries, policy measures in this area are justified on the basis that there are a number of barriers inhibiting the development of innovative new firms – intellectual property issues, lack of adequate premises, lack of pre-seed developmental and early-stage equity financing, lack of entrepreneurial and management skills, lack of interaction effects between possible innovations and potential entrepreneurs and lack of a dynamic environment to stimulate overall entrepreneurial activity. Policy measures to stimulate innovative entrepreneurship can be broadly captured within areas of the entrepreneurship policy framework but specific measures do have a different character and are targeted at a much narrower segment of the economy. The framework map of policy measures used to accelerate innovative entrepreneurship is presented in Figure 3-6.

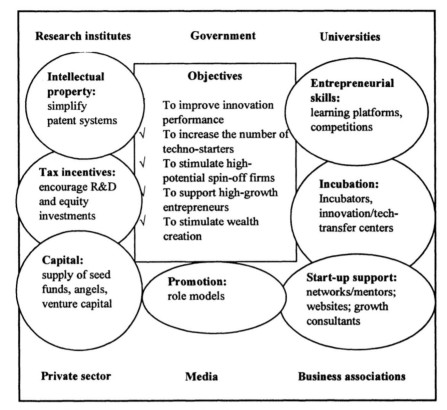

Figure 3.6. Innovative entrepreneurship policy: measures and partners

We saw that in countries such as Norway, the Netherlands, the UK and Australia, major pieces of the government's entrepreneurship policy agendas were embedded in innovation policy platforms. "Action 14" of the Dutch government's *Action for Entrepreneurs!* plan is a Techno-starter Programme aimed at removing bottlenecks for techno-starters. It includes a pre-seed facility to lower the barriers of innovative entrepreneurship; a seed facility to assist techno-starters in the challenge of raising sufficient venture capital; a university patents module to further develop the patent and licensing policy of universities so patents can be more easily transferred to techno-starters (and other innovative companies); and an information platform and coaching programme to help techno-starters grow quickly after start-up.[10] Other techno-starter supports are detailed in *Action for Innovation*, the government's companion innovation policy document, including the promotion of entrepreneurship in education and increased R&D tax breaks for the newly self-employed. The Australian government's entrepreneurship support is also included within the parameters of its *Backing Australia's Ability* innovation agenda.[11] The National Innovation Awareness Strategy, being implemented by the Department of Industry, Resources and Tourism, offers grants to support activities and initiatives that foster entrepreneurship and create awareness of the benefits of innovation across Australia. The Australian Young Entrepreneurs Programme is another case in point.

One of the key policy questions is "when is innovative entrepreneurship a good policy choice"? The likely answer is, it depends. But it is an important question because many governments want more entrepreneurial activity of the "innovative", high-growth potential kind. Is it an appropriate policy choice for all governments, irrespective of differences in level of economic development, business support infrastructure, entrepreneurial culture, and a broad range of other variables; especially in cases where the government opts for this policy path at the expense of building an overall climate for entrepreneurial activity?

Waasdorp (2002) raises the issue of how innovative entrepreneurship differs from "ordinary entrepreneurship". He suggests that these two types of entrepreneurship may result in different economic outcomes. The main contribution of ordinary entrepreneurship is job creation. The majority of business starts are by "lifestyle entrepreneurs" whose businesses will not grow beyond a very small size. Innovative entrepreneurship is more likely to lead to higher value-added jobs and wealth creation, their founders perhaps more compelled by the opportunity of the venture and its innovativeness. As well, innovative firms appear to have higher growth rates. This, in many instances, leads to the targeting of government support in the higher-growth potential, technology-oriented sectors. On the other hand, "ordinary entrepreneurship" can be the seed-bed for growth businesses as well as the incubator for more experienced, serial entrepreneurs.

Evidence exists to support the idea that innovative entrepreneurship is likely to be more effective in environments conducive to high levels of general entrepreneurial activity, that is, in environments where entrepreneurship is highly valued and supported by society. Kirchhoff (1994) makes the case that if there is a high density of firms with fewer than 20 employees that innovative, high-growth firms will emerge. Clarysse et al. (2000) found in their study of spin-off firms in different regions, that the entrepreneurial climate in a region, to a large extent, determined the number of start-ups and early growth research-based spin-off firms. In weak entrepreneurial environments, few opportunities are offered for external knowledge acquisition, starting entrepreneurs depend more on trial and error learning and the incubation phase of their start-ups often takes longer. Such environments create a lower incidence rate of high-growth ventures than supportive environments where entrepreneurs have the occasion to exchange experience, to make use of professional specialised services to build the business model and to access seed capital. Countries with the highest levels of economic creativity are countries that focus on access to technology *and* to a healthy entrepreneurial climate.

In addition to the possibility that the effectiveness of innovative entrepreneurship (or techno-starter) policy as a stand-alone "niche" policy may be impeded if the culture for entrepreneurship is under-developed, the density of business owners too thin, the full range of education support missing, and so on, policymakers should be aware of other risks in such an approach. A sole focus on opportunities in high technology sectors may well overlook growth opportunities in lower and non-technology areas. Balje and Waasdorp (1999) state that high-growth businesses form a kind of indicator for the capacity to innovate, but make the point that the growth of low technology, retail and service firms can be propelled by non-technological innovations in distribution, marketing and management or by the application of technology to aspects of production and operations. Since innovative entrepreneurship is targeted primarily at the better-educated segments of the population, other "niche" groups (e.g., under-represented groups) may become secondary policy targets and the economic opportunity from potentially successful entrepreneurial activity hampered (not that the two target groups are mutually exclusive). A techno-starter strategy does not necessarily incorporate efforts to integrate entrepreneurship throughout the education system and thus, the long-run benefits of producing a large number of competent future entrepreneurs will be lost. Governments seeking to increase the level of innovative entrepreneurship and the entry rate of high-technology and fast-growth firms should also pay attention to the strength of their entrepreneurial culture and their overall level of firm dynamism.

Authors of 2003 GEM country reports are critical of governments in both Ireland and Australia for placing a disproportionate priority on innovative entrepreneurship vis-à-vis their level of support for all start-up entrepreneurs. Fitzsimons and O'Gorman (2003) report that although Ireland's culture of entrepreneurship is strong[12], the TEA rate declined by 30 percent between 2002 and 2003. To them, this suggests that the government is focusing too narrowly on innovative entrepreneurship and ignoring other gaps in small business financing and entrepreneurship education. Hindle and Rushworth (2003) suggest that the policy of the Australian government is too heavily weighted towards innovative entrepreneurship while, at the same time, entrepreneurship education is not sufficiently embedded in Australia's public school system, there are few entrepreneurial role models, the TEA Index for women is very low, and there are shortcomings of policy in developing the innovative and entrepreneurial capacity of Australians. They suggest that these barriers are not being sufficiently addressed in the government's current policy. They also point out that, apart from the US, consistent "first tier" innovators such as Japan and the Scandinavian countries have been low scorers on the GEM TEA Index, suggesting that innovative capacity is not a predictor of entrepreneurial activity in terms of the number of business owners. Nor does a high TEA Index indicate high innovation capacity. Hindle and Rushworth (2003) further state that Australia GEM results consistently point to the general lack of capacity to commerialise ideas of any kind, not just those resulting from explicit R&D activities. They recommend a broader set of integrated and comprehensive policies to support an entrepreneurial culture.

Interestingly enough, the US government is criticised for not having a *strong enough* policy orientation in favour of innovative entrepreneurship. Entrepreneurship advocates in the US assert that the Small Business Administration and the Department of Commerce lack specific policies oriented towards fostering the start-up and growth of innovative, high-growth and technology-based enterprises and that the US will suffer competitive advantage if these are not put into place (National Commission on Entrepreneurship, 2000). Although the US can point to any number of good examples of programmes and initiatives, these are generally not the outcome of a cohesive, integrated national entrepreneurship policy framework. One might say they have policies for innovation, but not for innovative entrepreneurship. The same thing could be said of Canadian innovation policy.

We would argue that a "stand alone" innovative entrepreneurship policy may be an appropriate approach in an environment that already has a strong culture of entrepreneurship with a high density of SMEs and business owners. In an environment where there are cultural, regulatory, structural and other barriers to general entrepreneurship, then there may be an economic cost to focusing primarily on technology-based innovative entrepreneurship.

We therefore propose that policies in favour of innovative entrepreneurship (as a target approach) should be considered in the context of a "holistic" entrepreneurship policy framework which addresses all the other issues, such as societal support for an entrepreneurship culture, promotion of entrepreneurship, entrepreneurship education in the schools, general administrative, regulatory and legislative barriers to business entry, flexible labour markets and business support measures for the development of nascent entrepreneurs in their pursuit of any manner of business idea. This is the certainly the approach of the UK government which scores highest on both sets of policy comprehensiveness ratings.

Entrepreneurship Policy and Policy Structure

Structure is very important in entrepreneurship policy. We devoted an entire chapter to its discussion in Stevenson and Lundström (2002).[13] In this set of 13 countries, all of the governments have designated administrative units or agencies with a mandate for SMEs or entrepreneurship (see Table 3-8). In most, we could identify that an office existed somewhere within the national government with responsibility for directing, managing or delivering support to new entrepreneurs, even in cases where entrepreneurship policy, per se, did not exist. Most also had some level of horizontal communication or coordination mechanism to liaise with other ministries on at least some aspects related to our entrepreneurship policy framework; just over half appeared to have an advocacy arm inside government to promote entrepreneurship/SME policies and strategies. Most also managed a national delivery structure rendering support to nascent and new entrepreneurs at the local level.

Table 3-8. Percentage of countries with actions related to policy structure items

Policy structure for entrepreneurship	% of countries
Is there an agency or administrative unit within the central government with primary responsibility for SMEs/entrepreneurship?	100%
Is there an official responsible for entrepreneurship or enterprise development in the national/central government?	85%
Does the ministry/official responsible for entrepreneurship facilitate inter-ministerial processes to gain the horizontal commitment of relevant government departments to implement and enforce entrepreneurship policy elements?	77%
Is there an advocacy arm in the government to promote entrepreneurship and SME development policies and strategies?	54%
Is there a centrally-managed delivery structure for rendering support to nascent and new entrepreneurs at the local level?	85%

Governments with a more holistic entrepreneurship policy approach tend to adopt more horizontal structures for its development and implementation. This means that the ministry with lead responsibility for entrepreneurship builds collaborative relationships with other departments and ministries and other levels of government to promote a common vision and agenda. Achieving entrepreneurship policy objectives requires a government-wide commitment.

An important aspect of entrepreneurship policy is tracking and measuring developments and trends and monitoring entrepreneurial activity levels over time. All of the governments, to some extent and with varying quality and inclusiveness, track the level of business dynamics (the entry and exit rate of firms) on an annual basis, but some are much better than others in making this information readily available (see Table 3-9). Only eight of the 13 governments appear to publish an annual report on small business and entrepreneurship, and again, some do this more extensively than others. The US Small Business Administration, the Small and Medium Enterprise Administration in Taiwan, the Dutch Ministry of Economic Affairs, the UK Small Business Service and the Swedish Ministry of Industry, Employment and Communications (and NUTEK) are good practice examples of reporting on the state of their entrepreneurial dynamic. Governments are now more systematic about conducting reviews of existing support services and evaluating new entrepreneurs' needs. This is a big change since 2001.

Table 3-9. Overall country percentages for performance tracking items

Performance tracking	% of countries
Does the government have mechanisms to assess and track measures of "entrepreneurial climate" and "entrepreneurial culture"?	38%
Does the government evaluate and monitor the impact of its entrepreneurship policy measures and tools? Against pre-set, clear and measurable objectives?	46%
Does the government track and report on business dynamics (i.e., the entry, exit, survival and growth rates of enterprises)?	100%
Are self-employment, business ownership and business dynamic data disaggregated by gender, age, ethnic origin and region?	77%
Does the government support and/or publish research on and about its entrepreneurs?	85%
Does the government produce an annual report on the state of small business and entrepreneurship in the country?	62%

CONCLUSIONS

We see an overlap between Entrepreneurship, SME and Innovation policy in several countries. Innovation policy crosses over into Entrepreneurship policy in governments' efforts to stimulate greater numbers of innovative, technology-based start-ups. Traditional SME policy crosses over, in the "niche" E-policy area, aiming to increase the business ownership rates of under-represented segments of the population, and to some extent in the "New Firm Creation" policy set, where SME policy aims to address more of clients' needs for start-up supports (e.g., information, advice, counseling and micro-loans).

Governments have a choice of whether to use general ("everyone" benefits) or specific (selected groups benefit, but for the good of all) policy measures to achieve a desired outcome. In the areas of entrepreneurship, SME and innovation policy, we see both approaches. General framework policies to stimulate innovation would include things such as increasing the amount of R&D investment, improving the regulatory environment for approval of new products and technologies and emphasising opportunities for higher education in science and engineering. In SME policy, general framework policies would include such things as more open competition, fair taxation, and reduced administrative burden on smaller firms. In entrepreneurship policy, general framework policies would include such things as promoting entrepreneurship as an employment option for everyone, integrating entrepreneurship throughout the education system, and reducing the time and cost of starting a business.

Specific measures in each of these three main policy areas would focus much more on addressing systemic, market, and other failures. For example, in innovation policy, measures might be introduced to provide pre-seed funds to scientists to encourage them to develop prototypes and test them in potential markets. In SME policy, small firms are disadvantaged in capital markets, so governments implement loan guarantee or micro-loan programs for businesses meeting their definitional criteria. In entrepreneurship policy, specific policy measures might emphasise particular groups of the population under-represented as entrepreneurs, implementing special programmes for women, young people, and ethnic minorities.

We would argue that both general and specific policies are needed. If good general policy framework conditions do not exist, it will be difficult to achieve good outcomes from the specific policy actions. If it is difficult and costly to start a business, or if fair and open competition does not exist in the economy, or if entrepreneurship does not have social value in the economy, then efforts to increase start-up rates from among target group populations will be hindered. On the other hand, if the government's priority is placed on good general framework conditions without specific measures in key areas, then it may also be difficult to achieve good outcomes. Young people, ready and able to start businesses, may face barriers because they are not taken seriously by the financial community; women may not be encouraged to pursue entrepreneurship; and innovative entrepreneurs may not be able to source the expertise and risk-capital they need to develop their potentially-commercialisable ideas. We argue for policy convergence and more emphasis on an integrated entrepreneurship policy approach.

In this chapter, we have provided new insights into the nature and characteristics of entrepreneurship policy, including ways to categorise, measure and assess it. We have observed that governments demonstrate different levels of commitment to entrepreneurship policy and configure their policy measures in different ways. The entrepreneurship typology offers a useful way to classify these different approaches. We have discovered that governments in countries with lower business ownership and

TEA rates have higher commitment to entrepreneurship policy. Our entrepreneurship policy comprehensive instrument has been useful to explore overall as well as innovative entrepreneurship policy and to see how and why governments may diverge in these policy choices and some of the possibilities and risks of taking different policy paths.

In the future, it would be useful to extend the policy comprehensive scale into a measure of policy intensity – the depth to which governments are implementing actions in each of the policy framework areas. However, for the moment, we think it is equally important to explore in greater detail under what conditions different entrepreneurship approaches are appropriate, given a country's economic, structural and political context.

In Chapter 4, we present a conceptual discussion of this context.

---

[1] The self-employment rate for Spain is based on total employment figures taken from the OECD Labour Force Statistics for 2002.

[2] The unemployment rate is based on statistics obtained from the *OECD Employment Outlook 2004*, pp. 294-296.

[3] Described in *OECD Small and Medium Enterprises Outlook* (2002), p. 188.

[4] 30 and 38 business owners per 1,000 inhabitants respectively, based on 1998 figures (Wennekers and Thurik, 2001, p. 56).

[5] The percentage of total employment in SMEs for the latest year for which data was available (at the time we did our 2000-01 study) was 37 percent in the Netherlands, 30 percent in Finland and about 45 percent in the UK. This compared to about 42 percent in the US, 55 percent in Australia and 78 percent in Taiwan.

[6] The unemployment rate in Finland was 8.5 percent in 2003, according to data in the *OECD Employment Outlook 2004*.

[7] According to the CIA World Factbook report on the Netherlands (2004), real GDP growth in 2003 was –0.7 percent and the industrial productivity rate was –1.9 percent.

[8] See *A Government Action Plan for Small Business*, Department of Trade and Industry, 2004 (www.sbs.gov.uk/action).

[9] For example, the government's national action plan for employment would also include entrepreneurship and job creation as one its main policy lines of action, reinforcing the top priorities of the government.

[10] *Action Plan for Entrepreneurs!* Ministry of Economic Affairs, The Netherlands, 2004, p. 24.

[11] The innovation strategy is laid out in *Backing Australia's Ability*, Department of Industry, Tourism and Resources, Government of Australia.

[12] Three-quarters of the Irish population associate a high status with entrepreneurs and report often seeing stories about successful entrepreneurs in the media (Fitzsimons and O'Gorman, 2003, p. 3).

[13] See Stevenson and Lundström (2002), Chapter 3, pp. 67-95.

Chapter 4

CONTEXT - THE BASE OF ENTREPRENEURSHIP POLICY

INTRODUCTION TO CONTEXT

Creation of an entrepreneurship policy should take into consideration the specific conditions of a country or region. These conditions will vary from one country or region to another. One country may have a high unemployment rate, another a low female labour force participation rate, a third a high level of income dispersion, while a fourth may have a relatively low share of its total employment in the SME sector. Such is the case for the countries we have studied (Lundström and Stevenson, 2001, 2002; Stevenson and Lundström, 2001, 2002; Lundström (ed.), 2003). Because of these differences, one might not expect to find similarities in how entrepreneurship policies are developed or the problems they are meant to solve in different countries. "Necessity" entrepreneurship[1] is probably not a phenomenon in countries with relatively low unemployment rates or high labour force participation rates. Tax issues are perhaps less important in a country with high income dispersion, at least from an entrepreneurship policy point of view. This assumption could, of course, be questioned. For example in the US, which has a high degree of income dispersion, personal tax rates have been an important issue in recent years. Another example is illustrated by the Nordic countries, which have different conditions and problems, but where we see similarities in the choice of actual policy measures in the areas of entrepreneurship, SME and innovation policy (Lundström (ed.), 2003).

One could make a number of logical assumptions about why similarities and differences exist, depending on a country's economic and social conditions, as well as identify a number of logical reasons why behaviour in a country will not always be dependent on these conditions. This might be the case due to a lack of knowledge of alternatives, the fact that some problems have a low policy priority, the difficulty in changing an existing set of policy measures, or a lack of knowledge regarding how different outcomes will be affected by implementation of new policy measures.

The Importance of Context

Conditions, problems or possibilities are the starting point for a discussion of how to develop an entrepreneurship policy and what areas of the policy framework to emphasise because they are partly reflections of the existing "context" of a country. So what do we mean by the term "context"? In the entrepreneurship research literature, use of the word "context" is often associated with "social context" (Shane and Eckhardt, 2003; Shaver, 2003; Davidsson, 1989; Delmar, 1996) and primarily connected to an individual's perception. How individuals perceive their social context will affect the degree to which they choose entrepreneurship as an option and thus will determine the overall supply of entrepreneurship. This is an important point that we develop further in Chapter 5 when we discuss our conceptual model of the influences on someone's propensity to become an entrepreneur. In the conceptual model, we are interested in how the level of entrepreneurship is affected by a number of aggregate variables at an individual level. With such an approach both an individual and time perspective are needed. But in this chapter, we take a more empirical approach.

For the purpose of this analysis, "context" refers to a range of economic, social, cultural, attitudinal, and structural aspects of a country. It consists of three different aspects of the constraints and the possibilities that must be considered for a country or a region to construct an integrated entrepreneurship policy. We categorised these into three subsets: (A) "Outcomes variables"; (B) "Structure variables"; and (C) "SME/Entrepreneurial Vitality variables" (see Annex 4-1). Outcomes variables (Group A) consist of economic performance indicators, variables such as GDP growth, GDP per capita, labour force participation rates, unemployment rate, level of exports, and the industrial productivity rate. Structure variables (Group B) consist of demographic and industrial structure variables affecting opportunities for entrepreneurship (e.g., growth in consumer demand measured by size and growth of the population and level of income dispersion; the supply of potential entrepreneurs, measured by age composition of the population, the education level of the population and immigration rates; relative size of the service sector, where it is easier to start business; and constraints on entrepreneurial opportunities, measured by dominance of public sector employment and government taxation levels). SME/ Entrepreneurial Vitality variables (Group C) include measures of the level of entrepreneurial vitality in the economy, both in terms of density (e.g., proportion of SMEs, business owners, self-employed persons, and nascent entrepreneurs and SME employment share of total employment) and dynamics (e.g., annual growth in the number of SMEs and SME employment; and level of business entry and exit activity). Data for most of these variables is available from secondary sources and provides the opportunity to compare country contexts as a way of at least partly explaining their entrepreneurship policy orientations.

The most commonly used Outcomes variable in the area of entrepreneurship research is economic growth. The major research preoccupation is finding the link between economic growth and the level of entrepreneurship (Acs and Armington, 2003; Autio, 2002; Audretsch, 2002; Audretsch and Keilbach, 2003; Carree and Thurik, 2003; McGrath, 2003; Reynolds et al., 2004; Storey, 2003). A number of variables seem to be positively related to economic growth, including the number of business owners in the labour force at certain stages of a country's economic development cycle (Wennekers and Thurik, 2001), the level of necessity entrepreneurship (Reynolds et al., 2004), and a number of factors influencing the level of entrepreneurial activity (Autio, 2002). It is, therefore, of interest to comment on such correlations.

The weakest point of many of these findings is that they attempt to measure simple one-to-one correlations. Despite this, there does appear to be some sort of correlation between entrepreneurship and economic growth, but we are not exactly sure what the relationship looks like. We illustrate this by discussing two different approaches to measuring the level of entrepreneurial activity and economic growth. The first example is the approach used to determine the relationship between the level of nascent entrepreneurs, or the TEA index used in the GEM reports, and economic growth, measured as GDP per capita (Reynolds et al., 2004). In the 2003 GEM study findings, the Reynolds team found different values for two kinds of entrepreneurship – opportunity-based and necessity-based. The overall result is that there seems to be some form of correlation over time between necessity entrepreneurship and economic growth, while the relationship between opportunity entrepreneurship and economic growth is less measurable. One explanation for this could be that there is a positive effect on economic growth if people move from unemployment to self-employment. Countries with a low rate of necessity entrepreneurship, for example, EU member states, will see a less valid correlation between their entrepreneurial activity levels (TEA index) and economic growth. The second illustration is based on analysis of longitudinal business ownership data for 23 OECD countries (Wennekers and Thurik, 1999; Carree and Thurik, 2003). These researchers have discovered a U-shaped curve relationship between business ownership rates and country GDP per capita levels over time. Countries with low levels of GDP per capita (in earlier stages of the economic development cycle) have higher business ownership rates, but as GDP per capita increases (with economic development and growth) the business ownership rate declines. In later stages of economic development, there appears to be a positive correlation between the business ownership rate and GDP per capita.

If the business ownership rate illustrates the same phenomena as the TEA index or the prevalence rate of nascent entrepreneurs, then one could discuss the differences between observed relationships in the two illustrations of different approaches. What the U-shaped curve implies is that the business ownership rate will not always positively correlate with the variable for economic growth. On the contrary, during the first phase of economic development, there is a negative correlation, followed later by a positive one. In the GEM studies, nations with very different economic development stages are compared. The main result of this is a correlation between necessity entrepreneurship and economic growth. Now, if the share of necessity entrepreneurship is higher during the increasing part of the U-shaped curve, then the two sets of findings are comparable. Another explanation could be that the share of necessity entrepreneurs is highest for the pre-stage of the curve. It would, therefore, be of interest to know how the share of necessity entrepreneurship varies over the economic development cycle.

Summarising from these two research projects, one should not expect simple correlations over time between levels of entrepreneurship and economic growth. During certain stages of growth, the correlation is negative and during some other stages of the economic growth process, there does not seem to be any correlation. This latter observation is compatible with GEM findings for the relationship between opportunity entrepreneurship and economic growth. The explanation given for negative correlations during the earlier stages of economic development is industrial restructuring, while positive correlations in later stages of economic development are explained by the creation of new firms in different sectors, spin-offs, and so on. Our conclusion is that it is difficult to find simple and valid correlations over time and that there are problems in comparing economies in different development stages. This is one of the arguments for developing the context description in this chapter.

The context is about the structure of an economy, the performance or behaviour of the economy and the outcomes of that economy. The preconditions of an economy must be regarded when determining what emphasis to place on certain measures in a policy area versus others. Each government will formulate its own policy depending upon the preconditions in that country, at least from a logical point of view. There are, of course, other factors that must be taken into account here, for example, a government's view about the possible effects of policy actions taken or its view about what role a government could or should play in developing a policy area. Some governments are more positively inclined towards taking concrete policy measures than other governments. Different policymakers will behave differently to solve the same types of formulated problems. So even if there is consensus among countries on the policy measures to solve actual problems, this does not mean that the same types of measures will be selected to solve such problems. They will differ regarding policy measures taken, the type of general or specific approach, the type of organisations or service providers used and whether responsibilities are decentralised or not.

Another issue related to "context" is the use of best-practices and benchmarking approaches. As we have noted in previous chapters, the European Commission has produced a large number of documents and reports on good practices concerning how easy or difficult it is to start a firm in different member States or the state of entrepreneurship education in the school system, just to mention two areas that have been investigated. The OECD (1999) has made some comparative studies concerning the costs of regulations. The EU has also set some benchmarks stating the minimum or maximum level that member States should seek to achieve through certain policy measures. An example is the benchmark-maximum number of days it should take for an entrepreneur to start a company in terms of meeting procedural, administrative and compliance requirements (European Commission, 2002c). Best practice cases are built on an assumption that the experience in one country can be readily transferred to another. However, there are dangers with a best practice approach. A best practice could have been introduced to solve a very specific problem in a country which does not exist in another country. Or the factors that made it a best practice in one country are not present in another country. On the other hand, that does not mean that lessons cannot be learned from studying a number of good (as we prefer to call them) or best practices. The problem is that one normally does not know how sensitive the outcomes from such a best practice are to the context within which it was developed.

Similar arguments could be used to question the term "benchmarking" since, in these types of comparable studies, consideration is rarely given to the context in which practices are being developed. This also relates to the problem of comparing behaviour in different contexts. In general, we are talking about the difference between understanding (or evaluating) certain policy measures, and the desire to influence how certain processes should be carried out. It is not necessarily the case that by understanding policy measures we can decide how to implement them in other contexts. In the literature, one often sees a mixture of these two aspects. The negative implication of this is that a best practice is only valid for a certain time period in a certain context and does not say anything about the generalisability of such a best practice to other environments. However, the positive implication is that the best practice might be generalisable, but has to be proven first. If a best practice is more general, it could be regarded as a robust measure. These examples also illustrate the importance of considering context when evaluating different policy options and measures, a topic we will take up in Chapter 6.

Before entering into the detailed context descriptions, one additional perspective should be mentioned. A context is dynamic in the sense that it changes over time. Here one must be aware of the difficulties of comparing contexts using statistics for different time periods. Furthermore, the concept of "entrepreneurial dynamics" is really the concept of an ever-ongoing process. An individual can act entrepreneurially during certain periods of life,[2] and a country can change positions over time; yet, depending on at what point a statistical measurement is done, the individual or country could (or would) be judged as more, or less entrepreneurial. This is, of course, a general dilemma for most research carried out in the social sciences. In general, it is about attempting to study processes by taking a static view. By that we mean that most studies of processes are about studying certain occasions during such processes and but not the whole process. From that perspective, it is not obvious what the actual process looks like. On the other hand, we observe from our research that structures in different policy areas are not easily changed. This means that major shifts in policy orientation happen only slowly over time. In summary, one can see a lot of research attempting to study one-to-one relationships (see Annex 1-1 in Chapter 1), as well as a lack of consideration for the "time perspective".

CONSTRUCTING A CONTEXT DESCRIPTION

As described above, context clearly matters, but how can it best be understood and analysed? This is not an easy question to answer. We have attempted to construct a context model in two steps. The first step was to review the literature to identify variables stated as being important elements in the three dimensions we have described – Outcomes, Structure, and SME/Entrepreneurial, Vitality. The second step was to select a number of those variables for which reasonable comparable statistical data could be obtained. One could argue that this is not an optimal procedure to use to construct a context framework. This may, of course, be true, but we would argue that no such optimal way can be formalised and measured. Furthermore, even if this could be done, there is still no solution for how to find correlations between the different variables in the three sets of context groupings. To put it in another way there is no single alternative to explain economic growth, as we stressed earlier.

In fact, we believe that an economic growth measurement depends on the context in which it is measured, what part of the process is being analysed and what a country's Structure looks like. That does not mean that one context configuration is better than another in terms of generating economic growth. But the interactions and relationships between variables are much too complex for the simple correlation analysis used in many research studies. It is our belief that a better understanding of the importance of context will also help all of us to better judge the effectiveness and efficiency of measures taken in the entrepreneurship policy area. Complexity should be analysed and understood, not oversimplified. Summing up, we see our attempt, even if it is not an optimal description, as an improved way of better understanding measures taken, the reasons behind them, and possible outcomes.

Before moving to our context description, we want to make an additional observation regarding our definition of context. As we mentioned earlier, most researchers talk about context as a social matter, or mainly as perceived from an individual's point of view. In the coming section we develop the term context consisting of a combination of actual factors. The perspective of perceived factors is introduced in Chapter 5. One could argue that all factors should be perceived since actual factors, in some senses, will always be reflected in how they are perceived, but we think that such an approach will not ease our understanding of the term context. Firstly, individuals do not perceive things in similar manners. Secondly, it is not an easy task to "translate" the relationship between actual and perceived factors. Thirdly, individuals do not perceive factors independently; they are influenced by each other, meaning that one cannot know if a person is perceiving an actual fact or reacting to what someone in their surrounding emphasises is the actual case. If in a country the media always claims that it is difficult or easy to start a company, it is not the same thing as saying that this is actually true, for a number of reasons, but such statements could influence the behaviour of individuals. Therefore, one must present data and not only how data can be interpreted. In line with such reasoning, this chapter could be seen as the presenting of factors and data without regard for how such data is interpreted by individuals or policymakers.

In this remainder of this chapter, the context is developed as a model; in Chapter 5, we move one step further by constructing a conceptual model of entries and exits; and in Chapter 6, we explore issues of evaluating policies and measures.

Factors Influencing Entrepreneurial Activity Levels

In reviewing the literature, one realises that a number of factors have been identified as being related to entrepreneurial activity in a country or a region. Some factors are more commonly related than others, for example, ease of business entry or exposure to entrepreneur role models (Djankov et al., 2000; Reynolds et al., 2004). Other factors relate more to the results of entrepreneurial activity, e.g., economic growth, the density of business owners and the number of SMEs. There are also a number of factors that more describe the structure of a society and how certain structures promote or prevent entrepreneurial activity, such as the size of the public sector or level of income dispersion (Verheul et al., 2001; Storey, 1994; Davidsson and Henrekson, 2000; Arenius and Autio, 2001; Cooper, 2003).

In Table 4-1, we list a number of factors that are commonly described as being connected to the level of entrepreneurial activity in a society. These factors are organised in such a way as to combine our context approach with our entrepreneurship policy model. Related to our earlier mention of entrepreneurial behaviour being something episodic, one could also argue that entrepreneurial activity is something episodic. Even if this was the case, it would not change the fact that certain factors can influence or prevent these temporary or episodic activities. The context description is not about analysing individual behaviour at certain points in a process, but about modelling factors that hinder or stimulate such behaviour. These factors can be seen to describe Outcomes or Structures and be Opportunity, Motivation or Skills-related. One could debate how factors have been allocated to the quadrants of Table 4-1, but the intent is to provide an indication of the types of factors commonly presented in the literature. We discuss each of them in the next section.

Table 4-1. Factors influencing the level of entrepreneurial activity

	Opportunity	Motivation	Skills
Outcomes	Growth in GDP GDP per capita Unemployment rate Labour force participation rate Labour force participa- tion rate for women Exports as percentage of GDP Total industrial productivity rate		
Structure	Population size Population growth rate Immigration rate Ease of business entry Women's business ownership rate Access to start-up capital Flexible labour markets Size of the public sector Decentralized markets Ease of business exit Size and structure of industrial sector Age distribution of the population	Exposure to role models Exposure to entrepreneurship education Social security Inequities in tax treatment of the self- employed vs the employed Inequities in tax treatment of self- employment vs corporate income Favourable capital gains tax	Density of business owners Level of education
Behaviour	Positive supportive climate Government support	Tolerance for income dispersion Social and cultural norms Positive attitudes Entrepreneurship advocates Fear and stigma of failure	Public sector procurement

Outcomes

The Outcomes variables are all examples of objectives used in policymaking and are also of great theoretical interest when measuring correlations and results, especially, growth in GDP per capita. The general assumption is that high growth in GDP per capita will be in some way related to the level of entrepreneurial activity. Either increased entrepreneurial activity levels will produce growth in GDP or growth in GDP will produce opportunities for future entrepreneurship because of rising incomes and standards of living. If we accept the hypothesis behind the U-shaped curve theory, the relationship between entrepreneurial activity levels and GDP growth will differ over the economic development cycle for an economy, even if the growth measure itself is a derivative of the U-shaped curve.

The unemployment rate has been discussed as a factor in many research studies. Reynolds et al. (2004) discuss it in relationship to necessity entrepreneurship. Davidsson et al. (1994) considered the level of, and rapid change of, unemployment stating that a rapid change will be positively-related to the level of entrepreneurship, while a long-term high level of unemployment will be more negatively-correlated. We also know that only a small percentage of unemployed people will start their own business. Concluding, we see unemployment rate as a measure for Outcomes and Opportunity.

The labour force participation rate of the population is another Outcomes variable of interest. A high labour force participation rate means more working-age adults will have opportunities to be exposed to role models and relevant working experiences. On the other hand, it will also mean a higher share of opportunity-based entrepreneurship and lower share of necessity-based entrepreneurship. We use two measures of the labour force participation rate – the total rate and the rate for the female labour force. The reason for this is that the female labour force participation rate tells us something about the level of working experience among the women in a society, since working experience is normally an important factor in the decision to become an entrepreneur.

Total industrial productivity rate is of great interest for economists around the world, as are export figures. Productivity measures are very important in discussions of growth possibilities in an economy.

We will include all these variables in our context description for the countries in our study.

Structure

Population size is a structural factor in many respects. A large population base creates many possibilities for the establishment and growth of a viable enterprise in the domestic market. It is also often regarded to be of importance on a regional level. A large population increases the probability of more areas of density. One could expect that this factor will, therefore, be of importance in affecting the level of entrepreneurial activity. In our model, we see population size as a Structure variable influencing Opportunity for entrepreneurial activity. Population growth is also a Structure variable that, according to Reynolds et al. (1999) and Verheul et al. (2001), has a positive impact on entrepreneurial activity. We see these two variables as Opportunity-oriented.

Other Structure and Opportunity-oriented factors are net immigration rate (Verheul et al., 2001; Storey, 1994); ease of business entry (Djankov et al., 2000); women's participation in business ownership (Reynolds et al., 2004); access to capital (Reynolds et al., 2004); flexible labour markets and decentralised market economy (Davidsson and Henrekson, 2000); size of the public service (Arenius and Autio, 2001); and ease of business exits.

Another set of Structure factors is more Motivation-oriented, such as exposure to role models or entrepreneurship education (Hindle and Rushworth, 2003; Reynolds et al., 2000; Charney and Libecap, 2000; European Commission, 2003c); social security and tax inequalities (Verheul et al., 2001; Davidsson and Henrekson, 2000; NFIB, 2000); and favourable capital gains taxes (Davidsson and Henrekson, 2000).

The "density of business owners" is regarded as a Structure and Skills factor. One could argue that a higher density of business owners would impact positively on the creation of role models. It also is a sign of more entrepreneurial skills in a society. Similar arguments could be used for the educational level in the society.

Behaviour

Factors oriented more towards behaviour are also categorised into three different types. A positive supportive climate and governmental support are Opportunity-based factors (Birch et al., 1999; Zacharakis et al., 2000). Tolerance for income dispersion is a factor that is more Motivation-oriented (Reynolds et al., 2000; Verheul et al., 2001). Other similar factors are social and cultural norms that value and support entrepreneurship (Wennekers and Thurik, 2001; Reynolds et al., 2000; Verheul et al., 2001) and positive attitudes towards entrepreneurship, entrepreneurship advocates, and fear of failure (Vesalainen and Pihkala, 1999). Finally, public sector procurement is seen as Skills-oriented (Davidsson and Henrekson, 2000).

A number of these variables are used in our context description. The conclusion from Table 4-1 is that a great number of factors have been found to be important to the level of entrepreneurship. This means there are a lot of possibilities for creating a context description.

Creating a Context Description

One of the most interesting current issues in entrepreneurship research is determining to what extent factors contributing to entrepreneurial activity levels or the dynamic of the SME sector create certain Outcomes or influence Structure variables over time (Reynolds et al., 2004; Acs and Armington, 2003; Cooper, 2003; Carree and Thurik, 2003). There do not appear to be any simple correlations between performance and economic outcomes (often measured as growth in GDP per capita). In this section, we will demonstrate that it is also a choice of the variables used in such equations. Depending on the variables chosen, different results will be produced.

One aspect of the complexity is that the three subsets of variables that we have chosen are interdependent, which is also the situation in other studies and in evaluations. Such interdependencies are normally not taken into account in recent research in the entrepreneurship area. In Figure 4-1, we formulate our integrated context model.

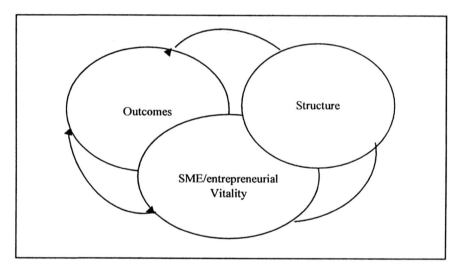

Figure 4-1. An integrated context model
Source: Lundström and Stevenson (2002), p. 63.

The three subsets of this context model are more or less consistent with those ones described in Table 4-1. However, the subset SME/Entrepreneurial Vitality is a new one and combines variables that are both structural and dynamic. We include measures for this subset because we are mainly interested in variables describing the entrepreneurial activity levels in different countries, as well as the structure of their SME sector. Furthermore, variables describing this subset can be statistically measured and data is available, an important consideration for us when constructing the context model.

We have already described the Outcomes variables in the previous section. Structure variables chosen for the context model include total population and population growth; net immigration rate; services sector output as a percentage of GDP; age difference in the population; education level; income dispersion; the level of government taxation; and share of public sector employment. Not all variables from Table 4-1 are included in our context model, the reasons being that some of them would be impossible to measure and others are reflected in the selected variables. Furthermore, some variables, like exposure to role models, are discussed in Chapter 5 where we present the conceptual model.

Variables chosen for the third subset, SME/Entrepreneurial Vitality, describe some aspects of the structure and dynamics of this part of the economy. Variables describing the structure (or density) include SMEs per 1,000 inhabitants, SME share of micro-firms, micro-firm share of employment, the self-employment rate, the business ownership rate, the TEA index, and the nascent entrepreneur rate. Dynamic variables include annual growth in the number of SMEs, annual growth in SME employment, and the annual start up and exit rates. We list all of the selected variables for the three different subsets in Table 4-2.

We have already shown how these variables are, in some sense, connected to the level of entrepreneurship. We have seven Outcomes variables, not independent of each other. One can assume that unemployment and labour force participation rates depend on each other. There are dependencies between the total labour force participation rate and the female participation rate. All of these variables, except the unemployment rate, are assumed to be positively-related to the level of entrepreneurship, so there are obvious connections between the Outcomes and SME/Entrepreneurial Vitality subsets. We also assume connections between Outcomes and Structure variables, for example between GDP variables and education level. Structure variables will also affect SME/Entrepreneurial Vitality variables. For example, a large public sector measured by share of total employment and level of taxation (as a percentage of GDP), will likely mean a lower TEA index because there will be fewer private sector opportunities, government employees are less likely to become entrepreneurs, and so on. However, the subset SME/ Entrepreneurial Vitality also affects the subset of Structure variables, for example, the level of services sector contribution to GDP. We will not describe all of these dependencies because we are more interested in the values for the different variables in each subset and in comparing these values.

Table 4-2. Variables used in context model description

Outcomes	GDP per capita
	Growth in GDP
	Unemployment rate
	Labour force participation rate
	Female labour force participation rate
	Total industrial productivity rate
	Exports as percentage of GDP
Structure	Total population
	Population growth
	Net immigration rate
	Level of income dispersion
	Education level
	Service sector output as percentage of GDP
	Age difference in the population
	Public sector employment
	Government taxation
SME/entrepreneurial vitality	SMEs per 1,000 inhabitants
	Solo-firms (percentage of all firms)
	SME share of total employment
	Micro-firms (percentage of all firms)
	Micro-firms employment
	Business ownership rate
	Self-employment rate (of total employment)
	Female self-employment rate
	TEA index
	Nascent entrepreneurship rate
	Annual growth in number of SMEs
	Annual growth in SME employment
	Start-up rate
	Start-up rate minus exit rate
	Start-up rate plus exit rate

Source: Revised from Lundström and Stevenson (2002), p. 60.

Data for each of the context variables was obtained for the 13 countries. We then ranked each of the countries on each of the variables. To rank the countries on each variable, we assigned the best performing country the ranking number of (1) and the lowest performing country the ranking number of (13). For the subset of Structure variables, low values represented better performance, except for public sector employment and government taxation. For the subsets Outcomes and SME/Entrepreneurial Vitality, low values indicated better performance for all variables. In the latter subset, the variable "exit rate" is only used to calculate the values for the net increase in the stock of firms (entry minus exit rate) and the level of turbulence or "Dynamism" (entry plus exit rate), since there is no consensus about the value of a low or high exit rate.

The list of variables, data used and all country ranking values from 1-13 are displayed in Annex 4-1. Each country is presented with its ranking values for each subset, including a calculation of the average values for each subset.

To deal with the rank-aggregation problem and to obtain a better rank-ordering, we next used the Borda ranking procedure (see Moulin, 1988). We used this ranking procedure to help overcome the number of well-known problems in doing international statistical comparisons (e.g., countries are at different stages of economic development; international statistical data are not completely comparable, and ordinal ranking systems do not take into consideration that two rankings can be more or less similar). Based on the average ordinal rankings for each of the three subsets of variables (and including the average rankings for the two categories of variables within the SME/Entrepreneurial Vitality subset), we assigned Borda ranking values from +6 to -6 to the ordinal rankings. An ordinal ranking of 7 was assigned the Borda value of 0; ordinal rankings below 7 were assigned values of +1 to +6; ordinal rankings above 7 were assigned Borda ranking values of -1 to -6. The average ordinal rankings for each subset of variables for each country appear in Annex 4-2 and the Borda rankings for each country and subset of variables in Annex 4-3.

In Annex 4-4, we categorise the average ranking values for each of the three subsets of variables for the 13 countries into three groupings, considering variable-ranking values of between 1 and 4 as high; values of between 10 and 13 as low; and values between 5 and 9 as average, in relative performance.

RESULTS OF THE CONTEXT DESCRIPTION

Data for the observed variables in each of the three different subsets illustrate the great variation among countries. The US has almost twice the level of GDP per capita as Spain; the US has a population of over 290 million compared to less than 300,000 for Iceland. We can also see great variations in ranking values for different variables for the same country. The US ranks as high-performing for many Outcomes and Structure variables, but relatively low-performing on exports/GDP and the unemployment rate.

In this section, we start by comparing the situation for all countries on two of the subsets of variables, Outcomes and Structure. In Figure 4-2, we combine the total ranking values for each country and subset, giving the value zero for the ranking value of 7 in each subset, meaning that there is a range of ranking values from +6 to – 6. All 13 cases are illustrated.

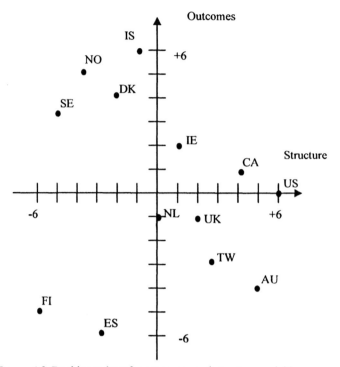

Figure 4-2. Ranking values for outcomes and structure variables

There are four different quadrants depending on whether the country has a positive or negative Borda ranking value for Outcomes and Structure. Canada and Ireland have positive ranking values for both subsets, while the US has an average Outcomes ranking value but ranks positive for Structure variables. The UK, Taiwan and Australia have negative ranking values for Outcomes variables and positive values for Structure variables. Finland and Spain have negative ranking values for both subsets, while the remaining Nordic countries have negative ranking values for Structure variables, but positive Outcomes ranking values. The Netherlands has ranking values close to average for both subsets.

One observation from this analysis is that there are great variations for different variables in the subsets. In relative terms, the US ranks very positive for GDP per capita and growth in GDP, but average or negative for the remaining Outcomes variables, and relatively high performing for all Structure variables. Norway, on the other hand, ranks fairly positive for all Outcomes variables, except growth in GDP and industrial productivity rate, but negative on most Structure variables. Another observation is that countries ranked negative on Structure variables are the Nordic countries and Spain, while all other countries have positive Structure ranking values.

We illustrate the relationship between the Outcomes and Vitality subsets in Figure 4-3.

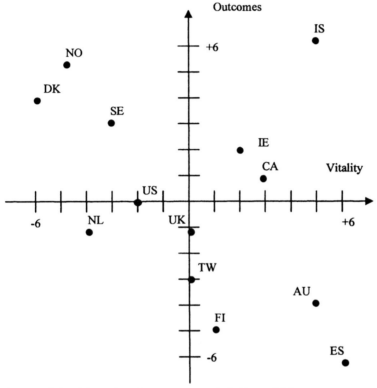

Figure 4-3. Ranking values for outcomes and vitality variables

Ireland, Canada and Iceland have positive values for both subsets, while the Netherlands has negative values for these subsets. Finland, Australia and Spain have positive values for Vitality and negative values for Outcomes, while Denmark, Norway and Sweden have positive values for Outcomes, but negative ranking values for Vitality variables. Three economies, the US, UK and Taiwan, have average ranking values for either Outcomes or Vitality variables.

As we described at the beginning of this chapter, a lot of research has been done concerning the relationships between SME/Entrepreneurial Vitality variables and economic growth. Obviously, there are a very limited number of cases in our study, even if we consider the relatively large numbers of variables for each subset. But if a simple correlation could be found, all countries, or most of them, should be in the quadrants with positive or negative values for both subsets of variables. That is not the case. Only four of thirteen cases are in these quadrants. One explanation is the variation among countries for different variables in the subsets. Ireland is a case in point. It has great variations in the ranking values for density variables in the Vitality subset but rather similar ranking values for the dynamic variables in the same subset. Denmark is another exception. It has relatively similar ranking values for most of the variables in the Vitality subset. One conclusion is that correlations will depend upon which variables are being used in their measurement.

Finally, in Figure 4-4, we illustrate the relationship between ranking values for the Structure and Vitality subsets.

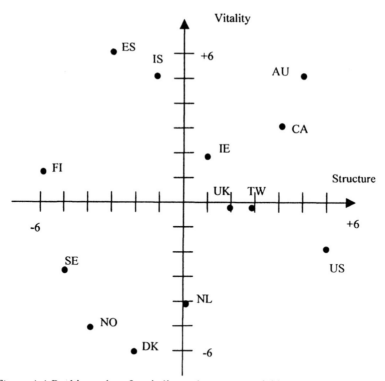

Figure 4-4. Ranking values for vitality and structure variables

In this case, Ireland, Canada and Australia have positive ranking values for both subsets, while Sweden, Norway and Denmark have negative ranking values for both subsets. Spain, Iceland and Finland have positive Vitality ranking values and negative Structure ranking values, while the opposite case is true for the US. Economies with average values for one of the subsets are the UK, Taiwan and the Netherlands. It is interesting that all economies, except Ireland and Canada, have changed quadrants when all values are taken into account. With the exception of Spain, there seems to be some type of correlation between the ranking values on variables for Structure and Vitality, with three of the Nordic countries having negative values for both. There are too few cases to do any real testing of this hypothesis. We assume, however, that Structure variables are very important in constructing an entrepreneurial society, variables such as, age distribution of the population, education level, public sector employment and services sector output, to give some examples. However, Structure variables are not discussed very much by policymakers in official government documents, with the exception of government taxation levels or the problem of an ageing population (even if the ageing population problem is more about future demands for health care).

In Figure 4-5, we present a more visually graphic illustration of the comparative differences between these 13 countries based on their Borda ranking values for our chosen Outcomes, Structure and Vitality variables.

One interesting observation from our analysis is that Structure variables seem to be more important than Outcomes variables in affecting the level of SME/entrepreneurial vitality. On the other hand, differences in Vitality variables influence Outcomes variables, even if it is not easy to say in what way and with what time lag. Outcomes variables make it possible to identify what changes need to be made to Structure variables, which then changes the presumptions for SME/entrepreneurship Vitality, and so on. The conclusion would be that it is of vital importance to Outcomes that a country has a dynamic and vital SME and entrepreneurial sector, but that to create such a sector, Structure variables are of outmost importance.

To simplify these conclusions, we suggest that more research needs to be done to explore all of these different types of correlations over time. The context model could be developed in a number of ways, not the least of which would be by including other variables. This approach has similarities with the GEM Conceptual Model (see Reynolds et al., 2004, p. 83). From a policymaker's point of view, we believe that it would be important to take an integrated approach, and above all, to discuss how a better structure for entrepreneurship can be created.

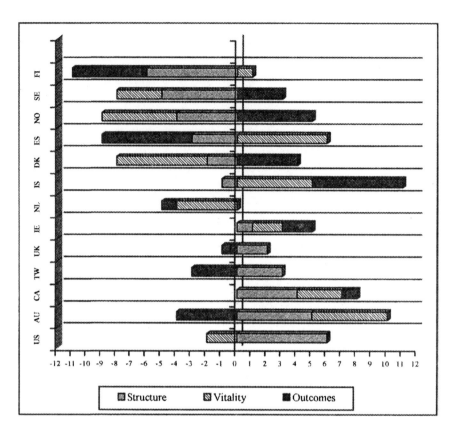

Figure 4-5. Country differences on outcomes, structure and vitality Borda rankings
Note: For the UK and Taiwan, the "Vitality" value is zero; for the Netherlands, the
"Structure" value is zero.

One of the problems with our context model is the great variation in
ranking values for each country and subset. This variation is not easy to
explain. No country or economy has high-performance ranking values for all
variables in a subset. For individual countries, there seems to be
contradictory results. Each individual country probably has its own path and
context model. In creating a context model, regional aspects should also be
included. It is important to continue to relate and learn from other countries.
These conclusions are further developed below.

No country or economy has high-ranking values for all variables in a subset
Some ranking values are not easy to explain when looking at a single
economy. Why does the US have such a high TEA index rating and nascent
entrepreneurship rate, but lower-performing ranking values for the business

ownership rate, the number of micro-firms, the employment share of micro-firms and the self-employment rate? Why does Sweden, on the contrary, have such a low value for the TEA index, but such a high value for the number of solo-companies? Why does Finland have a relatively high unemployment rate and also a high annual growth in SME employment? Unless contradictory results are due to statistical problems.

One way to deal with this would be to classify the ranking values into high, average and low, as is demonstrated for the three subsets in Annex 4-4. Even when this is done for all variables, we still see contradictions similar to the ones described above. How can we explain these contradictions? We will make an attempt in the next section to do a limited amount of this by commenting on the overall context model description for each of the countries in the study. Another way would be to group the different countries by their similarities in rankings. Except for Canada and Ireland, which have positive ranking values for all three subsets (one grouping), we can see that Denmark, Norway and Sweden have similar ranking values (see Figure 4-5). They would be in a second grouping. Finland and Spain would be in a third group. Furthermore, similar ranking values exist for the US, Taiwan, UK, Australia and the Netherlands and they would be in a fourth group.

Within individual countries there seems to be contradictory results

Some of the results for individual countries are contradictory. Even in cases where the Borda ranking values for SME/Entrepreneurial Vitality are low, one can find high ranking values for some Outcomes variables and vice versa. Or to put it differently, one can see positive Outcomes without positive values for certain variables describing SME/ Entrepreneurial Vitality; and one can see positive values for these without particularly positive Outcomes values. Now, as has been stated a number of times, we have few observations and cannot, therefore, draw general conclusions about these findings.

Each individual country has its own development path and context model

Another implication from our context model is that each individual economy has its own path for development. The possible combinations of actions taken to influence different variables are, among other things, dependent on the values that these variables have. For Structure variables it is about changing the industry structure or an ageing population or population growth, to give some examples. It is not obvious what alternatives to pursue. Will a higher labour force participation rate or lower unemployment rate be of equal importance, independent of how it is achieved? Is it start-ups or nascent entrepreneurs or micro firms or big SMEs that should be in focus? Each possible path taken will differ in results, resources needed, and over time. To construct such a path for an economy can only partly be done by examining international experiences.

In creating a context model, regional aspects also have to be included

Our context model has been based on national data. However, in practice we know that regional variations are of great importance. In several ways, the national data is an aggregation and an average value for these regional variations. One would, therefore, expect contradictory regional data as well.

It is important to continue to relate to and learn from other countries

Independent of the many problems in applying the context model presented in this section, we think that it is important to learn from other countries concerning actions taken and results. The experiences of other countries will provide examples for consideration and assessment, given the special context of an individual economy. We must learn more about possible correlations and how the context model we have described can be improved. The research society is still in the early stages of being able to explain the possible connections between a numbers of these variables.

   "In spite of over 100 years of theorizing, no theoretical link between (firm-level) entrepreneurship and national-level economic growth has been formally proven... Therefore, policy-makers should refrain from implying a direct link between entrepreneurship and national-level economic growth, because this may be prove misleading... It is the intertwined link between entrepreneurial activity and economic growth and dynamism that policy-makers should emphasise." (Autio, 2002, p. 11).

   However, one observable effect of learning from each other is that discussions will focus more on the possible policy measures than on how they fit a certain context and the policy constraints of finding this fit. One example of this is illustrated in the Nordic countries. They all have similar types of policy measures for SME and entrepreneurship policy, in spite of the fact that the context for the individual countries varies a lot (Lundström (ed.), 2003).

CONTEXT AND E-POLICY COMPREHENSIVENESS

   The context model illustrates the great variation in the different observed variables and their performance for different subsets and countries. In chapter 2, we introduced the entrepreneurship policy comprehensiveness index that measures how active different governments are in different areas of entrepreneurship policy. The obvious question is, can we see any connection between the context model and policy comprehensiveness? Is it possible to see that individual governments have taken into consideration any of the results demonstrated by the context model when they organise their different policy measures? This does not obviously seem to be the case. Ireland, for example, is not very active in Type 1 target group policy despite having a low female labour force participation rate and low female self-employment rate. Financing is the main policy area for the different countries, which is the more traditional measure of SME policy. Another interesting finding is that a number of the governments are not very active with efforts to track the performance of their entrepreneurship policy measures.

One way to demonstrate a possible relationship between the context model and entrepreneurship policy comprehensiveness is to compare the ranking values for each country in each of the subsets of the context model with their policy comprehensiveness ratings. We do this in Table 4-3.

Table 4-3. Ranking values for the context model and e-policy comprehensiveness

Economy	Outcomes ranking values	Structure ranking values	SME/Entrepre-neurial vitality ranking values	Entrepreneurship policy comprehensiveness ranking
Australia	11	2	2	8
Canada	6	3	4	11
Denmark	3	9	13	5
Finland	12	13	6	4
Iceland	1	8	2	13
Ireland	5	6	5	10
Netherlands	8	7	11	2
Norway	2	11	12	12
Spain	13	10	1	7
Sweden	4	12	10	6
Taiwan	10	4	7	9
United Kingdom	8	5	7	1
United States	7	1	9	2

What type of relationship should we expect to find? If we do, as before, and rank values in three groupings of high, average and low, we are able to explore some interesting connections.

Australia

Australia has a high ranking value for Outcomes, low for Structure and Vitality and average for policy comprehensiveness. (One must remember that low ranking values are seen as positive and high as negative in the context model). If we look further at the results in Annex 4-1, we can see that Australia performs relatively less well (has high rankings) for the unemployment rate, labour force participation rates, exports, education level, and annual growth in the number of SMEs. The Australian government is relatively active in areas like entrepreneurship education, business support for start-ups and early stage growth, and removing barriers to entry. Therefore, there is some logic between Outcomes and policy measures taken, that is, taking measures to increase the number of SMEs, improve the education system and encourage growth companies. This will likely have positive effects on the unemployment and labour force participation rates.

Canada

Canada has a relatively high unemployment rate and low annual growth in the number of SMEs. Furthermore, Canada performs relatively well on population growth (including for its net immigration rate), female self employment rate, the number of SMEs per 1,000 inhabitants, the share of micro-firms, the share of micro-firm employment, the annual entry rate, and the turbulence rate (sum of entry and exit rates). The government's main areas in entrepreneurship policy are SME financing and target group measures. These types of measures could have effects on the unemployment rate and the annual growth in numbers of SMEs. However, the low growth rate in the number of SMEs could either be a function of having both a high annual start-up and exit rate (thus minimal net growth in the stock of firms), or because there is already a large stock of existing firms. This could be a factor in Canada's low policy rating. We made this observation in Chapter 3; that countries with higher than average business ownership and TEA rates tend to have lower scores for entrepreneurship policy comprehensiveness.

Denmark

Denmark has negative ranking values for 13 of the 31 variables described in the context model. The country performs relatively well on only four variables: GDP per capita; labour force participation rates; the female labour force participation rate; and income dispersion (i.e., has low ranking values). All Vitality variables have negative ranking values. This could be a reason why Denmark is ranked as number five on policy comprehensiveness – they are working to improve their performance. However, they do not rank high for policy areas such as entrepreneurship promotion, policy for target groups or business support for start-up and early-stage growth. They seem to concentrate on seed financing, removing entry barriers and, to some extent, entrepreneurship education.

Finland

Finland has a situation similar to that of Denmark; scoring negative for 12 variables and positive for four variables (i.e., micro-firm share of employment, annual growth in SME employment, annual entry rate and the sum of entry and exit rates). They have the highest negative Borda ranking values of all the countries for Structure variables and the second most negative for Outcomes variables. Overall, Finland has a relatively high ranking for entrepreneurship policy, with higher scores than Denmark for all areas except the area concerning removing barriers to entry.

Iceland

Iceland scores low for all Outcomes variables, except one. They score low for 16 out of 26 measurable variables and high for five variables. They rank relatively less well (have high negative ranking values) for education level, service sector output, annual entry rate, the sum of entry and exit rates, and, of course, for the size of the population. They rank last in entrepreneurship policy comprehensiveness (13th place), which means this is not have a very well developed policy area (comparatively speaking), except for financing measures. Despite this, Iceland behaves fairly well concerning Outcomes variables. They also have a relatively high TEA index (ranking third) and nascent entrepreneurs rate (ranking second), which seems strange since they rank in eleventh place for annual business entry rate.

Ireland

Ireland has more positive ranking values than negative (15 against 8). The distribution of these variables among the three subsets seems to be rather equal. Ireland scores negative for labour force participation rates, education level, services sector output, size of the population, and the SME share of solo and micro-firms. It has low positive scores for industrial productivity rate (second place), population growth (first place), net immigration rate (second place), income dispersion (second place), entry rate (second place), and entry minus exit rates (first place). Ireland has a below average ranking value for the entrepreneurship policy comprehensiveness index, their main policy areas being seed financing and business support for early stages, but with a heavy emphasis on innovative start-ups with growth potential.

The Netherlands

The Netherlands has the most "average" ranking scores, for 18 variables; low rankings for only five (where it performs relatively well); and high negative scores for seven, such variables being: growth in real GDP; industrial productivity rate; public sector employment (illustrating a high share of public employment); the TEA index; the nascent entrepreneurship rate; the number of SMEs per 1,000 inhabitants; the SME share of total employment; and the SME share of micro-firms. Low positive rankings are for unemployment rate; exports; services sector output; female self-employment; and annual growth in the number of SMEs. These are the variables for which the Netherlands performs relatively well. However, if the number of SMEs is low, it is perhaps not so difficult to have a fairly high relative annual increase in that factor. The Netherlands ranks in second place on entrepreneurship comprehensiveness, having relatively high values for most of the areas measured, except for promotion of entrepreneurship.

Norway

Norway has many variables scoring low or high (12 against 9). It scores mainly positive for the Outcomes variables, performing relatively less well only for the industrial productivity rate and growth in GDP, which in some senses are not unimportant variables. Norway has high ranking values for most of the Structure variables, except for the education level, where it has a low value, and for some other variables, such as the age distribution where it has average ranking values. Norway only has three low ranking values among the Vitality variables: for the number of SMEs per 1,000 inhabitants (second place); the annual growth in the number of SMEs (fourth place); and the start-up minus exit rate (fourth place) On their entrepreneurship policy comprehensiveness ranking Norway came in 12th place, meaning that entrepreneurship policy is not well developed. To some extent, measures exist for seed financing and entrepreneurship education. However, the Norwegian government's main policy thrust is in the innovation area.

Spain

Spain has an equal number of variables with low and high-ranking values (10 of each). However, variables with high-ranking values are all Outcomes or Structure-oriented. It only has low ranking values for the size of the population and its relatively small size of the public sector. Spain has no high-ranking value for any Vitality variable, meaning that, according to the data for this subset, the country behaves relatively well (i.e., has a high business ownership rate and SME share of micro-firms). Regarding policy comprehensiveness, they rank 7th and score above average for policy measures in the area of seed financing, business support and removing barriers to entry.

Sweden

Sweden has 13 variables with high-ranking values and 7 with low positive ranking values. It mainly has negative values for Structure and

Vitality variables (performing relatively less well). The opposite is more or less true for Outcomes variables. Sweden has high labour force participation rates and export figures, a high education level, a high percentage of solo and micro-firms and relatively high annual growth in the number of SMEs. The size of the SME sector is small compared to some of the other countries, mainly due to a large public sector. Sweden has relatively high scores and ranking for entrepreneurship policy comprehensiveness. They place relatively more emphasis on target group measures, seed financing, business support, and promotion of entrepreneurship.

Taiwan

The data for Taiwan shows an equal number of variables with high or low ranking values (8 of each). Most of the negative values are for Outcomes and Vitality variables. Taiwan has a low labour force participation rate and a low self-employment rate for women, while it has a favourable age distribution, low taxation and a small public sector. The SME share of total employment is high, and so is the self-employment rate. Taiwan is active in entrepreneurship policy measures, especially in promotion of entrepreneurship, seed financing and business support.

The United Kingdom

The UK has six variables with high ranking values and eight variables with low positive ranking values. Outcomes variables with relatively negative values are exports and the industrial productivity rate; for Structure variables, they are population growth and the age distribution of the population; for Vitality, negative values are for annual growth in SME employment and start-up minus exit rates. Examples of variables with more positive values are the size of the total population, the size of the service sector, the size of the public sector and the level of government taxation. For Vitality variables, the UK has positive values (ranks in second or third place) for the number of solo and micro-firms, the micro-firm share of employment, and the sum of entries and exit rates. The UK government has the highest entrepreneurship policy comprehensiveness score and ranking and is active in all areas of the entrepreneurship policy framework.

The United States

The US has 8 variables with high-ranking values (where it ranks in tenth place or higher) and 14 with low positive ranking values (where it ranks from first to fourth place). Variables with positive values are mainly seen in the Structure subset. It has positive values for GDP per capita; growth in real GDP; all Structure variables, except the share of public employment (where the value is average); the TEA index; the nascent entrepreneurship rate; the female self-employment rate; and the number of solo-firms. On the other hand, it has negative values for the business ownership rate; the total self-employment rate; the SME share of micro-firms; the annual growth in number of SMEs; the annual growth in SME employment; and the entry minus the exit rate. It is, of course, peculiar to have positive values for the TEA index and negative values for the self-employment rate and business ownership rate. The US is seen as having the second highest entrepreneurship policy comprehensiveness policy score ranking high for all areas except for the area of entrepreneurship education.

Summarising, one does not obviously see that context variables are taken into consideration when formulating the entrepreneurship policy area. There seems to be a shared focus of priority interest in the areas of seed financing and business support. Considering the great variations in context among the economies, revealed through application of the context model, would expect to see greater variations in the future. This does not mean that all countries must concentrate equally on all of the entrepreneurship policy areas; in fact, we have emphasised the importance of formulating measures to address problems identified as part of the context description. However, how these measures are carried out in detail can vary. This is one reason why so many items were used to construct the entrepreneurship policy comprehensiveness index – it is based on a wide variation in current practice.

CONCLUSIONS REGARDING THE CONTEXT MODEL

This chapter has been about the importance of context in understanding entrepreneurial Vitality and its relationship to Outcomes and Structure. We have used a total of 31 variables, which were ranked from low to high across the 13 countries, with positive values given for lower rankings. We make five observations from the outcome of this analysis. The first observation is that the context model can be useful in assessing whether a variable has a positive or negative impact on the level of entrepreneurial activity. Using research findings from the literature presented in Annex 1-1 of Chapter 1, we find that for some variables, this is obviously true. A low unemployment rate is more positive than a high one. Higher levels of GDP per capita are preferred to lower levels. However, it is not true in every situation that we know the importance of different values for different variables. Many examples are given for the subset of variables illustrating SME/ Entrepreneurial Vitality. One cannot simple say that it is preferable to have many solo-firms rather than a few; or that a higher self-employment rate is better than a lower rate; or that higher income dispersion levels are always a positive thing; or that higher female labour force participation rates lead to higher levels of entrepreneurial activity. This just gives a number of examples concerning relationships demonstrated in the research about the effects on entrepreneurship activity levels. We can perhaps judge all of these examples, in themselves, as positive developments for any number of reasons. But if our main concern is to create a more entrepreneurial society, then we must take into account how different values for different variables affect the level of entrepreneurship. We take up this issue in the next chapter when we present our conceptual model. Here it is a more a question of which constraints one faces in developing such a society.

The second observation is that the context model, as presented, is only partly dynamic. We have not much discussed the time perspective or used it in describing variables, such as growth-oriented values. But we have shared some insight concerning the time perspective between values for SME/Entrepreneurial Vitality and how and when such values could affect Outcomes variables or values for Structure variables and how these then, in turn, might affect Vitality values. We really do not understand much about this because there is very little research in this area. Researchers in the GEM project have made some attempts and Thurik (2004) has demonstrated an approach. Since we emphasise the importance of the context of each individual country, these time dependencies are probably not similar for the different cases. However, a more general discussion of time and dynamics are made in our conceptual model approach mainly to distinguish between actual and expected performance.

The third observation is that the variables we chose for the context description could be questioned. The choices were based on knowledge from the research literature, but how many or few variables we should include is not obvious. If some other subsets of variables were chosen, this could also change the outcome results of the analysis, for example, values and rankings could change. While this may be true, above all, what we have done here is demonstrate the usefulness of such an approach.

The fourth observation is the importance of being able to find comparable international data. We know from a number of international research projects how difficult it can be to compare data across countries. We have experienced this problem in the undertaking of research for this book. Therefore, we used a ranking procedure for comparing countries, even if such a procedure has some obvious weaknesses. Data with similar numbers will be given different ranking numbers, to give one example; there are no possibilities for testing statistical correlations, to give another example. The GEM reports present their data using intervals for the TEA index, meaning that if the data do not differ more than the intervals, they are not of statistical significance. In our approach, this data would still be given different ranking numbers. However, we have divided the ranking values into three groups (high, average and low) and presented each value for each country in Annex 4-4.

The fifth observation is that in the beginning of the chapter we presented the terms necessity and opportunity-based entrepreneurship to illustrate some differences presented by Reynolds et al. (2004). We have not used such categories in our context model description since there is a lack of uniformity with respect to who belongs to which group for different situations and countries. In countries with social security systems, it is not obvious that unemployed individuals feel it is "necessary" to start a business. It is a puzzle. An interesting conclusion from the GEM reports is that there is a relationship mainly between necessity entrepreneurship and economic growth. However, one cannot see the connection between necessity entrepreneurship and technological change independent of how it is measured.[3] If this is true, one could estimate the relationships between opportunity and necessity-based entrepreneurship, technological change and economic growth, illustrated in Figure 4-6. This figure illustrates the difficulties in finding relationships between different types of entrepreneurship and technological change or economic growth. The context model is a model to illustrate the complexities in a much broader sense, which is demonstrated by the different ranking values for the different subsets.

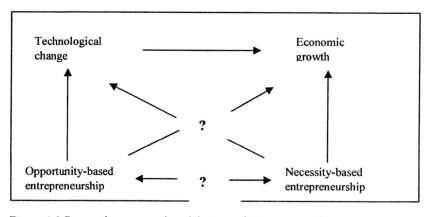

Figure 4-6. Perspective on growth and the type of entrepreneurship

Applying the Context Model Approach

Independent of whether there are currently few existing correlations between the entrepreneurship policy comprehensiveness index and the context model, we argue that such a relationship should exist and will be discussed in a broader sense in the future. The variables to be included in the different subsets in a context model can vary, so the first step will be to decide which variables a government would like to use to describe Outcomes, Structure and Vitality. In this chapter, we have used a number of the possible alternatives.

Step two would be to do an international comparative study of the chosen variables, ranking each country to compare the situation with the given country's values. This would present a picture of the relative positive and negative values and subsets.

The next step would be to assess existing policy priorities by using the entrepreneurship policy comprehensiveness index. Here one could discuss and analyse how different measures taken could affect different variables in the context model. From such an analysis, one could see if there were discrepancies and then discuss, in a more informed way, how to solve them with more appropriate policy measures. These steps may be repeated a number of times.

Finally, there should also be some decisions about how to evaluate the effects and efficiencies of the measures taken. Such decisions have to be dependent on more dynamic process approaches and also more knowledge about evaluation procedures, two issues we will discuss in Chapters 5 and 6.

ANNEX

Annex 4-1. Rankings for variables measuring Outcomes, Structure, and Vitality

A: Outcomes variables	AU	CA	DK	FI	IS	IE	NL	NO	ES	SW	TW	UK	US
*GDP/capita	7	6	3	10	4	5	8	2	13	11	12	9	1
*Growth in real GDP	3	8	12	10	4	6	13	11	5	8	1	6	2
**Unemployment rate	10	11	7	12	1	4	2	3	13	7	6	5	9
*Total labour force participation rate	10	5	2	9	1	12	7	2	11	4	13	6	8
*Female labour force participation rate	10	5	4	6	1	11	9	3	12	2	13	8	7
*Exports (f.o.b.)/GDP	12	7	6	5	8	1	2	4	11	3	9	10	13
*Industrial productivity rate	7	4	6	10	2	3	12	10	8	5	1	13	9
Average ranking score for Group A variables	8.4	6.5	5.4	8.8	3.0	6.0	7.5	5.0	10.4	5.7	7.8	7.5	7.0
B: Structure variables													
*Total population	6	4	9	10	13	12	7	11	3	8	5	2	1
*Population growth	5	3	9	11	2	1	7	8	13	11	6	10	3
*Net immigration rate	3	1	6	12	7	2	5	9	11	10	13	8	4
*Population age distribution (index)	5	6	9	11	1	3	8	7	13	12	2	10	4
*Education level	10	3	5	6	12	11	7	2	13	4	8	9	1
*Income dispersion index	3	8	4	12		2	6	11	6	10	9	4	1
**Government taxation/GDP	3	5	12	11	7	9	8	10	6	13	1	4	2
**Public sector employment share	3	4	11	9	8	7	12	10	2	13	1	6	5
*Service sector output to GDP	4	4	5	8	11	13	3	12	10	7	9	2	1
Average ranking score for Group B variables	4.6	4.8	8.0	10.0	7.6	6.6	7.0	8.9	8.4	9.8	6.0	6.1	2.4

Note: One star (*) means that a high level of the variable is considered positive for entrepreneurial activity. The highest ranking for the highest level of the variable is 1; the lowest ranking for the lowest level is 13.

Two stars (**) means that a high level of the variable is inversely related to entrepreneurial activity. The highest ranking for the lowest level of the variable is 1; the lowest ranking for the highest level of the variable is 13.

Annex 4.1. Rankings for variables measuring Outcomes, Structure, and Vitality (cont'd)

C: SME & Entrepreneurial Vitality variables	A U	C A	D K	F I	I S	I E	N L	N O	E S	S E	T W	U K	U S
Density (static measures)													
*Business ownership rate (labour force)	2	6	13	9	4	3	7	12	5	11	1	8	10
TEA Index	2	5	10	7	3	4	13	6	7	12	11	9	1
*Nascent entrepreneur rate	3	5	10	7	2	4	12	8	6	11	-	9	1
*Self-employment rate (% of total employment)	5	9	11	6	4	3	8	13	2	10	1	7	12
*Female self-employment rate	4	1	11	5	7	13	3	6	8	10	12	9	2
*SMEs per 1,000 inhabitants	8	3	9	12	1	7	13	2	5	4	11	6	10
*SME share of total employment	4	5	5	11	-	3	10	12	2	9	1	7	8
*Solo-firms (% of all firms)	5	7	8	-	-	10	8	11	4	1	6	2	3
*Micro-firms <10 empl (% of all firms)	5	1	13	8	3	11	10	9	6	2	7	4	12
*Micro-firm share of employment	-	3	6	4	-	5	-	7	1	8	-	2	9
Average ranking for density variables	4.2	4.5	9.6	7.7	3.4	6.2	9.3	8.6	4.6	7.8	6.3	6.3	6.6
Dynamic Measures													
*Annual growth in no. of SMEs	10	11	11	8	1	5	2	4	5	3	7	9	13
*Annual growth in SME employment	3	5	8	1	-	4	7	9	2	12	5	11	10
*Annual entry rate (to total firms)	-	1	12	4	11	2	6	9	3	8	10	3	7
*Start-up rate *minus* exit rate (net growth in firms)	-	8	11	5	3	1	7	4	2	9	6	10	12
*Start-up rate *plus* exit rate (turbulence)	-	1	10	2	12	5	7	11	4	8	9	3	5
Average ranking for dynamic variables	6.5	5.2	10.4	4.0	6.8	3.4	5.8	7.4	3.2	8.0	7.4	7.6	9.4
Average ranking score for Group C variables	4.6	4.7	9.9	6.4	4.6	5.3	8.1	8.2	4.1	7.9	6.7	6.7	7.5

Note: One star (*) means that a high level of the variable is considered positive for entrepreneurial activity. The highest ranking for the highest level of the variable is 1; the lowest ranking for the lowest score is 13.

Annex 4-2. Country rankings by average ranking scores for all Outcomes, Structure, and Vitality variables

	A: Outcomes variables	B: Structure variables	C: Vitality variables	C1: Density variables	C2: Dynamic variables
Australia	11	2	2	2	6
Canada	6	3	4	3	4
Denmark	3	9	13	13	13
Finland	12	13	6	9	3
Iceland	1	8	2	1	7
Ireland	5	6	5	5	2
Netherlands	8	7	11	12	5
Norway	2	11	12	11	8
Spain	13	10	1	4	1
Sweden	4	12	10	10	11
Taiwan	10	4	7	6	8
United Kingdom	8	5	7	6	10
United States	7	1	9	8	12

Annex 4-3. Borda ranking values for Outcomes, Structure, and Vitality variables

	A: Outcomes variables	B: Structure variables	C: Vitality variables	C1: Density variables	C2: Dynamic variables
Australia	-4	+5	+5	+5	+1
Canada	+1	+4	+3	+4	+3
Denmark	+4	-2	-6	-6	-6
Finland	-5	-6	+1	-2	+4
Iceland	+6	-1	+5	+6	0
Ireland	+2	+1	+2	+2	+5
Netherlands	-1	0	-4	-5	+2
Norway	+5	-4	-5	-4	-1
Spain	-6	-3	+6	+3	+6
Sweden	+3	-5	-3	-3	-4
Taiwan	-3	+3	0	+1	-1
United Kingdom	-1	+2	0	+1	-3
United States	0	+6	-2	-1	-5

Note: Values for the Borda ranking procedure were determined by assigning new values (from +6 to -6) to the average rankings (1 to 13) for each of the three subsets of variables in Annex 4-2. An ordinal ranking of 7 became 0 on the Borda ranking. Rankings above 7 were assigned negative values from -1 to -6 (with 13 = -6); rankings below 7 were assigned positive values from +1 to +6 (with 1 = +6).

Annex 4-4. High, average and low ranking values for Outcomes, Structure, and Vitality for each country

	A: Outcomes ranking	B: Structure ranking	C: Vitality ranking	C1: Density ranking	C2: Dynamic ranking
Australia	Low	High	High	High	Average
Canada	Average	High	High	High	High
Denmark	High	Average	Low	Low	Low
Finland	Low	Low	Average	Average	High
Iceland	High	Average	High	High	Average
Ireland	Average	Average	Average	Average	High
Netherlands	Average	Average	Low	Low	Average
Norway	High	Low	Low	Low	Average
Spain	Low	Low	High	High	High
Sweden	High	Low	Low	Low	Low
Taiwan	Low	High	Average	Average	Average
United Kingdom	Average	Average	Average	Average	Low
United States	Average	High	Average	Average	Low

Note: Ranking score: 1-4 = High; 5-9 = Average; 10-13 = Low

---

[1] For a definition and distinction between necessity and opportunity-based entrepreneurship, see Reynolds et al. (2004), where they explain how the two types of entrepreneurial activity are measured.

[2] See Shane and Eckhardt (2003) for a discussion considering the concept of entrepreneurial activity being something episodic.

[3] For a discussion of the measurement of technological change, see Audretsch (2002), p 18.

Chapter 5

A CONCEPTUAL MODEL FOR ENTREPRENEURSHIP
Perspectives for Individuals and Policymakers

INTRODUCTION

In this chapter, we expand on the conceptual model for the level of entrepreneurship that we introduced in Chapter 2 – the model describing Motivation, Opportunity and Skills. We introduce functions for measuring the level of entrepreneurship (LoE) and the level of entrepreneurial exits (LoEE). We build on our definitional use of "entrepreneurship" as a system that includes entrepreneurs (and potential entrepreneurs), institutions and government actions, the desired policy outcome of which is increased levels of entrepreneurial activity. Based on this definition, we are interested in the behaviours of individual entrepreneurs, behaviours that can be episodic, acted out in a team or individually, and demonstrated by developing ideas, taking initiative, and starting and managing a firm. We are also interested in the behaviours and motives of providers of support services to entrepreneurs (and their firms) and government policymakers. The perspectives of all three sets of actors must be considered in discussions about the level of entrepreneurship.

We consider that a measurement for the level of entrepreneurship (LoE) is broader than simply measuring the level of new business entries and should be able to capture more of the behavioural processes leading up to the business entry. To reflect the importance placed on entrepreneurial dynamics and "churning rates" (Davidsson et al., 1989; Reynolds et al., 2004; Stevenson and Lundström, 2002[1]), we are also of the opinion that it should encompass a measure for the level of entrepreneurial "failures" or exits. In our conceptual model, the entrepreneurial failure rate is a broader concept than measuring only the number of business exits. We include in the function a measure to also capture the "failure" dynamic of nascent entrepreneurs. This failure dynamic is defined as the LoEE rate and represents the level of entrepreneurial exits and the "failures" of nascent entrepreneurs to actually start a business.

Our basic assumption in describing the conceptual model is that simple correlations between entrepreneurship, entrepreneurial vitality and economic growth do not exist (Wennekers and Thurik, 1999, 2001; Lundström and Stevenson, 2002). Although attempts to measure one-to-one correlations are common in recent research studies (Acs and Armington, 2003; Audretsch and Keilbach, 2003; Reynolds et al., 2004), in our conceptual model, we intend to illustrate the complexity that exists around these relationships. We argue that it is important to start with the complex picture and from that formal description determine how this complexity could be simplified to make it more measurable and practically useful, more in line with the "eclectic" model approach developed by Verheul et al. (2001). Simplification is necessary for many reasons, but confusion can be created when contradictory results are produced from similar empirical approaches. One of the contributing factors to this confusion is how variables are defined, simplified and measured. Similar conclusions have been reached by Autio (2002), Audretsch (2002) and Storey (1994). This chapter is about complexity, not simplicity.

In the conceptual model, we define nine basic variables and describe their relationship to the level of entrepreneurship and the level of total entrepreneurial exit/failure. We develop the variables and their assumed connections and then analyse each of the variables at an individual and a sectorial level and from a time perspective. One effect of our conceptual model is the potential to describe the conflicting perspectives between entrepreneurs, service providers and policymakers. This is of importance since our main interest is entrepreneurship policy.

A CONCEPTUAL MODEL FOR THE LEVEL OF ENTREPRENEURSHIP

The level of entrepreneurship (LoE) depends on a number of variables related to the description of Motivation, Opportunity, and Skills, the foundation components of an entrepreneurship policy approach (Figure 2-1). We use three variables to measure Motivation: working experience, role models and dissatisfaction; four variables to measure Opportunity: profits, barriers to entry, concentration and growth; and three variables to measure

Skills: working experience, education and competence. The Opportunity variables were used earlier by Orr (1974) to measure new entries in the Canadian manufacturing sector. His based his model on the relationship between the number of entries in the sector and the level of profits in that sector (positively-related); barriers to entry (negatively-correlated); growth of the sector (positively-related); and concentration in the sector (negatively-related). We have constructed a more general conceptual model taking the Motivation and Skills variables into account and adding an individual and time perspective.

Our basic conceptual model is therefore:

$$LoE = f\,(X, BE, GR, C, YE, F, D, U, K)$$

where X stands for profits; BE is barriers to entry; GR is growth; C is concentration, YE is years of experience; F is role models; D is dissatisfaction; U is education; and K is competence. All variables except BE and C are assumed to be positively correlated to LoE, which we will explain later. We also introduce time (t), sector (j) and individual (i) dimensions to the model. This gives the general expression:

$$LoE = \sum\sum\sum f_{ijt}\,(X_{ijt}\, BE_{ijt}, GR_{ijt}, C_{ijt}, YE_{ijt}, F_{ijt}, D_{ijt}, U_{ijt}, K_{ijt})$$

where LoE is the sum over (i), (j) and (t) of all variables. We will further develop this general expression, demonstrating that not all possible variables are assumed to be of equal interest to individuals, service providers and policymakers.

The index (i) stands both for observed factors for individuals (e.g., education level) and perceived factors for individuals (e.g., barriers to entry or concentration). It could also stand for legal entities, in cases where a start-up has occurred. One could use an additional index for legal entities (notwithstanding the problems when two indexes are used), but for most start-ups, the individual and the entity are the same unit. Adding a time and an individual perspective adds value to the model because it can combine perceived and actual values for some variables. This issue of "perceived versus actual" has been noted in the entrepreneurship research (Shane and Eckhardt, 2003; Casson, 2003; Shaver, 2003, Davidsson, 1989), often in relationship to a discussion of perceived and actual opportunities.

The conceptual model is market-oriented since it takes into account specific sector factors, like growth, concentration, profits and barriers to entry. These are variables of particular interest to service providers and policymakers. Since the model also has a sector perspective, there are crossovers with research on clusters or industrial districts. We will discuss the model and its variables from the point of view of entrepreneurs, service providers and policy makers. The variables are related to dimensions of Opportunity, Motivation and Skills (Stevenson and Lundström, 2002) and combine individual and market perspectives (Delmar, 1996). In the next three sections, we discuss each of the sets of variables, including one for Opportunity-based variables, one for Skills-based variables, and one for Motivation-based variables. The conceptual model consists of these three sub-models, but they are not mutually exclusive, so the model cannot simply be divided into three independent parts. For example, one finds an interdependency between the working experience and competence variables.

The Level of Entrepreneurship and Opportunity-based Variables

In this section, our main interest is in the variables: profits, barriers to entry, concentration and growth. It is important to state that these variables are dependent on different sectors (j), different time periods (t), and different individuals (i).

Profits

To illustrate, we will start with the profit variable, X_{ijt}. Given the time perspective, profits could be real profits in the existing time period (t), previous profits in earlier time periods (t-1) or expected profits in the future (t+1). Real profits in the existing and earlier time periods is simply a sum of all individuals (i) in that sector (j) during the actual time period (the sum over i for $\sum X_{ijt}$ and $\sum X_{ijt-1}$). However, expected profits in the sector (j) will be the sum of all (i)s estimated to remain in or enter the sector during that period. Expected profits for nascent entrepreneurs will be of interest for time-period (t+1).

The representation (i) normally stands for individuals. Individuals could be either existing entrepreneurs in the sector (j) or nascent entrepreneurs in the gestation phase. The index (i) stands for individuals until a legal unity has been created, after which (i) stands for the legal entity. For the self-employed, there will be no difference. Since our interest is in the level of entrepreneurship, we focus on how individuals create entries during the studied time periods, as well as the profits of newly-started firms. So the term (i) could describe individuals in the gestation phase or legal entities in the case of start-ups and young firms.

Expected profits are probably also effected by some general profit level in an economy. The expression we have developed is

$$X_{ijt+1} = f_{ijt} (X_{ijt}, X_{ijt-1}, X_o)$$

where X_{ijt+1} is the expected profit for an individual or a firm (i), depending on which phase of the development cycle is being examined: the phase of thinking about starting a business or the phase of having a newly-started business in sector (j) during the time period (t+1). Expected profits could produce a different result depending on whether an individual starts a firm alone or in a team with other individuals; these two situations would not necessarily produce the same profit expectations. The idea of the LoE function is that expectations could be less dependent on actual and historical profits for some individuals, while for others, these factors could be of more importance. (X_o) could be a general profit value.

This type of equation points to a number of critical issues. First, there is the issue of the relationship between actual, historical and expected profits. It is not obvious that there is always a relationship. If a sector has historically produced high profits and continues to do so in the present, will there be high-expected profits in the future? The answer is no. As an example, we use the information and communications technology sector (ICT). During the "boom years" the emerging ICT sector did not show any previous or existing high profits, but it did produce a high level of expectations regarding future profits. A lot of investments were made from that perspective and a large number of new businesses entered the market. The motivation behind many of these start-ups was fast growth – this was more important than profits – with the expectation of selling the company or taking it public. So, obviously there are examples of only a small observable relationship between actual and expected profits or none at all. For other sectors, like the services sector for business consultants, we would expect a stronger relationship.

The second issue is related to the level of importance placed on profits by an individual planning to start a company. This factor seems to differ among entrepreneurs in different economies (European Commission, 2003c). However, we would like to argue that future expected profits should be an important factor affecting the number of entries in a sector. A sector could experience growth in actual profits, thus raising expected profits, or an individual or a new entrepreneur could establish a more efficient firm than the average one in the market in that sector and, again, raise expected profits. If a new entrepreneur believes he or she can produce a service or product at lower average costs than existing firms, then that will mean higher expected profits.

The third issue relates to the question of price structure and costs; whether an entrepreneur is a price-taker or whether a new entrepreneur can produce competing goods or services at lower costs. In such cases, the reaction of existing firms in the market has to be taken into consideration. We recognise that this is a classic issue, but will not develop it further in this discussion and analysis.

There is also the issue of whether historical data is a good predictor of future developments in a sector. According to Davidsson et al. (2001), such prediction possibilities are seldom at hand. However, we expect that from the service provider's point of view, historical profit performance of a sector is of great significance when making decisions about whether or not to invest in a new firm. For each new individual who is thinking of entering a sector, it is a question of how creative that individual is compared to existing firms in the sector. Service providers are more likely to see new entries as replicating what already exists in the sector. This is a possible conflicting interest between service providers and entrepreneurs (Hjalmarsson and Johansson, 2003). Another conflicting interest between policymakers and entrepreneurs could arise because expected profits are dependent on the tax structure. Policymakers need to generate revenue from taxation as a policy objective, while entrepreneurs have the objective of creating personal wealth.

From a competitive market point of view, a perfect market is one where little profit can be made by an individual entrant. According to the neo-classical model, a perfectly competitive market would mean less renewal as a result of new entries, but perhaps more innovation by existing firms (Baumol, 2002).[2] However, it is not easy to study whether such an effect exists, since the level of entrants also depends on barriers to entry and sector concentration.

From the individual's point of view, the issue of profits is most about the level of expected profits, where the relationship to earlier or existing profits varies by sector and, probably, over time. For individuals, it is also about how profits can be created, a question of "perceived" opportunity. This perspective is not as common among service providers or policymakers. According to us, expected profit is the first variable where one can see a differing emphasis or potential conflicting interest. This reasoning could lead to the conclusion that service providers and/or policymakers have a need for more sector expertise.

Another issue is the question of the degree of renewal of the base of existing firms in the sector, or the degree to which new innovations are transferred to the marketplace through new entries or existing firms. Innovations that would make a real impact on the future development of a sector will, of course, affect expected profits for both existing firms and new entries. So even if policymakers cannot normally create measures to influence expected profits, they can create new possibilities for such expectations by investing in innovations.

How is the issue of profits treated in the entrepreneurship policy area by the governments in our study? Many use the tax system to create incentives for firms by reducing their costs. This has the effect of increasing expected profits. Another set of measures relates to cost reductions, for example, labour, insurance, or financing costs. One special mechanism for increasing expected profits is tax policy that requires no taxation of income below a certain turnover level for start-ups or even zero taxes for the first years. These types of measures may be more psychological since many start-ups will not generate profits during the first year or two.

The issue of expected profits versus actual profits from the entrepreneurs' perspective would be an interesting future research area and also one of interest to service providers. From the entrepreneur's point of view, there should be at least a minimum level of expected profits, the question being, during which future time period? Since the cost structure differs between individual firms, expected minimum profits would also differ.

Policymakers do not likely discuss much about how their different policy measures will affect the profit potential for individuals and firms. For example, governments are often reluctant to decrease personal tax rates and government seed capital programmes sometimes carry relatively high interest rates. These actions on the part of governments could reduce the LoE, especially if individual entrepreneurs believe that previous and existing profits in a sector are an indicator of expected profits.

Barriers to entry

Barriers to entry (BE) is an aggregated variable that includes a number of aspects such as regulations (perceived and actual), cost structure, access to capital, technology development in the sector, and internationalisation effects, to mention some of the underlying factors. All of these factors will affect the level of entrepreneurship during a given time period. BE will, obviously, vary by sector. There will be higher levels of entry in sectors with relatively low barriers to entry. Thus, there will be more entries in the services sector than in the manufacturing sector. Concerning the time perspective, we assume that BE in previous time periods is of minor importance compared to BE in the existing time period, even if there is not much change between different time periods. Expected BE is probably of minor concern, except in specific instances where knowledge exists about new regulations coming into effect in the future. BE could be of interest to policymakers, since one of their aims is to reduce entry barriers. BE is also a variable reflecting aspects of the structure of an economy, for example in the situation where public sector activity itself creates high barriers to entry for entrepreneurs. This would be the case in countries where the government provides services to the public (e.g., home care services) that could otherwise be provided by private sector firms, thus creating BE in those sectors.

Research illustrates that it is very difficult to change structures over time (Lundström and Stevenson, 2002) and BE, as stated above, is part of that structure. The introduction of new sector regulations and increasing internationalisation may lead to increased BE over time. At the same time, innovations and new technology development could be forces working in the opposite direction. Both of these factors will affect the future level of business entry dynamics. Furthermore, one could question the degree to which nascent entrepreneurs are aware of (perceive) BE and to what extent it influences their decision to start a business. Much of this knowledge will be known for the first time only after an individual has started her or his company. Before the business is actually started, the entrepreneur's perception of BE is likely based more on prevailing popular wisdom that "it is difficult to start a business". In many of our country studies there was little evidence that BE is a big problem for new businesses. The bigger problem is for existing and growing companies who must comply with a large number of government administrative, reporting, and regulatory requirements. These requirements could be more burdensome in some sectors than others. BE (t) illustrates that existing BE is probably of more importance for existing firms than nascent entrepreneurs and new entries. However, this aspect of BE will vary for sectors (j) and, to some extent, for individuals (i). Many new entrepreneurs, some years after having started a business, will reflect on their experience by saying: "If only I had known...". This suggests that BE_{ijt} should perhaps be of more importance to new entrepreneurs.

From the policymaker's point of view, BE_{jt} is a variable of high priority. There has been increasing interest in recent years to measure the costs of regulations on new and existing SMEs and to reduce the number of regulations (OECD, 1999; European Commission, 2002c). One could question the actual outcome of all of these efforts, but there are no conflicting interests between policymakers and entrepreneurs with respect to the need to simplify the regulatory process for new entries and growing companies in different sectors. Exceptions to this could be in areas concerning health and safety regulations or labour rules, but that would depend on the country in question.

One possible reason why BE_{tj} seldom influences the number of entries is that few organisations in the services-providing sector have a complete knowledge of this variable. We have not been able to find any research that has actually investigated the degree of knowledge that service providers have about BE. If this level of knowledge is low, then one could not expect that entrepreneurs would have that knowledge either. Governments in many countries have recently launched internet-based information systems to provide easier access to information about government regulations and the requirements of tax authorities and other regulatory bodies.

Growth

Growth (GR), or growth potential, is a variable that is often considered when setting policy measure objectives.[3] Although interest in the growth variable is great (Autio, 2002), there is a lot of confusion about what is actually meant by "growth" or "growth potential". It is a complex variable (Davidsson et al., 2001; Storey, 2003). Is it growth in real turnover, in employment, in productivity or something else? Is growth in one area (e.g., revenue) congruent with growth in another (e.g., employment)? There also appears to be a weak correlation between historical growth and future growth for individual firms. Many research studies find that firms which have experienced rapid growth in previous time periods are likely to experience future declines in their rate of growth. This suggests that growth is episodic. Other results show that firm growth during early stages of development occurs as a result of internal growth, whereas, as a firm gets larger growth often occurs as the result of acquisitions or mergers. Furthermore, growth can be found in all sectors, although government policy often focuses more on stimulating growth in technology-based sectors, which, in fact, make up a small percentage of the overall economy. Few new entries will grow beyond a small number of employees, but the small percentage that do grow, will create a disproportionate share of employment growth. For example, Storey (1994) found that only 4 percent of new entries were responsible for up to 50 percent of all new employment over a 10 year period for the region of Cleveland. Similar results have been found for other countries and regions. Another result from the growth literature is that growth is not necessarily associated with a growth in profits. Davidsson et al. (2001) identified a number of more individually-oriented effects of growing firms that could influence an entrepreneur's decision about future growth. These include:
- Increases in the amount of work responsibility and burden;
- The range of tasks that have to be fulfilled;
- Challenges in maintaining employee satisfaction levels;
- The level of income for the entrepreneur;
- Changes in the entrepreneur's span of control;
- The degree of freedom the entrepreneur has;
- The capacity of the firm to survive a crisis; and
- The demands on product and service quality.

It is not obvious how all these factors will impact on the growth-orientation of an individual or a new firm. These factors have been the subject of various research projects, but mainly from the perspective of existing firms. We do not think that an entrepreneur considers all of these factors when deciding what type of business to start. Here, one can also see potential conflicting interests between the individual's perspective and the policymaker's perspective. All these factors are of importance from an individual perspective, while few of them are of priority interest from a policymaking point of view. Policymakers are likely more concerned about:

- Growth in employment (not growth in the entrepreneur's work demands or control issues);
- Taxation revenues gained from a growth in profits (not the entrepreneur's personal income level);
- Renewal of a sector (not the tasks of the entrepreneur);
- The potential for growth of new firms into "big" companies (not the episodic growth of a new company);
- The growth of individual companies (not the growing number of entries);
- The relationship between entrepreneurship and economic growth.

Next, we concentrate on the question of Growth as a variable for influencing the level of entrepreneurship. Growth rates will vary in different sectors over time and growth potential will differ within sectors. Growth will also be affected by differences between individuals and how they perceive growth potential. Among service providers and policymakers, previous and actual growth in a sector is of importance. Policy and programme support for the development of clusters is partly evidence of this belief that existing and previous growth is a good predicator of future growth. Even if this is not true from an individual perspective, it may be true for some sectors and some regions. Often the sectors chosen for cluster support are the more technology-based ones. Since significant investments are made in these sectors, one should expect to see the development of more technology-based business ideas and, consequently, the creation of more start-up companies. However, one of the problems with evaluating cluster performance is the "deadweight factor". We do not know what changes in start-up rates would have occurred as a result of causal or contextual factors regardless of the investments made in cluster support. Plus, there is some evidence that the scientists, engineers and technologists whose brilliant ideas are behind new technology businesses do not obviously make "good" entrepreneurs (Lundström (ed.), 2003).

GR_{ijt+1} is not always correlated to GR_{ijt-1} or GR_{ijt}. It is possible that the growth expectations of individuals are more connected to their perceptions of the potential of their personal business ideas than to any knowledge of previous or existing growth in a particular sector. However, their success in attracting financing for a business idea *is* probably correlated to prior and existing growth performance in a sector. Only a small percentage of all entrepreneurs appear to have a growth-orientation at the start-up of their businesses. This lack of an initial growth-orientation seems to be a factor in predicting low future growth for such start-ups (Davidsson et al., 2001). However, growth expectations could also be a function of how an entrepreneur judges the market potential.

We would expect that the sum of all individual growth expectations, the sum over (i) for GR_{ijt+1}, will exceed the actual growth that will occur in sector (j). This is one of the main reasons why the judgement about growth potential likely differs between individual entrepreneurs and service providers. If only a small fraction of all new entries develops into growth companies over time, then it is, of course, very difficult for a service provider to decide, among all applicants for assistance, which firms will grow. This is the major deficiency of the "picking the winners" strategy, a common strategy of government assistance programmes.

Concentration

Concentration (C) is a variable we introduced in the section on Barriers to Entry. One might say that Concentration is the effecting variable of the BE variable. Concentration effects exist in many different sectors, being one reason why there are fewer entries in these sectors. Much of the research on the effects of concentration has been done to examine the market efficiencies or deficiencies created by monopolies or oligopolies. This concentration behaviour in certain sectors is one that many governments, as well as the European Commission, attempts to discourage through competition policies, deregulation policies and other types of market regulations. This is the essence of the "internal EU market" concept. The aim of these policies is to prevent companies from achieving monopolistic control over a market or a sub-market. Concentration effects could be altered by the introduction of new technology or specialisation in smaller "niche" market segments. Foster (1986), among others, has studied how the dominant actors in certain sectors have changed over time.

How would we expect the C variable to affect the level of entrepreneurship? As far as we know, little research has been done on the effects of concentration on the levels of entrepreneurship. It would be interesting to know what kinds of promising business ideas are not developed by nascent entrepreneurs because of market concentration problems. One implicitly concludes that higher sector concentration will mean fewer new businesses in that sector. We expect that existing C_{jt} will continue into the future unless something is specifically done to alter it, i.e., that normally C_{jt} is equal to C_{jt+1}. However, the perceived C_{ijt+1} for an individual entrepreneur (i) will vary. One entrepreneur will see high concentration as a competitive challenge and enter the market anyway, while another will see it as an insurmountable barrier to starting a business. Therefore, C_{jt} will not be equal to the sum over (i) for C_{ijt+1}.

Summarising this section on LoE and opportunity-based variables, what are the main findings?

1. There is interdependency between the described variables. Profits depend on Barriers to Entry and Concentration, and Concentration is an effect of Barriers to Entry. So the function describing Opportunity-based variables is not a set of independent variables.

2. There are conflicting interests between policymakers, service providers and entrepreneurs. Growth is probably a more important variable for policymakers than profits, while growth for entrepreneurs is generally not as important as profits. Growth for an entrepreneur is more about turnover than employment, and the opposite is true for a policymaker.

The Level of Entrepreneurship and Motivation-based Variables

In this section, the variables of interest are: working experience, role models and dissatisfaction.

Work experience

In the research, Work experience (YE) is normally measured in terms of whether an entrepreneur has experience working in the same sector as the business he or she would like to start. The main finding is that it seems to be important to have working experience in the same sector (Bridge et al., 1998; Audretsch, 2002). However, we still do not know much about how many years of working experience seems reasonable if this experience is to have a positive impact on the outcome of a new business. It may well be that the length of working experience differs, depending on the sector.

Why is working experience in the same sector important to future performance of the entrepreneur's firm? Through working experiences, potential entrepreneurs learn about the market conditions in that sector and also build networks for future business relationships. Experiences create knowledge and possible connections. If this is the case, entrepreneurship should depend on what type of working experiences we are discussing. If an individual has experience working in a large company doing administrative work, this will be a very different experience than the experience gained by an individual working in a small company with lots of external contacts. The position and type of work an individual has should be of importance here. We assume that working for a small firm would enable the development of more general knowledge than doing specialised work in a large firm. Therefore, working experience as a variable will depend on the type and size of firm in a specific sector where the experience was gained and the position held in that firm or firms. Furthermore, one can assume that there is a positive relationship between the length of working experience and entrepreneurial performance, but we do not know the optimal number of years of this experience, or whether there are diminishing effects to years of experience beyond a certain length of time. The number of years of working experience in sectors with rapidly changing conditions might need to be longer in order to produce an incremental impact on entrepreneurial performance compared to that required in very stable environments and sectors.

The variable (YE_{ijt}) is of importance here, but not expected work experience in future time periods. The sector perspective (j) and the effect on individuals (i) are also of importance. The number of years of working experience and the type of work position are both factors in determining the value for the variable. If there is going to be a start-up (a business entry), then there are several possibilities to gain entrepreneurial experiences: as an individual entrepreneur; as part of a team of entrepreneurs; or by seeking expertise from advisers or board members. Most new businesses are started by individual entrepreneurs, although Delmar and Davidsson (2000) found there are some advantages in doing pre-start-up planning as part of a work team, at least in certain sectors.

What does this mean from the policymaker's or service provider's point of view? One implication could be to require potential entrepreneurs to work for a number of years in existing firms before attempting to start a company. In fact, the advice often given to young people who want to start their own businesses fresh out of school is, "work in someone else's business for five years first, learn the ropes, and then start your own business". This, however, would be a difficult policy position to take. Another possible option would to make previous working experience in the same sector a criterion for obtaining start-up assistance from service providers. In some senses, this is already a subtle criteria applied to inexperienced entrepreneurs when they try to obtain financing. A more reasonable policy option would be to implement programmes to provide mentoring to new entrepreneurs as a way of bringing experience into a start-up firm.

One could also discuss the effects of "knowing too much" from working experiences. Too many years of experience may have inculcated an acceptance of existing business practices and behaviour, whereas, successful entrepreneurship should involve the creation of new ideas and management practices. It is possible that the degree of creative destruction diminishes over time (Aldrich, 1999; McGrath, 2003). We expect that many individuals would placer lower importance on the need for a certain number of years of working experience than service providers might. Finally, we should not forget that working experience provides the opportunity to accumulate savings and to create some wealth that can be used in the start-up, even if research has not been able to find any clear relationship between entrepreneurship and the level of wealth acquisition (Kim et al., 2004).

Role models

The variable role models (F) is one of great interest in the research literature (Reynolds et al., 2004; Audretsch, 2002). The Annex in Chapter 1 makes reference to a number of studies that reinforce the importance of role models to the emergence of entrepreneurship in a society. There can be different kinds and levels of role models. Close role models are usually members of the same family – a father or mother or sister or brother who has started or is running a business. Many research findings confirm the importance of this connection to a close role model, but we have not been able to find a study of the relationships between the "entrepreneurial outcomes" of the close role model and the effect of this on another family member's motivation to start a business (i.e., how successful a mother or father has been in their business or whether they have had failure experiences). The assumption would be that it is the learning process, in general, both for negative and positive experiences, that seems to be of most importance in role-modelling effects. Research exploring whether the role-modelling effect is about general or specific knowledge would be interesting to do. Another interesting question to explore would be whether the individual enters a similar business in the same sector as that of the close role model (i.e., copies the business idea) or does something completely different. This is more or less the same question regarding general or specific knowledge. If the knowledge from such role models is general in nature, then the sector perspective may be of lesser importance, but if it is specific knowledge, then the sector perspective should be taken into account.

Individuals will react differently to entrepreneur role models. Otherwise, more or less anyone with a close entrepreneur role model would become an entrepreneur. But that is not the case. Furthermore, what about all the individuals who start businesses who did not have *any* close role models? As well, the share of the population of nascent and new entrepreneurs who have been exposed to close role models differs across countries (Reynolds et al.,

2004). The effect of role models as an influencing factor in an individual's motivation to start a business has to do with earlier time periods.

If this is an important issue, what can be done from a policymaking point of view to expose more of the population to close role models? The common response in many countries seems to be to initiate the integration of entrepreneurship education in the school system. One rationale for doing this is to expose students to general and specific knowledge about entrepreneurship over the long period of schooling years. In some respects, this produces a role-modelling effect, especially when links are made between the educational experience of entrepreneurship and the community of entrepreneurs. It also produces a learning effect and entrepreneurship, as a set of behaviours, can be learned. In recent years, many of the governments in our study have initiated such programmes, as we described in Chapter 2. We can also see that these programmes are being introduced at the very early levels of the educational system.

Role models can also be promoted by profiling good examples of entrepreneurs through advertising campaigns, awards programmes, media profiles, and so on. These initiatives create more awareness of the benefits of being an entrepreneur, but do not create the same effects of the "closeness" aspect emphasised in the research. Entrepreneurship awards are becoming very popular. We know from the research that awards are important for the winners as an acknowledgement of their work, but it does not tell us very much about the importance of such measures for the level of entrepreneurship. There is no international comparative research testing the correlation between the number of awards, or the importance given to awards programmes by policymakers, and the level of entrepreneurship. Similar things can be said about the importance of media coverage. If there is a positive effect from media profiling of entrepreneurs, we believe that it may be rather short-term, i.e., that its impact is mainly felt for the period (t).

The role model variable, in the broader sense described above, is of importance to policymakers but not the close role model perspective. This variable probably has low awareness among entrepreneurs.

Dissatisfaction

Dissatisfaction (D) has been created as an aggregate variable. There are a large number of research studies measuring the motivational aspects of a person's decision to start their own business. Many of these aspects could be seen as the lack of possibilities in an existing circumstance, thus, a form of dissatisfaction (e.g., unemployment or the risk of being unemployed). Dissatisfaction could be caused by a number of things: job dissatisfaction, the need for more independence, the desire to be in control of decision-making, better salary prospects, the will to develop an idea that an existing employer organisation has little interest in and so on. The assumption is that if the aggregate dissatisfaction variable is of a certain size, there will be an increased probability that the "dissatisfied" individual will start her or his own business. An alternative interpretation of the Dissatisfaction motivation is that it offers the possibility of future satisfaction.

In their study of entrepreneurship in 23 OECD countries, Wildeman et al. (1999) found their measure of dissatisfaction to have a positive impact on the number of start-ups. In our conceptual model, Dissatisfaction is assumed to be positively-related to entrepreneurship. This variable will vary by sector, depending on the working conditions and future prospects in that sector. However, we think that the variable is primarily about the existing time period (t) for different individuals (i). Since Dissatisfaction is mainly perceived by individuals, it would be interesting to do international research concerning the correlations between general employment and working conditions in different sectors and the level of entrepreneurship.

For policymakers and service providers, this is not a variable of high consideration; however, in our policy case studies, we do see examples of measures to encourage unemployed individuals to start their own businesses.

The Level of Entrepreneurship and Skills-based Variables

Variables describing Skills include education, competence and working experience. We have already described working experience (YE) in the previous section. Therefore, we elaborate on the education (U) and competence (K) variables.

Education

Education (U) has been a variable of great interest to researchers for many years, evidenced by the large number of statistical surveys from different countries regarding the motives of individuals to become entrepreneurs (referenced in Annex 1-1). One finding from this research is that entrepreneurs tend to have higher educations than the average adult population. However, for people with university educations, the percentage of entrepreneurs declines. Education is mainly a variable for (t) and (t-1).

One could question the construction of the education variable in earlier research studies, which mostly measure the *level* of education, but not the *content* of that education. As with the discussion regarding role models, is education for entrepreneurship about general or specific knowledge? Or to put it differently, does higher education provide the necessary general knowledge or does it mainly offer specific knowledge? If the school system below the tertiary level provides more general knowledge and the university system emphasises more specific knowledge, one could argue that it is general knowledge that seems to be of importance for the level of entrepreneurship. If so, one should not expect to find a relationship between the number of university-educated people and the level of entrepreneurship. Another explanation could be the nature of the education model. For example, in the basic school system, a wider variety of education models is used, compared to the models used in higher education.

If general knowledge seems more important, then the sector perspective (j) is of minor interest. The idea here is that the school system creates knowledge of how to do it, but not where to do it. However, there are a lot of initiatives at the university level to stimulate entrepreneurship among students. There is also new research concerning so-called "academic entrepreneurship", which illustrates that some areas of the university produce relatively higher levels of entrepreneurship (Delmar et al., 2003). Whether this is a question of the type of education or the type of markets being entered by graduates from different university programmes is not obvious.

Education is an important issue for policymakers, as we can see in our 13 cases. The question of whether or not entrepreneurship can be taught and learned, which was prevalent in the research society for a number of years, is no longer as frequently challenged. Governments have taken some measures to support the introduction of entrepreneurship courses for all students at the university level and not only for students in business degree programmes.

From the individual's point of view, the education issue is probably of minor interest, while it could be of importance to service providers.

Competence

The competence variable (K) is a combination of different factors: personal networks; job training; education; tacit knowledge; and learning experiences. This type of variable has been of considerable interest to researchers for a number of years. An expanding area of research is to measure the competence of existing firms as a function of the cumulative individual competencies of their employees. This collective competence is seen to be of great importance when judging the performance of an individual firm. Another example of emerging research interest is in connection to theories about the changing behaviours of the same individual in different surroundings and different time periods. This means that an individual's competencies cannot be easily summarised. Another research issue is how individual competencies are used and developed within a firm. Most of these effects will probably not affect the level of entrepreneurship, but if not, could affect the level of individual Dissatisfaction (D) or the variable Working Experiences (YE). The Competence variable will, however, be of interest in trying to understand the competencies needed for starting a new firm in different sectors (j). It is mainly about what has happened during past time periods, meaning that the number of entries in future periods will probably be affected by the competence factor for individuals in earlier periods.

From a policymaker's point of view, it would be of general interest to know more about how the competence factor develops in different sectors across countries. Service providers would be more interested in knowing what competencies are needed for new entrants in different sectors.

Influencing the Level of Entrepreneurship – Some Conclusions

In this chapter, we constructed a conceptual model with nine different aggregated variables determining the level of entrepreneurship. We described the different variables and related them to existing research. We also discussed the sometimes-conflicting interests between policymakers, service providers and entrepreneurs. The general model can be formulated as:

$$LoE_{t+1} = f\ (\Sigma\Sigma X_{ijt+1},\ \Sigma\Sigma\Sigma BE_{ijt},\ \Sigma\Sigma GR_{ijt+1},\ \Sigma\Sigma C_{jt},\ \Sigma\Sigma\Sigma YE_{ijt},\ \Sigma\Sigma F_{it-1},$$
$$\Sigma\Sigma D_{ijt},\ \Sigma\Sigma U_{it},\ \Sigma\Sigma K_{ijt})$$

where X_{ijt+1} stands for the expected profit for the sum of all individuals (i) and sectors (j); BE_{ijt} stands for existing barriers to entry for the sum over all individuals (i) and sectors (j); GR_{ijt+1} stands for expected growth for the sum of all individuals (i) and sectors (j); C_{jt} stands for existing concentration for the sum of all sectors (j); YE_{ijt} stands for the existing number of years of experience for the sum of all individuals (i) and sectors (j); F_{it-1} stands for the earlier experience of role models for the sum of all individuals (i); D_{ijt} stands for existing dissatisfaction for the sum of all individuals (i) and sectors (j); U_{it} stands for existing level of education for the sum of all individuals (i); and K_{ijt} stand for existing competence for the sum of all individuals (i) and sectors (j).

The model illustrates the relationship between individuals, time-periods and sectors. For some variables it will be more important to discuss expected outcomes (e.g., concerning profits or growth possibilities), while for others, such as education or role models, the discussion will be more about existing and past time periods. Another aspect will be factors influencing the selected variables. We illustrate the different variables related to Motivation, Opportunity and Skills in Figure 5-1.

We believe conflicting interests exist for profits and growth. Profits are of high interest to individuals, but not to policymakers. Growth, on the other hand, is of high interest to policymakers, but of less importance to individuals, especially if growth is measured in terms of job creation. Other conflicting interests could exist between service providers and individuals regarding work experience and the use of past and present profits as indicators of future profits. We see barriers to entry (as defined in our conceptual model) being more of a factor for existing firms than for start-ups.

In Table 5-1, we attempt to rank-order clusters of variables according to their level of importance for individual entrepreneurs, service providers and policymakers. One could argue about the order in which the different sets of variables should be ranked, but the intent of Table 5-1 is more to illustrate that the order of ranking probably differs for different types of actors. If Dissatisfaction is very important to individual entrepreneurs, but not regarded as very important by service providers or policymakers, then the types of measures introduced may not ease the problems of dissatisfaction. A similar argument can be made for the growth variable, which would probably be of less importance to the individual entrepreneur, depending on how it is measured. The growth variable will be treated differently by the different actors. For policymakers, it will be about making predictions for sectors based on existing growth and taking into consideration barriers to entry and sector concentration. This is probably one explanation for the great interest in initiating clusters. Growth for individual entrepreneurs is based much more on their individual business ideas and the confidence they have in their ability to exploit the market potential. For service providers, it is about business ideas, skills, competence and years of experience variables. So, expected growth will be looked upon very differently by these types of actors. Policymakers will "keep the structure", service providers will "change the structure at the margins" and entrepreneurs will create new structures and market opportunities. Judgements about the different types of needed measures will, therefore, also differ.

Figure 5-1. Variables influencing level of entrepreneurial activity

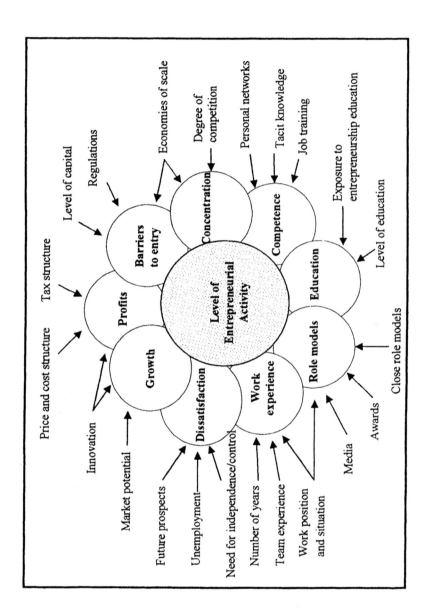

Table 5-1. Conflicting priorities between different actors

Individuals	Service providers	Policymakers
Profit	Growth	Growth
Dissatisfaction	Profit	
	Competence	Barriers to entry
Barriers to entry	Education	Concentration
Concentration	Working experience	
Growth		Education
	Barriers to entry	Profit
Education	Concentration	
Working experiences		Role models
Role models	Role models	Work experience
Competence	Dissatisfaction	Dissatisfaction
		Competence

The model is dynamic in this sense, since it takes into account some structural factors. If there are many small firms in a sector, there are likely low barriers to entry and, by definition, low concentration. Both of these aspects will, according to the function, produce positive effects on the level of entrepreneurship. Higher population density or population growth will probably increase expected profits and growth expectations and also increase the level of entrepreneurship. Referring back to the list of factors influencing the level of entrepreneurial activity in Table 4-1, we can observe how these factors might affect different variables in our conceptual model. Population growth and growth in GDP could affect profit expectations. High immigration rates affect population growth and, eventually, population density, and, therefore, profit expectations. Tolerance for income dispersion will eventually affect the prevalence of role models and the level of dissatisfaction. Social and cultural norms that value and support entrepreneurship could be expected to affect role models, and positive attitudes towards entrepreneurship would affect role models and exposure to role models.

Similarly, there are relationships between our context description and the conceptual model. For example, the unemployment rate will affect the level of dissatisfaction; total labour force participation rates will affect working experience and competence variables; service sector output in percentage of GDP will affect the number of SMEs, which affects the number of role models, working experiences, and competence; and all variables describing the vitality of the SME and entrepreneurial sector will affect many of the above variables.

A CONCEPTUAL MODEL FOR THE LEVEL OF ENTREPRENEURIAL EXITS

In line with the model for determining the level of entrepreneurship, we need a conceptual model for entrepreneurial exits. This is not our main objective in this book and not an issue that we have looked into very deeply when analysing the policy position of the 13 governments. However, there is emerging research interest in doing more in-depth studies of "failures", not only in terms of numbers and exit rates, but in terms of what happens to the entrepreneurs and their business ideas after the closing down process (Delmar et al., 2003). We also know from statistical data that, although a large percentage of firms do not survive their first four to five years after start-up, only a small percentage of exiting firms actually end in bankruptcy.

In this section, we briefly discuss the subject of failures measured as exits, that is, the number of nascent entrepreneurs who cease to continue the development of their business ideas plus the number of start-ups and young established firms that fail.

One of the major findings from recent research is that in an entrepreneurial economy, it should be easy to start up and wind down a business. Another major finding is that the turbulence rate, measured as the sum of start-ups (entries) and exits, is an important sign of a dynamic economy. This measure of turbulence provides more insight about what is really happening in the economy than the static measure of annual net growth in the stock of firms (entries minus exits).

To construct a conceptual model for entrepreneurial dynamics (or turbulence), we start by describing LoEE. The basic expression is:

$$\text{LoEE}_{t+1} = g\ (\Sigma\Sigma\Sigma X_{ijt},\ \Sigma\Sigma BE_{jt},\ \Sigma\Sigma\Sigma GR_{ijt},\ \Sigma\Sigma C_{jt},\ \Sigma\Sigma F_{it},\ \Sigma\Sigma YE_{it},\ \Sigma\Sigma D_{it},\ \Sigma\Sigma\Sigma U_{ijt},\ \Sigma\Sigma\Sigma\ K_{ijt}\ ).$$

We employ the same approach as earlier, but represent the function by the sign (g). This expression is partly an inverse of the earlier one (e.g., expected profits are negatively-correlated with growth possibilities). We assume the same effects for profits in earlier periods of time, years of experience, role models, education and competence. Barriers to entry would have a positive correlation, while Dissatisfaction could be both positive and negative, which we will explain below.

Profits, or lack of profits, is more about what has happened in earlier and existing time periods for individuals (i) and sectors (j). From an individual's point of view, there would always be an interest in expected profits (partly independent of earlier or existing profits). However, a lack of profits could pose financial constraints affecting a firm's survival; a lack of expected profits could affect whether or not a formal business is actually started. Different individuals will be more or less optimistic. Profits are also needed to produce a positive outcome for the business. If alternative activities, such as paid employment, are seen as more profitable, then this will likely increase the probability of an exit.

We see a difference between starting up a business and closing one down. When starting a business, there is limited knowledge of the actual situation concerning profit possibilities, while once in the market, the experience from running a business in a certain sector will produce a higher level of knowledge about what is realistic. The level of low versus high profits will vary across with sectors (e.g., between a business in the ICT sector and a traditional service business). Even if the business generates relatively low profits, the entrepreneur could still be earning a higher income than by working part-time as an employee.

Lack of growth will produce a similar set of implications because it will decrease the possibility of making profits in the long run. The profit variable is about the difference between expected and real growth, that is, actual development for the time (t) compared to the expectation of future growth held in an earlier period (t-1).

Other problems that could occur are obsolescence of products or services or a lack of innovation and renewal.

Barriers to entry (BE) could change over time due to market dynamics or innovations. There could be a miscalculation of what this variable actually consisted of when entering a market. For existing start-up firms, there is also a concern about barriers to exit; about the extent to which the penalties to failure are too high. The ease of closing down a business, especially in cases of insolvency, is seen as an important issue in contemporary entrepreneurship research. In a situation of diminishing markets, a start-up or small business would encounter fewer exit difficulties than a large company in the same situation.

Other reasons for failure or closure of the business could be lack of competence, an increasing dissatisfaction with the entrepreneurship situation compared to alternatives, or lack of use of education, experiences and tacit knowledge. These types of variables would be discussed mainly from present and future expectation perspectives, and also from sector and individual perspectives.

In the areas affecting LoEE, there are likely to be a number of conflicting interests between service providers and entrepreneurs where one could expect more optimism among entrepreneurs about future developments. So what is really meant by "ease of exits"? If entrepreneurs would like to continue to be in business longer than service providers would advise, then it is the individual entrepreneur that prevents "ease of exit". Or is it only when an entrepreneur has finally decided to quit that the formalities should be easy? This is also a question of the relationship between the quality of business ideas and the individual characteristics of entrepreneurs. In Table 5-2, we present possible outcomes from entrepreneurial activity based on the interaction effects of the quality of the entrepreneurs and their business ideas.

Table 5-2. Business ideas and entrepreneurs – possible business outcomes

Individual characteristics	Business ideas		
	Excellent	Imitating	Poor
Very good	success	survival	failure
Fair	survival	survival	failure
Poor	failure	failure	failure

If success, survival and failure are the possible outcomes, we can expect deviations between interests of individuals and the interests of society. In two out of three cases, society would benefit from excellent business ideas if the competence of the individual entrepreneurs could be better developed or if a more competent entrepreneur could be found. If one could "use" a very good entrepreneur for the execution of better business ideas that would also theoretically improve the situation from a societal point of view. The point of this illustration is to show that, when considering failures and successes, it is best to think both from the point of view of the characteristics of the individual entrepreneur and the quality of the business idea. When judgements are made about future viability, one should at least consider whether the business idea has real market potential, independent of the quality of the individual's characteristics at (t).

Discussions could also focus on the question of whether innovators generally make good or poor entrepreneurs. To what extent are they more likely to fall into the quadrant of excellent ideas but poor individual characteristics? If this is the most common case, the conclusion could be that, independent of the type of business idea developed by the innovator, the probability of survival and success on the market would be low. This is likely one reason why there is an increasing interest among governments in several economies to more closely integrate the entrepreneurship and innovation policy areas. Furthermore, only one out of nine cases of new product development will find success in the marketplace, a logical explanation for the very small number of successful innovative start-ups.

This is not an area of interest from the policymaker's point of view, but it is for service providers. In addition, one can assume that entrepreneurs and service providers will not come to the same judgement concerning the individual characteristics and the quality of the business idea. To judge the business idea, one can use a number of methods, including potential market share, the level of investment required, price and cost relationships, competition, and so on, most of the data coming from earlier time periods. The bigger challenge is being able to judge the quality of individual characteristics in combination with the quality of business ideas. If judgements could be done, we predict that service providers would support cases in at least four of the nine quadrants in Table 5-2. If they were necessity entrepreneurship individuals, probably all nine cases would be supported, depending on the level of dissatisfaction in their current situation.

Perspectives on Dynamics and the Effects of LoE and LoEF

So far we have discussed the variables for the level of entrepreneurship (LoE) and entrepreneurial exits (LoEE) separately. One observation from our analysis is that most of the variables for LoEE are the inverse of the same variables for LoE. In research and practice, discussions stress the importance of ease of entry and exit in producing a "dynamic" that will contribute to renewal and innovation in the economy. Research results demonstrate a relationship between entries and exits (Reynolds et al., 2004), but the nature of this relationship is not well specified. According to our conceptual model, it is not obvious what level of dynamic should aim to be created in an economy, the reason being that variables giving rise to entries will simultaneously give rise to exits, although likely at different rates. To describe aspects underlying this dynamic in an economy, one could refer to a number of things. One could assume that it is about real or expected profits, or about low or high individual competence, as two examples. Taking into consideration the variables used, one could expect that there will be some conflicts between the number of exits and entries. Also, there will be an effect on existing companies in the market and a time dimension. A high number of entries in a certain sector (j) during the time-period (t) will increase competition in the market and the level of renewal, thereby placing pressure on existing firms to innovate. One outcome of this could be an increasing number of exits in the period (t+1) for the sector (j).

According to our conceptual model, an increase in entries in time period (t) and sector (j) would probably decrease profits for (t+1) in the sector (j) or increase the demand for competence, to give two concrete examples. If this was the case, there would be a positive outcome for that sector. However, if new entries are the result of lower cost structures from government subsidies or grant assistance, then positive outcomes for the sector could be questioned. The point is that it is important for policymakers to assess how all variables will be affected by different policy measures to ensure that chosen measures do not distort or change market conditions for different sectors over time.

In Table 5-3, we attempt to show the connection between the possible effects on LoE (entries) and LoEE (exits) of measures taken to influence each of the variables in our conceptual model. Entrepreneurship education will affect role models, the competence factor and, perhaps, the education variable. The effects are expected to be positive for LoE and negative for LoEE due to the higher level of competence and education of entrepreneurs. In this case, the time lag between measures taken and potential effects is very long, meaning that the effects on LoE and LoEE may not be produced until some time in the future.

Seed financing could be provided in the form of equity financing, loans, grants or loan guarantees, the argument being that new entries encounter difficulties attracting private capital due to perceived higher risks, a lack of collateral and a limited track record. Assuming this argument is valid, there could be two outcomes from government assistance. If seed financing is offered in the form of grants or equity capital to strengthen the capital structure of an entrepreneur's firm, the effects would be positive; if, on the other hand, it consists of loan schemes with high interest rates, the effect would be higher costs and lower expected growth and profits, thereby producing a negative outcome. This could lead to higher future exit rates. We conclude that effects on the entry/exit dynamic should be analysed for different types of seed financing measures. The time lag for effects from financing measures will be much shorter than for entrepreneurship education.

Less regulatory burden will mean lower barriers to entry, perhaps less concentration in a sector and, therefore, a higher probability of growth. This will produce positive effects on both LoE and LoEE. However, we lack knowledge regarding how soon such effects would produce observable outcomes as well as the level of the effects. There will also be a time lag between the positive effects on LoE and LoEE. Fewer regulations mean lower costs for entrepreneurs and, therefore, higher profits. However, if more entrepreneurs enter the market segment, expected profits will be reduced for all entrepreneurs, producing a question mark for both variables.

Table 5-3. Entrepreneurship policy measures and their effects on different variables

Measures	Variables	Type of effects
Entrepreneurship education	Role models Competence Education	Entrepreneurship (+) Exits (-)
Seed financing (public)	Profits Growth	Entrepreneurship (?) Exits (?)
Regulation (less)	Barriers to entry Concentration Growth	Entrepreneurship (+) Exits (+)
	Profits	Entrepreneurship (?) Exits (?)
Tax reductions	Profits Growth	Entrepreneurship (+) Exits (+)
Counseling Information	Competence	Entrepreneurship (?) Exits (?)
Networking	Competence Growth	Entrepreneurship (+) Exits (?)
Target groups	Role models Competence	Entrepreneurship (+) Exits (-)
Promotion	Role models	Entrepreneurship (+) Exits (?)
"Innovation"	Growth Competence Education	Entrepreneurship (+) Exits (+)

Tax reductions have an impact on profits and growth, affecting LoE and LoEE positively. In the long run, this means increased competition in the marketplace and more renewal in the economy. There are many studies concerning the effects of measures related to the provision of counseling and information (Hjalmarsson, 1998; Storey, 2000). This is an area where many measures are taken, but about which there is limited knowledge regarding total effects. We, therefore, question these effects on LoE and LoEE. If there is an effect, we assume it would increase the competence factor, leading to fewer exits and more entries. Networking will affect competence and create higher growth potential, producing higher levels of entrepreneurship. The impact of this on LoEE is a question mark because little is known about the relationship between networking, competence and exits. However, if competence increases, one would expect exit levels to decrease. Similar arguments could be used for target group and promotion measures. Innovation would probably affect a number of factors such as growth potential, competence and education. Here one could expect a higher level of entrepreneurship, but also a higher exit rate due to increased competition.

We will also see differences between the perspectives of individuals, service providers and policymakers. Individual entrepreneurs would not tend to see a lack of competence as a reason for failure, more likely attributing failure to market-oriented problems, such as diminishing markets, barriers to entry and competition. Service providers will look into the individual competence factors and the actual structure of the firm (e.g., the product or service, the financial structure and so on). The three categories of actors will have different perspectives and focus of interest. The expectations of service providers will have much more to do with the entrepreneur or about the lack of entrepreneurship. Policymakers will be less interested in individual performance and emphasise market behaviour. They could be interested in the general lack of competence in a sector or the lack of competition. They may not regard the market effects of the measures taken, instead viewing their public investments as stimulating an expansion of existing markets and developing the markets of the future. Individual expectations are likely to focus on future profitability issues.

CONCLUSIONS FOR ENTREPRENEURSHIP POLICY

This chapter has described a conceptual model for the level of entrepreneurship and illustrated the complexity of this system. It is important to see the total complexity and not to always seek simple correlations between actions taken and results obtained. We do not argue that one cannot learn a lot from simple correlations, but that one should try to understand the complexity of the system before making assumptions about linear independent correlations.

We have used many variables in the conceptual model with detailed definitions of each one of them, including different time periods and sectors. We have illustrated that the described variables are aggregated ones consisting of a number of influencing factors. Each one of these variables has potential to be more fully developed in an extensive research programme.

Why is it of interest to discuss a conceptual model that, according to us, could not be used to measure variables and test correlations? Perhaps it is as simple as being able to use the method to consider the implications of some of the results highlighted in Table 5-3. The discussion of conflicting interests is also an area where this conceptual model approach could be used. The model further illustrates that increases in entries and exits could be impacted by a number of combinations of policy measures. However, there is still a lack of knowledge regarding failures and the connection between exits and entries, despite the general conclusion that such correlations exist. There are also interesting possibilities for exploring the differences between necessity and opportunity entrepreneurship based on the variables in the conceptual model.

In conclusion, we believe that this approach can be used as a tool to stimulate a more general discussion of economic problems in an economy and the possible ways to deal with those problems. However, in the future, we also believe it would be useful to "translate" this conceptual model into a more heuristic one so actual outcomes could be tested. We will come back to this issue in the final chapter where we bridge connections between the context model, the conceptual model, the entrepreneurship policy typologies, and the evaluation approach.

We move in Chapter 6 to a discussion of evaluation issues and the problems of measuring performance impacts in the entrepreneurship policy area.

---

[1] See Stevenson and Lundström (2002), p. 499.

[2] See Baumol (2002) for a discussion concerning the need for routinised innovations.

[3] See Autio (2002) for an overview of the results of much of the research literature on growth.

Chapter 6

EVALUATION PROBLEMS AND PERSPECTIVES

Implementation of SME and entrepreneurship policies requires an appropriate delivery structure and a commitment of human and budget resources. In many cases, the investment of public funds is substantial with the potential to affect the economic system in various ways. Therefore, policy and programme evaluation issues need to be considered. Issues of evaluating SME policies have been well articulated by Storey (2000, 2003), the NFIB (2000) and Bridge et al. (1998). International organisations, such as the OECD and the European Commission, are increasingly emphasising the importance of proper policy and programme evaluation and working with member States and countries to develop more systematic approaches. Evaluation issues have been much in focus during the recent process of assessing the overall impact of the EU Structural Funds Programme. There is a growing commitment on the part of governments in developed countries, including the countries we have studied, to evaluate their policy and programme actions (Stevenson and Lundström, 2002). The major reason for this attention is the need to improve the effectiveness and efficiency of government expenditures in the area. Knowledge from evaluation studies will theoretically, at least, be able to determine the outcome of specific measures and to provide useful input for future policy and programme planning. Evaluation findings will assist policymakers in making the next set of decisions about what actions to take and in making refinements or adjustments to existing initiatives. Ultimately, this will lead to a better allocation of public funds. At the same time, evaluation in the area of entrepreneurship policy is an underdeveloped area with many outstanding issues to be taken into account.

In this chapter, we highlight some of the important evaluation issues for the entrepreneurship policy area and, to some extent, the area of SME policy. In fact, in formulating this chapter, we draw heavily from the existing knowledge base in the field of SME policy evaluation. The major reason for this is that the entrepreneurship policy area has not yet been explored much in the literature. However, the theory applied and methods discussed for the SME policy area are often applicable to the entrepreneurship policy area.

The first section deals with the more theoretical aspects of evaluation, starting with a general discussion of how to approach the problem of formulating objectives and choosing an appropriate evaluation method, and the strengths and weaknesses of the different approaches. We draw some conclusions about the application of evaluation approaches, using concrete examples to illustrate a number of issues. Finally, we summarise key issues and aspects to be considered in evaluation of the whole policy area.

THE PROBLEM OF IDENTIFYING POLICY MEASURES

There are two basic questions of great importance in deciding on specific policy measures in any area of public policy: i) what are the priority problems that need to be solved; and ii) to what extent should public spending programmes be used to solve these problems (Boter et al., 1999). The application of these questions will help in defining the domain of publicly-financed small business and entrepreneurship policy. These fundamental questions have not been substantively dealt with in evaluation theory with the exception of contributions by Hjalmarsson (1998), Storey (1994) and a small number of others. Hjalmarsson (1998) and Hjalmarsson and Johansson (2003) conclude that the answers will depend on which theoretical approach is used by policymakers to guide their economic decisions. The application of different macroeconomic theories will point to differing public policy roles. While it is beyond the scope of this book to go into this problem in great detail, we believe it is an important one.

The evaluation approach used by Boter et al. (1999) was to conceptually redesign the Swedish SME policy system using a zero-based approach. Starting from the conceptual position of no policy and no programme delivery structure, and given knowledge about the problems faced by the SME community, what should the optimal policy look like? In order to determine how to reconstruct such a policy area, a theory regarding the problems to be solved and the domain of possible policy options will be needed. Evaluation literature documents well that decisions regarding policy choices and the level and type of public investments depend on the use of macroeconomic theory. Macroeconomic theories describe how markets function and provide guidance as to when, where and why public interventions should be made in the market system. These are fundamental questions in evaluation exercises. Very little research has related evaluation theory and macroeconomic theory. Hjalmarsson (1998) discusses the different results for public policy measures depending on whether a neo-classical theory or Austrian theory approach is used. The results from applying these different macroeconomic models could have quite different implications for how the domains of a policy area are determined.

Isolating the problems to be solved

The first question of determining the priority problems that need to be solved in the SME/entrepreneurship policy area requires research-based analysis of the most important problems faced by small businesses and entrepreneurs, given their experience. For this reason, a bottom-up perspective is necessary. However, from their review of existing research, Storey (1994), Audretsch (2002) and Autio (2003) conclude that bottom-up approaches seldom produce similar results. One likely problem is the heterogeneity of the small business population. Problems experienced by small business owners or start-up entrepreneurs will differ depending on, among other things, the size of the firm, the stage of the firm's development and the type of business. Consequently, many policy measures are often developed from a top-down perspective. The problems to be solved within the policy area are defined by the system of business support providers and institutions, and among policymakers and business and employer organisations. We see similar problems in the entrepreneurship policy domain, evidenced by our 13 case studies.

The second question regarding the use of public funds in solving the problems is crucial from a policy point of view. Storey (1994) argues that even if problems are formulated, it is not always obvious that they should be solved by government policy measures. More theoretical thinking is often needed to properly justify different policy actions. Using a neo-classical approach, the motives for policy interventions are grounded in theories about the role of market forces. Justifications for public intervention are based on external effects, the need to improve competition in different markets, information asymmetries and various other kinds of market failures. Hjalmarsson (1998) argues that the process of identifying these market failures is one thing, but determining whether the public or private sector has the major role to play in mollifying these failures is not always clear. He uses the example of publicly-funded information systems. On the one hand, lack of information could have a negative external effect; on the other hand, the need for information systems could be a potential market opportunity for the private sector. He concludes that not everyone would agree that publicly-funded information systems should be an area for government intervention.

A discussion of these two questions is an important starting point in developing a proper foundation for policy analysis and determination. Since the specific problems faced by entrepreneurs and SMEs will vary across countries, context must be considered. Since the nature of these problems will likely change over time, policy flexibility is also important. Existing policy measures should be evaluated on a regular basis to assess their effectiveness in addressing those market failures identified in earlier time periods. At the same time, organisational stability is important, since the competence among service providers is built up over time.

So the first step in designing effective policy and measures is assessing the nature of problems experienced by small businesses and entrepreneurs and then deciding which of those problems are best solved by the public versus the private sector (Figure 6-1).

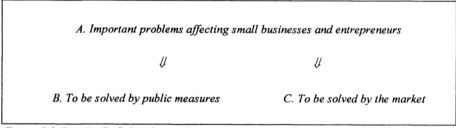

Figure 6-1. Step 1 – Defining the problems to be solved

Defining policy objectives

The second step would be to define objectives for the different policy measures to be taken, given the specific nature of the problems to be solved. What objectives should be met by possible policy measures? If there is a problem that is supposed to be solved with policy measures then someone also has to decide when that problem is solved. For what time period should the policy measure be in force to ameliorate the problem? Take as an example the situation where a government determines there are too few business start-ups to meet the projected need for employment or economic renewal in the economy. If the policymaking system decides that a 10 percent increase in the start-up rate is needed to solve or ease the problem, then when that target is met, a new set of policies will have to be considered. The policy analysis cycle will begin again. We realise how difficult it is to set quantitative objectives, such as the 10 percent target mentioned above, but it is hardly a better approach to set an objective to "improve conditions" or "generate higher benefits" for start-ups or to create more employment from start-up activity and new firms. Such targets could be measured, but they will not indicate much about whether the problem has been solved or eased. On the other hand, qualitative statements could be the basis of never-ending policy measures. That said, it is not sufficient to set a quantitative objective without describing the consequences that such an objective will have on the economic system. An increase of 10 percent in the number start-ups where all start-ups are solo-firms will produce a very different effect than if the increase is due to new start-ups with growth ambitions. The many problems of quantifying objectives have been discussed by Storey (2000). Sarasvathy (2001) and Sarasvathy et al. (2003) examine the merits of applying more qualitative approaches to objectives-setting. There are different opinions about whether evaluations should question the objectives set for different programmes and projects, even when comments are made about the appropriateness of their quantitative versus qualitative nature (Storey, 2000, 2003).

One of the observations we make from our review of government policy in the 13 countries is that the majority of stated objectives within the areas of entrepreneurship policy are more qualitative in nature. In some senses, qualitative objectives produce more positive evaluation results, the reason being, they are less precise. It is much easier to hit a qualitative target when many possible solutions could have produced it than to hit a target that is defined by a quantitative objective. So if the objective is to increase the start-up rate by 10 percent and it only increases by 2 percent, then the result is not that good. But if the objective is to "improve" the start-up rate, then an increase of two percent might be considered good. Or to put it more generally, the subset of improved results includes all positive values over zero. Or to make a political conclusion, it is more favourable for policymakers to use qualitative objectives than quantitative ones. The requirement of being able to determine the future outcome of the implemented policy (the situation at t+n) and to describe how the problem has improved should rationally motivate a quantitative objective. Many attempts to formulate such objectives have recently been made by the EU and member States. A reminder caution is that any one quantitative objective could be decomposed into a number of sub-objectives.

There is also a question of the number of objectives set. Storey (1994) demonstrates the problem of conflicting objectives. An objective in one area of policy could actually counteract the objective in another area of policy, thus potentially solving one problem but creating another. He suggests that policymakers need to take this possibility of conflicting objectives into consideration when designing policy measures. Even if objectives are not conflicting, it is still possible that one set of policy objectives could pose constraints on the attainment of another resulting in a cancelling-out of positive policy outcomes.

The process after Step 2 is reflected in Figure 6-2.

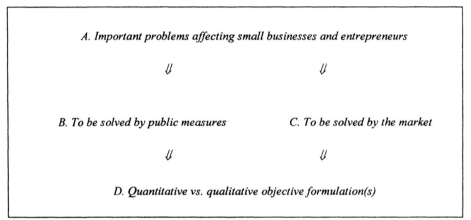

Figure 6-2. Step 2 – Defining policy objectives

Making the selection of measures

After identifying the objectives, the next step in the process will be to discuss possible policy options, resource requirements and resource allocations. There are several alternative ways to achieve a stated objective, often through a combination of different measures. In the entrepreneurship policy area, a number of common measures can be employed depending on the type of problem to be solved. Table 6-1 highlights some of these options, indicating the type of problem motivating each type of measure, the level of research-based confirmation that the problem exists, and the types of objectives set for each policy measure. It points to some important issues with respect to entrepreneurship policy formulation in many countries.

Our first observation is that each type of measure attempts to address its own particular problem. In other words, a general problem formulation could be missing. Our second observation is that objectives set for the different problem areas are mostly of a qualitative nature, such as "increase awareness of entrepreneurship as a career option". Our third observation is that not many of the stated problems have been well verified by research. Many of them could be myths and not actual problems or, at least, possible problems not verified so far.

Table 6-1. Entrepreneurship policy measures: stated problems, objectives and research basis

Type of measures	Problems stated (Examples)	Knowledge from research	Objectives (examples)
Administrative burden	Too many High compliance costs	Limited but increasing	Decrease regulations by (x) percent Increase transparency
Seed financing	Lack of seed capital Relatively high costs	Extensive but conflicting	Increase amount of seed capital (in different forms)
Entrepreneurship education	Lack of role models Lack of awareness Lack of knowledge	Limited	Increase awareness of entrepreneurship as a career
Tax incentives	Increase expected profits	Limited	Increase the number of start-ups
Counseling and information	High cost of private services Lack of competence	Limited and conflicting	Increase competence Increase access to information and advice
R&D and innovations	Need for renewal More technology transfer	Limited and conflicting	Increase innovative entrepreneurship
Exporting support	Low degree of internationalisation Lack of competence	Limited	Increase number of SMEs in international markets
Target groups (e.g., women entrepreneurs)	Too few	Some, mainly statistically-oriented	Increase the level of start-ups among under-represented groups
Promotion activities	Lack of awareness and role models	Limited	Create more positive attitudes for entrepreneurship
Networking	Lack of individual competence and resources	Limited	Create more networking opportunities

Source: Revised from Lundström and Stevenson (2002), p. 23.

Our final comment is related to the integration of measures. Suppose that a government has an objective to increase the number of start-ups by 10 percent a year. This could probably only be achieved through a combination of measures, for example, by improving access to financing and advice *and* reducing barriers to entry *and* creating networking opportunities. In the government policies we examined, objectives are often set for each of these areas. Evaluations, when they are done, tend to focus on each specific policy measure in isolation of the effects of the whole policy area – a form of disaggregated evaluation approach. If there are many different financing initiatives, a large number of regulations, and several initiatives for different target groups, the range of possible policy measure combinations will be very high. This creates obvious evaluation problems. De-composing the evaluation process (i.e., focusing on the evaluation of finite, individual measures) could potentially result in more positive evaluation results than evaluation of an overall objective that includes a combination of measures. However, decomposition of the problem is not an obvious optimal solution.

This brings us to the completion of the step-process illustrated in this section (Figure 6-3). This is a rational, step-process for a certain time period.

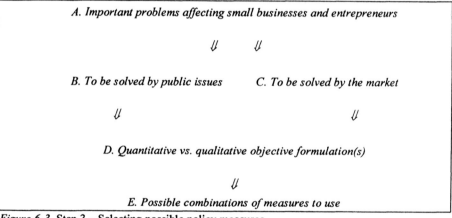

Figure 6-3. Step 3 – Selecting possible policy measures

We are aware that some researchers in recent years have questioned the rational approach to setting objectives and then trying to meet them with different measures. Sarasvathy (2001) discusses effectuation; Ahl (2004) refers to the alternative use of discourse analysis; and Hjalmarsson and Johansson (2003) refer to clientification approaches. There is a difference between really trying to understand entrepreneurs and discussing how policymakers formally behave. It would not be acceptable for a policymaker to set policy without objectives or to implement policy measures without indicating an anticipated outcome. Even if such a trial and error process might be a possible approach, it is not realistic in a situation of limited public resources to invest and competing policy demands for an allocation of those resources. At the same time, there seems to be some apathy for more systematic evaluations of the policy measures in place. This could be due to the fact that formulated objectives are not of great importance or that the results from previous evaluations have not proven that useful.

THE PROBLEM OF CHOOSING AN EVALUATION METHOD

We now discuss the problems in choosing a method for evaluating the effectiveness and efficiency of different policy measures. The assumptions we made in the previous section must be kept in mind, otherwise the tendency may be to assume that measures taken and their objectives are valid. In developing policy, it is not feasible to take into consideration all of the possible variations of the different measures for solving certain problems, but researchers and policymakers should at least be aware of the possible range of options and alternative approaches for solving the problem. This is necessary input for informed policy development. It should also be considered a part of the policy evaluation process, although in many instances, there is not an extensive discussion of the precise nature of the problem to be solved and how it is being approached. Given that the combination of implemented measures should be the focus of evaluation, the problem of isolating the effects of particular measures is an important one. We illustrate the difficulty of doing this in Figure 6-4.

An individual entrepreneur's firm is influenced by a range of factors during any given time period. Changes to the firm may occur as the result of hiring a new person to chair the board of directors, obtaining a new loan from a bank (that is secured by a government loan guarantee programme), accessing business-related information from a public service provider, developing a new product or gaining a new customer, as examples. If it was important to measure the precise effects of the government loan guarantee on the performance of the business, there would be problems. First, it would be impossible to isolate the impact of the loan guarantee on the firm's performance from the impact of other actions that took place inside the firm over a period of time. The proposed solution to such a problem is normally to find a control group company with similar characteristics in terms of size, sector and years in business, and similar factors influencing its development, except for the one factor, i.e., the loan guarantee. Every existing entrepreneur/firm could be regarded as unique if they were studied in detail, so the problem of identifying a control-group firm is challenging. If this cannot be done, it will not be possible to "isolate" the effect under review. Although there may be some difficulties with the control-group approach, it is one alternative to examine the difference made by the loan guarantee to the outcome of the assisted firm.

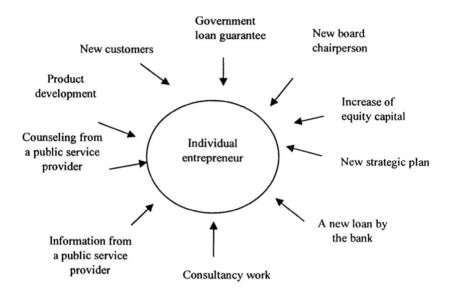

Figure 6-4. Factors influencing the growth of a single start-up or young company
Source: Revised from Lundström and Stevenson (2002), p. 25.

However, another problem is even greater. Changes in the behaviour of the firm have been caused by the range of activities occurring in a certain period; they cannot be assumed to be independent of each other. The normal assumption is that factors are independent and, therefore, that different combinations will produce different results. In our example, some ten actions occurred including the loan guarantee. If there had been a different set of actions, the loan guarantee, in combination with these actions, may have produced a totally different result for the firm. If one of the evaluation measures attached to the loan guarantee programme was job creation, and if the entrepreneur increased total employment by 10 people within the evaluation time frame, it could be said that the loan guarantee resulted in ten new jobs. However, this employment growth could have also resulted from the new customer gained over the same period of time. In cases where a small firm receives assistance through a number of government programmes each one could claim the increase in employment as an outcome. In theory, the employment effect would be counted several times. Summarising, the two main problems are first to isolate the factor of interest and then to determine how such a factor is influenced by all other factors. Storey (2000) and OECD (2003a) have examined these types of problems in detail.

Another problem in evaluation is measuring the total effect of the assistance programme on the sector or economy. Fully or partly public-financed assistance programmes may create a more favourable situation for some entrepreneurs in the market than others. Even if the individual entrepreneur referred to in Figure 6-4 did not access government assistance, the position in the market of his or her firm could have been indirectly affected by the actions of a competitive firm that did receive such assistance. If the outcome for the unassisted firm is negative, then the positive effects of assistance to the assisted firm may be cancelled out. The same argument could be used for measures like publicly-funded counseling or training programmes.

The evaluation challenge is to find appropriate methodologies and indicators that will enable the study of effectiveness and efficiency of a defined policy area, in this case, small business or entrepreneurship policy. Because individual policy areas are not independent of each other, the optimal approach would be to evaluate the whole policy area within a country. This would be an overwhelming task so, in our view, the systems approach we are discussing is at least a step forward, even with its limitations. With a systems approach there will be opportunities to improve the total effects of assistance measures by changing some or a number of the measures taken in the policy area. One option could be to reduce the number of measures simply to get a better overview of the system.

THE PROBLEM WITH EXISTING EVALUATIONS

A positive development in recent years is the growing emphasis on programme evaluation. More or less every programme of a certain magnitude will undergo an evaluation review. Even so, the learning effects from this may be limited. A general problem in the area of entrepreneurship policy evaluation is that the field is relatively new, meaning limited information exists about performance indicators and appropriate evaluation methods. Few policy benchmarks exist.

The governments in our case studies have collectively done many evaluations to determine the effectiveness and efficiencies of single measures taken in the area of small business and entrepreneurship policy. Some of these employ comprehensive evaluation approaches, whereas others use follow-up methodologies. There are a variety of possible evaluation methods, each with its own of set of strengths and weaknesses. Irrespective of which method is selected, a number of problems may be encountered.

The first problem is one of "dependency". Often agencies responsible for a policy or programme measure will also be responsible for conducting the evaluation review, even if they enter into a contract with an external consultant to perform the work. We refer to this as a "dependent" evaluation as opposed to an "independent" evaluation. An independent evaluation is one where there are no formal agreements between the organisation responsible for the measure taken and the organisation performing the evaluation. The general result will be that dependent evaluations give more positive results and independent evaluations more negative (or critical) results (Table 6-2). This is a preliminary result from a limited number of observations, (Lundström (ed.), 2003). There are, of course, a lot of reasons for such potential behaviour. If a consultant has a contract with an agency that could lead to additional contracts in the future, there may be a tendency for the consultant to carefully weigh critical comment on the outcome of the evaluation, especially if results are negative. The contracting agency's reaction to a negative evaluation outcome could be that the consultant showed a lack of understanding of the system or the problem and this could jeopardise the consultant's chances of being awarded another contract.

In cases where evaluations are done by independent organisations without a contractual obligation to the agency client, the outcomes tend to be more negative. Government agencies have a natural interest in doing programme/project follow up, but there is a general need for more independent evaluations.

Table 6-2. The relationship between "dependency" and evaluation results

	Positive results	Negative results
Dependent evaluation	Mostly	Seldom
Independent evaluation	Seldom	Mostly

Source: Lundström (ed.), 2003, p. 280, revised.

We often find dissatisfaction among policymakers on different levels concerning the use of evaluation results. The learning effect seems to be very limited. One reason for this could be that, even if a "good" evaluation is done from a methodological point of view, the results from it could be questioned - the time when the evaluation was done, the specific circumstances during which the programme was launched, the lack of general conclusions, and the limited insight about why the programme was more of a failure than a success (if that was the outcome).

The second problem concerning the way evaluations are done is whether an ad hoc or process perspective is taken. The ad hoc perspective means that the evaluation is done at a certain time period, often halfway through (ex nunc) or after a program has been completed (ex post). This will lead to the problem of retrospectivity. Ex-post evaluations are not able to track after-the-fact developments without running into the problems of having to redefine or reconstruct important aspects or events. Process evaluations often start during the preparation phase of an intervention and estimates of the expected outcomes of the intervention are measured beforehand. However, a process evaluation also has some limitations since one cannot always know in advance what activities or events will be of importance in the future in terms of producing the project or programme outcomes. The problem is one of generalising individual actions taken in different time periods.

Policy measures are about affecting individual behaviour during a given time period. But every individual will be affected differently, meaning that it is easier to understand each individual's behaviour than the total effects of all such behaviour. We propose that one has to differentiate between the actual events (e.g., the number of start-ups or failures, and so on) in terms of the resources invested and find explanations for why these events have occurred. We see a lot of confusion between these two aspects. For instance, from an evaluation perspective, total outcomes could be positive even if measures are seen as negative for a number of individuals. It is not obvious that there should necessarily be consensus in an effective system of policy measures. One possible way to move forward could be to combine research with discussions among researchers, policymakers and service providers regarding achieved results. To have a more intensive dialogue in the future will likely be of great importance.

On-going developments in the field of evaluation

Although it has become more common for governments in different countries to conduct evaluations of their major programmes and projects, there is a great deal of variance in the methods used and approaches taken. The OECD is now constructing models to be used in descriptions for individual economies and trying to compare the results of such approaches in order to promote policy and programme benchmarking (OECD, 2002b). The intent of their policy benchmarking for firm creation and entrepreneurship exercise is to develop comparative performance data for measures of entrepreneurial activity, start-up rates and churning rates that will lead to a policy model for the domain (OECD, 2002b, pp. 6-7). The major approach is to inventory and describe interesting programmes for different policy areas and countries without aiming to formally evaluate identified measures. The European Commission is using a similar approach in the "best practices" and benchmarking initiatives referenced throughout this book. In their series of best practice reports, the EU relies heavily on project descriptions from individual countries. It is not obvious how many of the projects have undergone formal evaluation.

A more rational type of evaluation approach is that employed by the Atlantic Canada Opportunities Agency (ACOA), a regional development arm of the federal government responsible for small business and entrepreneurship development in one of Canada's regions. In ACOA's programme development, goals and objectives for new programmes are set before approval of any resources (Thomas and Landry, 2001). An evaluation framework is developed before the programme is launched, stating how goals are to be achieved and how programmes results will be evaluated. This is a classic example of dependent evaluation, independent of which organisation will carry out the evaluation in practice. It is also a programme type of evaluation because every programme has its own objectives and evaluation methodology. However, this approach does offer the possibility for policymakers to judge whether resources spent were worthwhile and also to question the programme delivery approach and how it is evaluated. Another example of a rational evaluation approach is illustrated by the ALMI group in Sweden, which delivers business and financial assistance to SMEs as part of the national government's SME policy. ALMI uses official statistics and control groups to compare the effects of assistance on client-firms versus non-assisted SMEs. ALMI also uses a number of other approaches to try and measure external and internal efficiencies. In addition, we could mention all types of evaluations of individual programmes and projects carried out by the EU or by different service providers in different countries or by more independent organisations. Finally, different approaches are used to generate discussion among members of the policy system, for example, the *European Observatory for SMEs*, government White Papers that are produced in many countries, and the GEM reports.

It is not our purpose to judge or rank these types of evaluation or follow-up studies. One problem, however, is the lack of comparability between different studies. One can see very different data for the same measure in different reports. Often more attention is paid to positioning countries according to their performance on comparative indicators than to generating substantive discussions on issues of policy and programme effectiveness and efficiency. The lack of resources invested in evaluation, compared to the level of resources invested in programmes, is a limiting factor in trying to increase knowledge about programme impact. As well, only a minor share of resources will be used for learning activities based on these evaluations.

Our main conclusion is that there is no single optimal method for doing evaluations in a policy area that has many programmes and projects. Reasons include the problem of interdependencies between variables, the lack of dynamic approaches (which are seldom used), the retrospective nature of ex-post approaches and the limited comparability of international data.

Even if such factors could be taken into consideration, there are still a number of problems. For one, the magnitude of the challenge. There could be over 100 different types of programmes and financial measures in a country, with a myriad of measures in other policy areas. Given this reality, it is easy to understand the daunting challenge of trying to evaluate the total policy system. If we think about the entrepreneurship policy area, there are financial measures, target group initiatives, counseling and information services, regulations, and networking and motivational measures, each one potentially involving a large number of possible combinations of existing measures. This is the major reason why the scope of most evaluations is of an individual programme or project. Given that it is probably impossible to take a systems approach to evaluation in an optimal way, one must consider second-best solutions.

EVALUATION ISSUES FOR ENTREPRENEURSHIP POLICY

In this section we use examples from the entrepreneurship policy area to illustrate different types of evaluation problems. These problems could exist even when each area is evaluated separately. In particular, we highlight the special problems of evaluating measures in areas where: 1) there are long-term effects (entrepreneurship education); 2) there are a high number of alternatives (administrative burdens); 3) special groups are targeted (target groups); the area has a modest amount of invested resources (entrepreneurship promotion); 4) it is difficult to define the unit for evaluation (networking); 5) there are market externalities (counseling and information); and 6) there is an "over-supply" market (seed financing). We describe these examples below.

Understanding the impact of entrepreneurship education - the problem of long-term effects

The area of entrepreneurship education as a policy area is accelerating rapidly in the 13 countries we have studied. It is one of the most popular emerging areas of entrepreneurship policy. However, there is still a lack of complete consensus among economies about what is meant by "entrepreneurship" education. Differing views are held about what should be included in the content of this area, at what level it should begin to be taught in the school system, and whether it should be integrated across the curriculum.

Courses in entrepreneurship are being taught at a number of universities in our case countries. There is general agreement that entrepreneurship should be offered as a course to students in all disciplines, but there are very few incidences where this is actually being done. Similar tendencies can be seen at the high school level. There are many new initiatives to expose elementary school children (at a very young age) to entrepreneurial behaviours and concepts. Across countries, but not necessarily within all countries, activities are ongoing at all levels of the school system, even if the amount invested in the area differs among governments. In cases where national entrepreneurship education policies do not exist, we see a lot of efforts taking place at the local and regional level (e.g., in Canada and Sweden).

So why has this area of entrepreneurship policy become so popular? Obviously, results measuring attitudes among young people and students towards entrepreneurship has increased as a result of actions taken. On the other hand, there is a growing awareness of the importance of preparing young people for a changing labour market where different attitudes, skills and behaviours are required at different levels. Introducing every student in the education system to the possibilities of working as an entrepreneur rather than being employed and giving them the opportunity to gain a better understanding of the conditions for entrepreneurs is seen as important exposure and knowledge, independent of their future career orientations.

There are two different views about this development in the education area. One view is that it is a core area of general knowledge, like mathematics or geography. One will note that we rarely discuss the effects of the knowledge that such education creates. The other view is that it is a special subject introduced to create better attitudes and, in the long run, to produce more entrepreneurs in the system. In this latter case, more emphasis should be given to improving attitudes, developing skills, and discussing aspects related to renewal of the future industrial structure in an economy.

Entrepreneurship education poses a special type of evaluation problem, mainly because of the long-term time period between the education experience and the ultimate action of starting a business, if this is the expected outcome. Many objectives in the area of entrepreneurship education are about increasing awareness of the option of becoming an entrepreneur rather than being an employee. The implication is that by increasing this awareness, the level of entrepreneurship will increase. It could take 20 years to see such a result from measures taken to introduce entrepreneurship to students in the elementary school system. In the meantime, there will be a huge problem in finding any correlation between entrepreneurship education and the level of entrepreneurship. On the other hand, if entrepreneurship education is on-going throughout the whole school system one could perhaps see it as something similar to having close role models for individuals. Even so, it will be very difficult to see a direct relationship between measures taken and results obtained. This is a rather typical process evaluation problem, but in the case of entrepreneurship education, evaluations are generally more ad hoc.

How is this type of problem dealt with in the 13 case countries? In some cases, governments are measuring changes in attitudes among young people who have been exposed to entrepreneurship education in the school. These studies find a positive result regarding a change in attitudes. In other cases, studies are done to determine if people starting business have had entrepreneurship education in schools. Both approaches will produce a lack of certainty concerning relationships between actions and results because a one-to-one correlation is being examined. Even if a control group was to be used in these studies, it would be difficult to know with certainty that the "correct" type of correlation was being studied.

Administrative burden – a high number of alternatives

More or less every economy gives a high priority to the issue of reducing administrative burden, as do organisations like the European Union and the OECD, and for a number of logical reasons. Entrepreneurs, SMEs, business and employer associations, and research organisations all express concerns about the increasing number of regulations over time and the level of different taxes affecting developments in the private sector. This debate is similar across countries, independent of the actual situation.

We discussed earlier that administrative burden is an area mainly in the SME policy domain. However, there is some overlap with entrepreneurship policy in areas affecting the ease of starting a firm – whether there is a single point of entry for business registration matters; the time and cost of meeting business start-up requirements; the perceived administrative burden for nascent entrepreneurs; and so on.

One of the major evaluation challenges in the area of administrative burden is the huge number of regulations. Governments seeking to reduce the number will often set more quantitatively-oriented objectives for their policy measures, such as reducing the number of regulations by a fixed percentage within a certain time period or reducing the costs of regulation to SMEs by a fixed percentage (or amount) by a certain year. In fact, this is one of the primary areas in entrepreneurship policy where one can see examples of this type of quantitative statement.

Governments in several countries have started the work of calculating the costs of administrative burden and are seriously trying to reduce the number of proposed new regulations by demanding cost calculations of the impact of these new rules on SMEs and entrepreneurs. However, to put it simply, it is likely easier to implement changes in the tax system than to reduce the total number of government regulations. Since the number of regulations, in quantitative terms, is so large, it is very difficult to know which one(s) are presenting the major barriers to business entry, survival and growth. Furthermore, the importance of regulations differs by sector. There are few regulations that apply in a general way to all new or existing firms. In other words, there is a lack of generality in this type of work. There are some paradoxes in this area as well. The regulations that are the easiest to change are likely the ones of least importance for business development.

No one person or organisation in the system has knowledge of all the regulations. Therefore it is also difficult to understand the impact of new regulations. Some of these regulations will be agreed upon on at the EU level which makes it difficult for individual European countries to work independently in this area. Such work could potentially be regarded as a barrier to entry from the perspective of the EU internal market.

Government actions to calculate the costs of regulation and administrative burden on SMEs and entrepreneurs have occurred in a number of countries (e.g., Denmark, Sweden, the Netherlands, Australia, and the US). The commitment is to track the development of these costs over time. The OECD has tried to compare countries by using a cost-model approach and to do this on a longitudinal basis. However, there are problems in collecting comparable data across countries. The fact that there are so many regulations makes it difficult to isolate precisely why certain countries have higher costs than others. One way to ease this problem would be to look at a very specific sector or a particular phase in the development of companies (e.g., start-up regulation costs).

Furthermore, individual firms or entrepreneurs lack knowledge about all of the relevant regulations affecting their type of business. One effect of this is that they manage their companies without taking into consideration the full range of regulations affecting them.

In this administrative burden policy area, we see measurement problems, awareness problems, time and costs problems, and perceived attitude problems. Even if some governments try to work closely with different types of advisory groups to provide regulatory information to groups of entrepreneurs and SME owners, the situation for all entrepreneurs or for different SMEs are seldom taken into account. The presence of lobby groups which might have differing opinions about the value of certain government regulations means negotiations for even small changes in the system take a long time. What can be done in a situation like the one described? First, it is important to obtain a good estimate of the total costs of administrative burdens over time. Second, restrictions should be placed on the introduction of new regulations. Third, government departments and agencies having a number of regulations should be required to describe the total effects of these regulations on SMEs and entrepreneurs. Fourth, governments should work with tax reductions as a more general tool. Finally, the area should be entered into with a totally new approach, ideally on an international basis within the OECD or the European Commission. The idea would be to take a zero-based approach building up from the conceptual position of "no regulations". A number of cases or typologies could be formulated for different types of entries, SMEs in different sectors, or businesses in different stages of development. Discussion would focus on the regulations and rules that would be needed if they were forced to be created from the point of view of health and safety, security, working conditions, or environmental considerations. "Optimal cases" could then be used as a basis against which to compare the actual situation in different countries. A new form of objective would be one stated in terms of deviation from the optimal case, e.g., the cost of administrative burden imposed on SMEs should be no greater than a certain percentage. This means that the focus would be more on the demand side than the supply side of the regulatory issue.

Target groups – selecting special groups

During the last decade, a number of programmes have been established to encourage entrepreneurial activity among different target groups. It is becoming a policy area of increasing interest among governments with many initiatives to increase start-up rates among target groups. The most common ones are young people, women and ethnic minorities, groups that tend to be under-represented in the population of business owners. The number of potential target groups is much greater than this. In Chapter 2, we outlined the range of target group measures being undertaken, such as counseling and information services.

Compared to their share of the total population, women and young people have a low representation in business ownership and self-employment. There are a number of explanations for this situation. One is the lack of entrepreneurial opportunities for women, either because of the nature of their working experience, the lack of role-models, or the lack of cultural reinforcement. We see in the Nordic countries that women are much more likely to be employed in the public sector where they are less likely to gain working experience that prepares them for entrepreneurial activity. If that is the case, one could ask what actions are best suited to increasing their share of business ownership. Would it be to create more opportunities for women to increase their knowledge of becoming an entrepreneur in a different sector than the one in which they have acquired their experience? Or would it be better to privatise certain government services, such as home care, and offer women the opportunity to do this as a private business? The latter is not happening in the Nordic countries to much of an extent so the former option is the only one left. If a person starts a business in a different sector than the one they have experience in, there are potentially higher risks. They means they may start smaller, invest a minimal amount of resources and grow very slowly as they gain knowledge of the sector and develop their entrepreneurial management skills. It is a structural problem where fewer opportunities exist to become entrepreneurs in sectors where women are mostly employed (again, the Nordic example). This is a situation of lack of role models and opportunities for entrepreneurship. The conclusion would be that one has to focus policy on Opportunity as well as Skills and Motivation in an integrated fashion. For young people there are problems of lack of experience, limited personal resources to invest and a lack of credibility.

Objectives in this area will be about increasing the number of start-ups among different target groups. There are several possibilities to evaluate measures to improve the level of entrepreneurship for these groups. From a general systematic policy evaluation point of view, one option would be to assess whether the resources invested to achieve this type of objective could be better used in other areas within entrepreneurship policy. In some instances, supporting select target groups may not be the most efficient use of invested resources, but that depends on what other objectives are being met through these policies, for example, labour market integration, social integration, gender equality, reduced unemployment and so on. As well, because the target is individuals, it is one of the most precise areas of entrepreneurship policy. However, the opportunity to evaluate such initiatives, from a rational point of view, could be questioned.

Entrepreneurship promotion - an area with modest investment

The objective of entrepreneurship promotion is to increase the motivational factors for individuals to become more entrepreneurial, to improve social acceptance of entrepreneurship and to increase interest among the adult population in becoming entrepreneurs. Much of these efforts are at the core of entrepreneurship policy.

One of the spill-over effects of promotion efforts is the creation of role models. Creating role models can be done in a number of ways, e.g., through media coverage of successful entrepreneurs, promotional material and information, awards, books and articles, and so on. In most countries, promotion of entrepreneurship in this sense is not a main priority of government policy initiatives. However, entrepreneurship promotion is an area where there is interest from the research society and business organisations and where there are many private sector initiatives. We mentioned a number of concrete examples of policy measures in Chapter 2, examples of weekly television programmes in Canada, media coverage in the US, and awards and mentoring programmes in Taiwan. The most common type of measure is support for entrepreneurship award programmes. If the objective is to create a more entrepreneurial society, two of the things that should be measured are the extent to which policymakers are involved in these activities and how they refer to entrepreneurs in their public presentations and documents. More could be done to promote entrepreneurship activities within existing organisations, either by exposing employees to the possibility of becoming an entrepreneur or by trying to provide good quality services to entrepreneurs in the society.

With minor exception, the level of resources invested in promotion of entrepreneurship is small. This presents another problem for the evaluation area. It is not easy to make a comparison between the value of investments made in a lightly-resourced area (e.g., promotion) with those made in an area which has been significantly resourced (e.g., start-up financing). It will be difficult to isolate the effects from relatively small investments or to understand precisely what impact they are having. It is also likely the case that observed effects will not be sustained over a long period of time. Instead, there could be a short time-period effect, meaning that the result from an evaluation could be misleading with respect to how persistent the observed changes would be over time.

Networking - defining the unit to be evaluated

There are many service providers in each economy working in different areas related to entrepreneurship policy. In many cases, these service providers have developed their own networks for various kinds of professional and experience exchanges at the EU level (e.g., Euro Information Centres; Innovation Relay Centres; and Business Innovation Centres) and country level (e.g., regional networks of professionals in the areas of research, counseling and information). The idea behind these networks is to increase the competence of their members, to make it easier for entrepreneurs to make use of all participating actors in a network, to promote the exchange of experiences, and to be independent of the physical location of a service provider or research organisation. The Internet has been a phenomenal impetus for development of these types of networks, making it easy to gather and spread information. Internet-based network systems are another popular policy measure. Governments use web portals to provide information on regulations, sources and types of financing, and steps to starting a business, and to promote other forms of exchange, such as that between entrepreneurs and angel investors.

Networking mechanisms can be publicly, semi-publicly or privately-financed. We have seen examples of all three types in our country studies. Their forms vary from one country to another; some are publicly financed and others by the private sector. Building networks between existing smaller organisations is becoming an alternative approach to creating large service provider organisations. In networks, different organisations can also be specialised.

The evaluation problem would be in comparing the effectiveness and efficiency of such networks with alternative organisational structures in terms of solving similar problems. If consideration is not given to this, then the efficiency of delivering services in this way cannot be judged. Another problem is being able to separate the evaluation of delivered services from how they are produced in the networks. A network could be very effective in producing the services, but less effective in delivering them and vice versa.

Counseling and information – measuring external effects

We see the entry of new types of actors in the entrepreneurship policy area, but demand still exists for the more traditional service providers who offer information, training and counseling to entrepreneurs. The motives for this type of policy measure are mainly to reduce negative external effects and to increase the competence of entrepreneurs. With better information and more advice, it is assumed that assisted entrepreneurs will achieve better market performance, leading to increased probability of survival and growth. Evaluation of this area of entrepreneurship policy attempts to measure both market externalities and also the competence factor. How can such effects be measured? First, if one is interested in the effects on the competence factor, one must know the changes that have taken place at the individual level during a given time period and be able to estimate how any changes have influenced firm survival rates. In the case of information provision, some type of measurement will need to be done concerning how information has been accessed and used by individuals. The evaluation approach will have to be able to measure how individual behaviour has been influenced and the effects of that influence. Such an evaluation will be very difficult to carry out even if a process perspective is taken. It would be almost impossible to identify a control group of individuals with similar competence or information levels at the beginning of the process.

In reality, evaluations in this area stop short of asking clients and users for their opinions about the level and quality of services received (i.e., let individuals estimate the market effects). More extensive evaluations of the impact of counseling efforts are difficult because some interventions with clients could be very intensive over a period of time, while others involve only a brief encounter on one occasion. Another evaluation issue has to do with the competence and experience level of the counselors and their capacity to help entrepreneurs gain the competencies needed to be successful in start-up efforts. An age-old question is whether these counselors and advisers should, themselves, have experience as an entrepreneur.

A broader evaluation issue relates to the extent to which government resources invested in business advisory services prevent the development of private sector services and the development of this counseling area as a business opportunity. To determine the total impact of advisory services, one should also be able to assess how the situation has changed for entrepreneurs who did not receive any counseling or use the offered information systems. Objectives in this area will be of a more qualitative nature, such as increasing the client's competence and individual ability. If an unemployed person is given a grant to start a business, they might be required to first take some start-up training. Arguments used for this type of measure include the need for increased competence and the inability or lack of willingness of entrepreneurs to use private consultancy firms due to affordability and value issues. However, there are few research projects proving the validity of such statements. The case for government intervention in the area of advisory services should be reviewed to make room for the use of private consultancy firms in providing such services.

Since the limited research on this topic cannot provide answers to the critical questions stated above, it is difficult to indicate options for action. This brings us back to the issue of doing evaluation in an individual policy area, not for the whole policy area. One alternative approach would be to examine other possible uses of the resources currently invested in this area. If service providers should be financed with public money, what would be the optimal set of activities for them to be offering, given the objectives to be achieved in this policy area?

Seed financing – the dilemma of an "over-supply" market

It is accepted among governments in our case countries that there is a need for public-financed seed financing programmes of various kinds. Whether myth or reality, policymakers, service providers and entrepreneurs more or less agree there is a role for government in filling financing "gaps". At the same time, in most of these countries, the commercial financial market is well developed and a private sector venture capital industry exists (although to varying degrees). Why is the supply of existing private capital not meeting the demand? The underlying problems of supply versus demand and of availability versus accessibility are not clear.

One of the arguments used to justify government intervention in the area of seed financing is that existing capital is not being allocated to entrepreneurs and firms in the start-up and very early stages of firm development. The perceived risk factors in financing these early phases of a new firm are often judged by conventional lenders as being too high. This is particularly problematic for new technology-based firms. Even private sector venture capital investments tend to favour later-stage companies because the growth trajectory is easier to predict. Some arguments have been presented that if an amount of public funds is invested in the system, it will act as an incentive for additional private investment. There is no way of knowing whether the effect of the additional government investment replaces private investment (i.e., private investment is withdrawn from the market), whether the private investments would have been made anyway, or if any positive effects from the public investment actually means those resources were efficiently used in this manner.

Research findings on the issue of SME financing are extensive and conflicting. Most of this research has studied the financing problems of existing firms. Other projects have studied how existing firms finance their businesses noting a variety of options and instruments (Landström (ed.), 2003). One of the research conclusions is that access to financing is a perceived problem for only a small share of existing SMEs. Another is that only a limited number of firms and entrepreneurs state they have major problems in financing their business ideas. Service providers, central agencies and policymakers have a different opinion. They believe that access to financing is one of the most severe problems for entrepreneurs, especially for SMEs in the early phases of development. So, in some way, there seems to be a knowledge gap between researchers and policymakers.

As we described in Chapter 2, many different types of public or semi-public financial support exist in the countries we have studied. There appears to be a general lack of knowledge about the types of firms who make use of all these financial programmes and the actual incremental impact of that assistance on the firm's performance and on the economy. When evaluations are done, they are generally limited to measuring the impact on the market of a single financial support programme or the financial programme of a single organisation. In some cases these evaluations use a control group to measure such things as deadweight and additionality; however, we previously mentioned the problems in finding matching control-group firms.

A systems approach to evaluating all such programmes that exist in a country, as far as we know, has not been undertaken. By this we mean a study of the whole area of seed financing. If a hundred different government financial assistance programmes existed in a country, consisting of loans, grants, loan guarantees, and some form of risk capital, it would be almost impossible to measure the total effect of the system or to judge whether programme "23" was better than programmes "87"or 92". One of difficulties in measuring the impact of the total system would be that the same client might have accessed several programmes. Secondly, if higher-risk loans carried higher interest rates this would increase the cost structure of the assisted-business and reduce future profits, meaning that the public financing ended up supporting less profitable business ideas. However, it might reveal very useful insights. For example, one financial programme could have some weaknesses, but perhaps relative to other measures taken, it produced quite good results. Furthermore, its weaknesses could have been the result of other measures taken. In evaluations, one should also discuss the role of public financing and the competence needed to deliver these programmes.

We are left with an obvious question. What can be done to redirect a share of the existing supply of private capital to investments in early-stage firms, if a financial gap truly exists in that segment of the market?

CONCLUSIONS

Policy evaluation is seen as an increasingly important area for governments in almost all of the countries we have studied. The major needs are to gain better insight about how the system can be improved, to know more specifically about the extent to which the stated problems and objectives have been reached, and to assess whether new measures are needed. The rational perspective would aim to achieve objectives through a combination of implemented measures over a certain time period. Ideally, we advocate for more efforts to do evaluations of the whole policy area. Doing this in the area of entrepreneurship policy would provide more complete knowledge about the overall impact of the results of individual policy measures. Attempts in this direction for the SME policy area have been carried out by Boter et al. (1999).

In this chapter, we have pointed to some of the major issues in the evaluation field as discussed and experienced by researchers (e.g., Storey, 2000; Lundström et al., 1998; Sarasvathy, 2001; Sarasvathy et al., 2003), international organisations, such as the EU and the OECD, and government agencies. We have stressed the importance of doing evaluations to provide informed input to policy decisions in such matters as: identifying key areas for intervention, setting objectives, determining the best combination of possible policy options and measures to achieve those objectives, and allocating public resources. We suggested that a bottom-up perspective should be used in formulating the nature of problems to be solved, and that objectives should be as precise as possible in order to limit the number of possible solutions that could be associated with achieving the objective(s). We pointed out that more general formulations of objectives are much easier to fulfil, but much more difficult to measure. We have presented a step-by-step illustration of some of the problems with evaluation and used examples from the entrepreneurship policy field. We also indicated the need for more research in the entrepreneurship policy area, because in many of the policy measure areas, there is limited evidence of the precise nature of the problems to be solved. In most of the presented areas, limited research has been done. Some of the problems as stated could be more "myths" generated within the institutional structures of service providers and policymakers than reality. The word myth is used here since it is not obvious that problems stated are based on the actual and existing problems of entrepreneurs. We need to know more about this.

To formally conclude this chapter, we make a few additional comments.

- There are very few evaluations of a whole policy area like entrepreneurship or SME policy. The more probable evaluation approach is to use methods describing single programmes or projects. This leads to fragmentation which we believe could be one reason for the low learning effects about systems evaluation.
- Policy and programme objectives are seldom quantified or easy to measure. Objectives such as: "to improve access", "to make it easier", or "to create a better regulatory environment" are very common. The reason for using more qualitative objectives is understandable but their lack of specificity makes it difficult to isolate the impact of a policy measure in producing the intended result compared to more quantitatively stated objectives.
- Many evaluations are static measurements of the situation at one point in time and conducted after the fact (i.e., retrospective). There are few examples of the more process-oriented evaluations initiated at the same time the measure is introduced. The latter approach is more sophisticated and would produce better information but is more time consuming and costly. This seems to the trade-off.
- It is important to recognise the time-lag that could exist between the implementation of a measure and its results. An obvious example is in the area of the entrepreneurship education, where the time-lag for outcomes will be much longer than to see the effects from the delivery of an advisory service. From the policymaker's point of view this

could be a problem, especially if the immediate economic objective is job creation or business start-ups. When working with entrepreneurship education or innovation systems, there will be a weak short-term observable relationship to such objectives, even if the knowledge factor is seen as a very important variable for economic development.

- Evaluation results could be influenced by who does the evaluation, the responsible agency or an independent organisation. Independent evaluations may produce more objective and critical results.
- Relatively limited resources are invested in programme and policy evaluation, both in terms of budget and human resources. This means a lack of comprehensive evaluation research and inadequate opportunities for methodological development and the transfer of learning effects. This has led to the use of simple evaluation methods and an insufficient supply of researchers in the evaluation field.
- The area of evaluation has not been taken up much by the research society so we know very little about the types of evaluation problems we have presented in this chapter. This lack of knowledge within the research community has opened up a lucrative market for consultancy firms instead.
- Another evaluation problem is created by changing structures and programme initiatives. This could be seen as a problem of reallocating resources between existing measures and new proposals, a much more difficult problem that one would expect.
- Small variations in a policy area means there is a lack of renewal in the policy system. At the same time, this means there is an opportunity to build up the competence of different organisations, because for some measures, one cannot expect short-term results. In any policy area, there is a need for many types of service providers, not few. It is easier to make changes in smaller organisations than in bigger ones. We also see an opportunity for competing organisations in the field. It is not obvious that if a few organisations have all the resources that they will be more effective, although we realise that it is easier from a policymaking system point of view to have fewer contacts in a policy area. One solution could be to develop more specialised service providers.
- There are probably no simple correlations between resources invested and results. If one type of action taken seems to produce positive results given the amount of money invested in the activity, it does not mean that more money invested will produce even better results. On the contrary, if there are negative results, this does not mean that less money invested will produce better results or that more money

invested would not produce better results. The lack of linearity is a vast problem here. One reason is the constant change that is taking place from a process perspective. So the challenge is to distinguish between results obtained and actions taken. This is one of the major problems concerning evaluation – the results from evaluation and the propositions from such an evaluation.

In terms of reflecting on what would be successful evaluation measures in entrepreneurship policy, we draw from questions often discussed in the evaluation literature (Storey, 2000, 2003; OECD 2003a, 2002b; Hjalmarsson and Johansson, 2003; Sarasvathy, 2001). One criterion would be a high demand for the measure or many users. However, this would not necessarily be a success criterion. The measure might have high demand because it is an attractive grant offering, but the outcome from the grant activity may or may not be favourable. Another criterion would be good effects or results. In spite of good outcomes, these results may or may not be associated with an efficient use of resources, which could possibly have been better used in another way. Another criterion could be high impact. This means the assisted firms pursued actions that they would not otherwise have done. Again, this is not the same thing as saying the result was the best alternative for either the firm or the individual. Another criterion could be improving market imperfections, defined as barriers to entry, lack of information or lack of capital, as examples. However, even if it could be shown there was an improvement in terms of overcoming the market failure, this still would not necessarily mean the resources were used in the optimal way. This is a very challenging area for policymakers. Good evaluation is very hard to do.

Programmes within a policy area are interrelated. Even if all programmes were independent of each other and could be evaluated with control group methodologies and take into account the personal influence effect (Storey, 2000), it would not mean that individual programmes could be ranked, because each of them would have different resource allocations, different process aspects, and so on. So even with all this knowledge it would be hard to see how it could be useful in terms of making decisions about resource reallocations between programmes or projects or coming up with new combinations of programmes in the entrepreneurship policy area.

There are increasing demands for knowledge about the effectiveness and efficiency of government policies. Simultaneously, there is a lack of appropriate evaluation methods and independent evaluation reviews. Process-oriented and systems evaluations are rare. The optimal, more holistic approach of evaluating a whole policy area with its various combinations of policy measures would be very difficult to undertake because of the complexities. However, it may be that evaluation problems cannot be solved in an optimal way. That does not mean that we should not continue to search for better solutions. The bottomline is that evaluations cannot be solved in an optimal way so we should develop a number of criteria for making them at least acceptable. The use of more heuristic models should be explored and in this book we provide some tools that may be helpful in doing this.

Chapter 7

COMPLETING THE E-POLICY JOURNEY
The Transition to an Integrated Entrepreneurship Policy

Entrepreneurship has been described as the driving force of the 21st century and crucial for the transition from factor-driven growth to more innovation-driven growth (Balje and Waasdorp, 2001). Virtually every country is now seeking to increase their level of entrepreneurship. As governments begin to realise the significant implications of business entry and exit ("turbulence rates") and the dynamism of the small business sector for innovation and growth, it will be hard for them to ignore the need for enhanced entrepreneurship support in many areas of policy. In this era of rapid technological change, globalisation, and virtual mobility of money, ideas and people across borders, governments must adopt new approaches to fostering entrepreneurship, innovation and growth.

Since 1998, the studies, reports and policy-oriented documents of the OECD and the European Commission have significantly raised the level of awareness and knowledge we have about the kinds of policy measures needed to promote higher levels of entrepreneurship. Both are encouraging the practice of benchmarking country performance against entrepreneurial activity levels and working to harmonise and standardise country data so better comparisons can be made. But the process of developing entrepreneurship policy has not, until now, been well articulated.

In this final chapter, we bring together the entrepreneurship policy framework, the policy comprehensiveness scale, the policy measure framework maps, the context and conceptual models and the evidence of practice from the 13 case studies to articulate an integrated approach to the entrepreneurship policymaking process.

Entrepreneurial activity levels vary widely across countries, the 13 countries in our study an illustrative example. A country's share of nascent entrepreneurs (the potential pool of future entrepreneurs) also varies widely (Reynolds et al., 2004). We have seen in earlier chapters how governments take different approaches with respect to an entrepreneurship policy orientation. One could say they are at different points in the entrepreneurship policy process. Governments in countries with high business ownership and TEA rates, more likely than not, simply do not see the need to be concerned about increasing the level of overall entrepreneurial activity as a priority policy target, at least not in the short-term. The emergence of entrepreneurship is almost assumed; any increase in entrepreneurial activity rates is more a by-product of macroeconomic policies or those in favour of small business or innovation. In countries with lower than average business ownership and TEA rates, governments are keener to improve the level of their entrepreneurial dynamic and more advanced in their entrepreneurship policy formulations, as we saw in the case of the Group 2 countries in Chapter 3. On a country-by-country basis, governments have their own rational and practical reasons for assuming the policy positions they do. But even in highly prosperous countries, there are compelling reasons to become more strategic in their entrepreneurship policy positions to ensure long-term sustainability of that prosperity.

The countries in this study have diverse structures, diverse philosophical underpinnings, diverse ideologies and diverse economic and social goals. Some are led by conservative or republican governments, some by liberal governments, and some by social democrat or labour governments. They fall along the continuum from right to left; from "entrepreneurial economy" to more "managed economy"; and from individualistic to collective society. But regardless of these differences, they are all somewhere along the road to entrepreneurship policy. All are, in some way, exploring what they need to do to produce a more "entrepreneurial economy".

We have defined entrepreneurship policy as that which is:
- aimed at the pre-start, the start-up and early post-start-up phases of the entrepreneurial process,
- designed and delivered to address the areas of Motivation, Opportunity and Skills,
- with the primary objective of encouraging more people in the population to consider entrepreneurship as an option, move into the nascent stage of taking actions to start a business and proceed into the entry and early stages of the business.

Within that policy definition, which assumes a process perspective, there are four broad policy challenges: 1) influencing a stronger entrepreneurship culture from which higher levels of entrepreneurial activity can emerge; 2) introducing people to the concept of entrepreneurship as a personal choice and instilling entrepreneurial know-how at an early age; 3) effectively facilitating the conversion process from intent to action to start-up; and 4) supporting new entrepreneurs through their vulnerable first three to four years of development.

1: Building an entrepreneurship culture

The first challenge is to influence a stronger environment from which entrepreneurship will emerge. More governments are talking about the need to have a more "entrepreneurial economy" and aiming to create a stronger entrepreneurial culture and climate, but it is actually rare to see strong and comprehensive policy measures in place to achieve this, that is, promotional/awareness measures that will enhance the social legitimacy of entrepreneurship within the broader society. We noted more strategic government policy actions in a small number of countries, highlighting some examples in Chapter 2 and profiling a number of good practice initiatives in Stevenson and Lundström (2002). Ironically, we find that countries with the strongest entrepreneurship cultures are the ones with the most entrepreneurship promotion activity. Generally, we conclude that more work needs to be done to link promotional efforts with changes in attitudes towards entrepreneurship and to establish the relationship between favourable entrepreneurial attitudes and the incidence of business entry.

2: Creating nascent entrepreneurs

The second challenge is to create favourable conditions for the emergence of entrepreneurship so people will be encouraged to explore the entrepreneurial process. One way to do this is by providing more education-based opportunities for people to learn about entrepreneurship and to practice entrepreneurial skills so entrepreneurship is seen a more feasible career choice and employment option. Most countries now recognise that "we must put entrepreneurship education in the school system", but there are still few systematic (although increasing) efforts to do this. One of the problems is that education is most often not a mandated responsibility of central governments; it is a delegated responsibility of state or provincial governments. As well, there is often a lack of communication between Ministers for Education and those for Industry/Economic Development who rarely come together to discuss policy issues. However, these challenges can be overcome, as we see from the examples highlighted in Chapter 2. Good practice governments have begun the process of integrating entrepreneurship components at each level of the education system from kindergarten through post-secondary levels in a cross-disciplinary fashion. Although educators are increasingly becoming accepted as central actors in entrepreneurship development, considerable work remains to be done before entrepreneurship is fully accepted as a discipline or offered across all disciplines and areas of study.

One of the supporting arguments for early exposure to entrepreneurship is that it will lead to better preparation, which will lead to stronger start-ups, which will result in higher survival and growth rates. More of this kind of strategic support during the early phases of the entrepreneurial process may act to reduce the trial and error experience of new entrepreneurs by increasing their level of competence and accelerating their learning path through knowledge-transfer and a supportive environment. The additional policy challenge in this phase of the entrepreneurial process is to remove career and employment choice disincentives that may be embedded in the country's social and institutional arrangements, particularly in the taxation, social security and regulatory regimes.

3. Converting nascent entrepreneurs: facilitating the start-up process

The third challenge has to do with policy actions to facilitate the actual start-up process − to accelerate the gestation process and to increase the rate of conversion from the nascent stage to start-up. At any point in time, there are a number of the people in any population who are involved in some activity leading to the start of a business. Reynolds et al. (2004) estimate that this number could be as high as 300 million people worldwide. In the past, start-up support consisted primarily of measures such as self-employment training programmes or micro-loan funds. But we know from recent studies of nascent entrepreneurs that a broader set of policy measures is needed. Given that new firms are important for the economic development of countries and regions, and that nascent entrepreneurs are important for the foundation of new firms, information about nascent entrepreneurs and their behaviour is important for understanding crucial aspects of the economy (Wagner, 2004).

As a result of the GEM studies and the Panel Study of Entrepreneurial Dynamics we know that the share of nascent entrepreneurs differs widely between countries. Using the eclectic framework of determinants of entrepreneurship levels, van Stel et al. (2003) found four major determinants which may account for some of these differences in the level of nascent entrepreneurship: the stock of incumbent businesses (positive correlation with density); the innovative capacity (negative correlation); social security costs as a percent of GDP (negative correlation); and whether the country had previously been under communist rule. In his review of the findings from country studies of nascents' behaviours, Wagner (2004) observes that there is no fixed set of pre-start-up activities or a uniform sequence of undertaking them. He concludes that industry, region and personal factors (like gender, skills, and financial reserves) all matter in determining what a nascent entrepreneur does, and when. Factors that significantly differentiate nascent entrepreneurs from the general population of adults include: knowing someone who is an entrepreneur; perceiving a good opportunity for business; the presence of business skills; being employed; and living in a higher income household.

Early evidence from these studies indicates that from one-third to one-half of all nascent entrepreneurs actually start businesses (Wagner, 2004). In this context, it is as important to ask why they don't start businesses as it is to ask why they do. Investing in research to discover more about the pre-start-up nascent stage of entrepreneurial activity will provide useful information to policymakers as they seek to understand more about the obstacles hindering a higher conversion rate of nascents to new entrepreneurs.

Measures to create a more munificent environment and increase conversion rates might include mentoring initiatives, horizontal networks, business assistance entry points (one-stop shops), start-up assistance web portals, and taxation incentives. Flexible competition policies may also promote the creation of more entrepreneurial opportunity. Governments in various countries are already starting to assess their system of small business support with the goal of providing better and more appropriate services to meet the needs of potential and nascent entrepreneurs. They are also adopting more strategic and tailored approaches to increasing the start-up rates of particular target groups of the population, whether they be currently under-represented as business owners or among the segment of the population with high potential for becoming innovative entrepreneurs. Many governments are paying more attention to entry and exit barriers created by administrative, regulatory, legislative, labour market and tax burdens. This is a newer area of policy development – one that should be embraced as a critical delineation of an entrepreneurship policy focus.

However, there is still a lot we do not know about the relationship between nascent entrepreneurial activity and business entry and the precise points for policy intervention that would be most effective in increasing the conversion rate.

4. Supporting the survival and growth path

Entrepreneurship policy measures are also needed to address the needs of early stage entrepreneurs, those within the first 42 months of a new business. This is a particularly vulnerable period for new entrepreneurs and the period during which the failure rate is highest. New entrepreneurs have not yet had enough time to gain the know-how and credibility they will need to fully develop their businesses, nor are they able to attract bank financing due to an unproven track-record. The Motivation, Opportunity, Skills framework is highly relevant to this stage of the entrepreneurial process as well – motivating new entrepreneurs to think more strategically about how to realise the potential of their businesses, providing access to the right mix of business supports and learning opportunities, and offering incentives to encourage them to pursue innovation and growth. We saw examples in our case studies of government support for networks for high-growth entrepreneurs, business development advisory services, mentoring and incubation initiatives, and seed capital programmes.

In order to address the policy challenge of early stage survival and growth, focus has to be placed not only on the economic opportunity factors, such as access to money and information on government programmes, but on the social opportunity factors, such as cultural support for entrepreneurs through promotion, and opportunities to gain knowledge and skills through entrepreneurship education and mentoring.

STEPS IN THE E-POLICY JOURNEY

The policy imperative is to ensure a future stock of new firms to replace exiting firms and the jobs shed by exiting and downsizing firms. The rapidity with which the structure of the economy is changing is accelerating. We know that the majority of the firms that exist today will not still be around ten years from now. The example we shared in Chapter 1 is illustrative of the effect of this rapid churning (Parsley and Dreessen, 2004). The entrepreneurship policy journey has two major outcomes – an increase in entrepreneurial activity levels and an increase in the percentage of new, young firms that grow. The base objective of entrepreneurship policy is to increase the supply of entrepreneurs. The unit of focus is the individual entrepreneur or potential entrepreneur. Because many people have the potential to become an entrepreneur, policy measures are both broad and general at the beginning of the entrepreneurial process and more specific as people become nascent entrepreneurs and enter the actual start-up and early-development stages. Different policy measures will be required for different stages of the process, depending on the national or regional context.

Taking the lessons we have learned from the policy practices in the 13 countries in combination with research-based knowledge, we have constructed an integrated and systematic approach that can be followed by other governments seeking to implement entrepreneurship policy. Although the specificities of each country will differ, as we have seen in our case studies and demonstrated through the context model, we believe that entrepreneurship policy offers the potential for both short-term and long-term impacts on the level of entrepreneurship and entrepreneurial activity in a society and, therefore, its future economic prosperity.

The nine-step process we describe in this final chapter will make use of the policy frameworks, conceptual models and assessment tools we have developed in the preceding chapters. Completing the process will ultimately require a considerable amount of analysis on the part of governments in cooperation with the research society and the business support community. All of the necessary information and data to enable a full completion of each step may not be immediately available for this purpose but we argue that this more systematic approach to finding the path to an optimal configuration of policy measures will produce favourable results.

In the next sections we describe each of the nine steps in this process:

1. Examine "context" – take-stock of aspects of the Outcomes, Structure and SME/Entrepreneurial Vitality dimensions of the economy that have the potential to impact on higher or lower levels of entrepreneurial activity.
2. State the priority problems and issues resulting from the context analysis and set overall policy objectives.
3. Assess the state of affairs with respect to the foundations of entrepreneurship policy, i.e., level of Motivation, Opportunity and Skills relative to entrepreneurial activity.
4. Review possible options for entrepreneurship policy measures from areas of the collective framework.
5. Configure the policy measures into a comprehensive policy orientation using the typology framework as a guide.
6. Align policy development, implementation and delivery structures to achieve objectives set by the policy formulation.
7. Identify performance indicators and evaluation measures to track and monitor short-term and long-term impacts.
8. Develop the action plan and identify resource requirements and partners.
9. Allocate budget and implement.

At the end of each of these steps, the resulting analysis should lead to identification of the major issues, priorities and objectives to be addressed. In the process of completing the initial steps there will likely be a need for research and perhaps consultations with stakeholders in the entrepreneurship support field. This input will help guide the next steps in the process.

1. Examine "Context"

The first step along the journey to entrepreneurship policy involves a stock-taking description and analysis of country characteristics related to Outcomes, Structure and SME/Entrepreneurial Vitality. In Chapters 4 and 5, we referred to a number of factors identified in the research literature as being associated with the level of entrepreneurial activity in a country or region, acting as either promoters or inhibitors. These studies provide an appreciation of the many factors influencing entrepreneurial behaviour in a society; however, given the large number of possible influencers, it is difficult to ascertain the precise impact of any one factor on a country's level of entrepreneurial activity. We know very little about how these factors and influencers, individually or in combination, work to produce a certain level of entrepreneurial activity relative to another country with a different combination of those factors and influencers. Although we have concluded that it is difficult to identify the precise relationship between the level of entrepreneurial activity in a country and economic outcomes, such as growth, our study indicates that in making entrepreneurship policy, "context" matters.

Governments must take stock of where they are in terms of being an "entrepreneurial economy" before they can more deliberately determine what is needed to become a stronger one. Not all will be starting from the same base because of differences in their industrial structures, their current economic/industrial policies, the current role of new and small businesses in their economies, the state of their business support infrastructure, and their cultural and social values. We saw a great deal of variability in the descriptions of context variables for each of the 13 countries, as well as in how they combined. For example, a country could have relatively strong economic performance and yet not have a high level of business entry and exit activity or a particularly dominant SME sector in terms of overall employment share. The reverse could also be seen.

As we have pointed out, there are indications that Structure may matter moreso than Outcomes (e.g., growth in GDP, the level of unemployment, and labour force participation rates) in directly affecting the level of entrepreneurship. Demographic and industrial structure variables affect the scope and level of opportunities for entrepreneurship. Population size and growth rate, age composition of the population, the immigration rate and the relative size of the public sector and the services sector are among the factors that could impact on the supply of entrepreneurs and the level of entrepreneurial activity in positive or negative ways. Privatisation or competition policies are examples of policies related to removing structural barriers. But overall, the importance of context for entrepreneurship development is still poorly understood. We know there are relationships between the three Variables groupings but do not know precisely what they are. However, it is quite clear that, depending on the description of the current context, the "entrepreneurship policy gaps" to be filled will differ. Therefore, we suggest one of the starting points of setting comprehensive policies in this area is to conduct a description and assessment of the context variables.

It is also important to understand what is going on within the structure of the SME sector. Although SMEs contribute to employment share, the level of this contribution varies considerably between countries, as does the net change in the stock of firms and employment due to entry and exit rates. There is research evidence that the density of SMEs and the dynamic created by start-up and exit rates matter. Wagner (2004), for example, reports that the start-up rate in a region tends to be positively-related to the share of employees working in small firms in the region, or to the proportion of small firms among all firms in the region. One of the reasons for this is that working in a small firm provides employees with more relevant experiences for starting a business. He also highlights research findings indicating that the propensity to be a nascent entrepreneur is higher for people who live in more densely populated, fast growing regions with higher rates of new firm formation. In other words, dynamic environments produce density and both produce higher levels of entrepreneurial activity. A greater density of SMEs leads to a higher share of SME employment and higher levels of entrepreneurship. Countries with higher shares of overall employment in large public and private-sector firms may have lower entrepreneurial activity levels.

The critical questions to begin with might include:
- Is the business entry rate too low? Too high?
- Is the percentage of growth firms too low?
- Are there a large number of solo-entrepreneurs who cannot overcome the threshold to hire their first employee?
- Is there under-representation of business ownership among some segments of the population? Which ones?
- Are there regional variations in enterprise density?

- Are market, social, labour market, education and other structural or systemic failures impeding the level of entrepreneurial activity and if so, what are they and in what ways are they doing this?

A feasible way to approach the context description may be to first do an assessment of the existing situation regarding SME/Entrepreneurial Vitality variables, then to examine Structure variables to identify possible opportunities or impediments, and thirdly, to examine the relationship between Outcomes and SME/Entrepreneurial Vitality. Focusing analysis and discussion on the variables included in the context model will help identify where certain structural weaknesses may exist and point to possible policy solutions. Minimally, it will create more awareness among policymakers of some of the trade-offs being made as a result of contradictory policy choices.

2. State the priority problems and set objectives

After completing the context analysis, governments will have identified any number of economic, structural or social problems that need to be solved and the degree to which developing entrepreneurship is a contributing solution. If a connection can be made between start-up rates and the government's desired projections for employment increases or between start-up rates and economic growth projections, then this could form the basis for an overall entrepreneurship policy objective. If estimates can be made about the number of new firms needed over the next five-year time period in order to replace the stock of firms and jobs lost due to exiting and downsizing, that would also provide the basis for an overall entrepreneurship policy objective.

The end goal of entrepreneurship policy is an increase in the level of entrepreneurial activity, defined in terms of higher start-up rates, more new businesses and more new entrepreneurs. We see concrete expressions of these overall objectives in governments' entrepreneurship policy documents. However, in the process leading up to this final quantitative outcome, a government will often state other more qualitative and difficult to measure objectives, such as, "to strengthen the entrepreneurial culture" or "to increase the entrepreneurial behaviour of the population". We will deal with the issue of performance indicators later in this chapter, but for now, we will focus on the quantitative policy objectives.

More use can be made of statistical data on the SME sector to understand its structure, its changing dynamic, and the implications of this dynamic for future growth. Analysis of this kind will help to underpin entrepreneurship policy formulation. Governments with more "holistic" entrepreneurship policy approaches recognise the importance of increasing turbulence to the stimulation of economic renewal, innovation and future productivity growth.

Based on good data, they can make projections about the number of new businesses needed over a future period of time to achieve certain levels of economic growth. Using these projections, they can make determinations about start-up rates and the number of new entrepreneurs needed in the pipeline to create these new firms. It is also possible to make an estimation of the impact of increased start-up rates on productivity increases (NUTEK, 2003)[1] and to measure the cost of failure to society from start-ups that failed (Balje and Waasdorp, 2001). In countries where good economic outcomes exist, unemployment is low, and prospects for future economic growth look promising, a government may not immediately consider its entrepreneurial activity level a priority issue in the current time period. But through an analysis of the dynamic changes in the stock of firms and growth prospects for the base of firms in future time periods, it may bring the entrepreneurial vitality issue into more present focus.

New businesses are needed to replace exiting businesses. New and growing businesses are needed to replace jobs lost due to exiting and declining firms. An analysis of the change in the stock of firms on an annual basis along with an analysis of the employment changes caused by new, exiting, growing and declining firms (of all sizes) will allow a government to project its need for new entries. One or more new entrepreneurs are needed for every new firm (many new businesses are started by two or more people). A useful projection would be of the future supply of entrepreneurs needed to meet the minimum level of demand for new business entries. By combining data on the number of nascent entrepreneurs (from GEM studies), the number of nascents who plan businesses in teams, and nascent conversion rates, it would be possible to make an estimate of the number of people in the population who should be seriously exploring entrepreneurship in the current time period. So if 1,000 new businesses are needed in the future time period (t+n); each new business has an average start-up team of 1.8 people; and 33 percent of nascent entrepreneurs actually start businesses within a year, then 5,454 nascent entrepreneurs should be in the development cycle in the current time period to meet this demand.[2]

Then the question becomes, how can that supply be ensured? What are the things within the contextual scan that will either potentially hinder or encourage the development of this future supply of entrepreneurs? Is there something about the structure of the labour force (employment in the public versus the private sector), the age distribution of the population, opportunities available (free and open competition for private enterprises), or the role of government (level of taxation, other quiet disincentives) that could be adjusted? What better conditions are needed to motivate more people to explore the entrepreneurship option? What about the quality and preparedness of this future supply – what is being done to ensure a higher quality of entrepreneurial and management skills? What about the level of support for entrepreneurs in the society and their access to required resources and know-how?

In Chapter 5, we introduced the concept of measuring the level of entrepreneurial exits. This may not be a direct policy objective but we see "easing exit" as an entrepreneurship policy imperative of many governments. In most cases, the policy solution is to simplify bankruptcy legislation and insolvency procedures to give the entrepreneur more time to restructure a troubled business or, in cases where the business cannot be saved, to reduce penalties so the entrepreneur can be a re-starter. That said, concerns may be raised about the role of government in encouraging more people to start businesses, knowing the survival rates are low during the first year (although this rate varies by country). Is there a cost to society of using public resources to foster entrepreneurial activity? And if so, what is it? First of all, at the macro-level, there is evidence that high entry and exit rates are associated with long-term increases in employment creation and productivity increases. Secondly, many of the entrepreneurs who do not succeed in their first business try again in a higher opportunity business taking with them the skills they learned in the first venture. Thirdly, most businesses that cease to exist do not create a negative impact on society. This question of benefit-cost to society was explored by Balje and Waasdorp (2001) who estimated that, for Dutch firms started during the 1994-1998 period, the contribution made by these new firms in terms of value-added and employment was equal to more than three percent of total gross value-added of the private sector. Calculating the sum of unpaid debts of the start-up companies that went bankrupt and the capital losses of companies that stopped their activities during the period, they estimated total costs of about 10 percent of gross benefits. In other words, there is a highly positive outcome from policy to promote entrepreneurship – the benefit to society far exceeds the cost.

Given that there has been very little research on to what extent "exit" is good or bad, it is difficult to design policy around exits. Policy can, however, address the issue of improving survival rates, particularly by providing services to assist nascent entrepreneurs in assessing business opportunities and increasing opportunities for them to gain knowledge and skills prior to the start-up experience. In terms of increasing the conversion of nascent to start-ups from its current one-third to one-half (Wagner, 2004), it would be helpful to know more about the percentage that gave up or abandoned their idea (part of LoEE).

3. Assessing Entrepreneurship Policy Foundations

An important step in assessing what needs to be done is to examine the relevance and impact of existing small business policy and programme measures on people who are actually in the nascent, start-up and early development stages. But before that can be properly done, it is important to understand more about the behaviour of the population towards entrepreneurship, the conditions and circumstances that lead to a start-up, including motivational aspects and the nature of disincentives or incentives for this behaviour in the system. This understanding will help in designing policy measures and institutional structures to create a favourable environment for the emergence of entrepreneurship. A framework for this is provided by the conceptual model in Chapter 5, which describes factors related to Motivation, Opportunity and Skills, the building blocks of an entrepreneurship policy. Although there are many problems in trying to measure levels of Motivation, Opportunity and Skills, some key areas of questioning will be helpful in identifying where policy actions in each of these areas might be taken. To determine where gaps may exist, one might ask questions such as:

- Are the attitudes towards entrepreneurship in the population positive or negative?
- Are attitudes towards entrepreneurship favourable, but business entry rates low?
- Do fears hold people back from considering entrepreneurship? If so, what are those fears?
- What do people consider to be the trade-offs between paid employment and unemployment versus self-employment?
- Are certain groups or regions under-represented in the business ownership or self-employment statistics? What are the possible explanations for this?
- Is entrepreneurship seen as an attractive option among young people and students?
- What level of confidence do students and young people have in their ability to start a business?
- Does the country have an abundance of credible entrepreneurs as role models?
- Is the media favourably disposed to the "entrepreneurial" story?
- Are there lots of places where people can learn and develop entrepreneurial skills?
- Does it take a long time and a lot of money to register a business? To incorporate a limited liability company?

- Is it difficult for entrepreneurs to restart after a business failure? How can these difficulties be reduced?
- Is there sufficient community support for entrepreneurs, particularly at the start-up stage?
- Is it difficult for people to gain support for their business ideas, including technical assistance and financing?
- To what extent are nascent entrepreneurs giving up on their plans to start a business? Are any of the perceived obstacles ones that can be lifted through policy actions?
- Are innovative entrepreneurs able to secure financing for the developmental stages of their project ideas?
- Is there a sufficient base of quality entrepreneurs in the economy to maximise opportunities vis-à-vis the commercialisable potential of R&D outputs?
- Are private sector venture capital markets oriented to meeting the needs of entrepreneurs?
- Are there a lot of opportunities for people to start new businesses in the Services sector?

Answers to these questions will provide guidance as to where there are weaknesses in the system and how these might be adversely affecting overall levels of Motivation, Opportunity and Skills.

4. Reviewing Collective Framework Options

The next step is a policy self-assessment against the Framework of Entrepreneurship Policy Measures presented in Figure 2.4 in Chapter 2. In this exercise, the policy comprehensiveness checklist can be used as a tool for analysing what entrepreneurship policy measures are currently underway in the areas of promotion; education; regulatory barriers to start-ups; access to seed-capital and start-up financing; start-up support services (including networks); and target group initiatives, and for focusing discussion on possible gaps where further actions are required. The outcome of this assessment can be matched against the gaps and opportunities identified in the context description and the analysis of Motivation, Opportunity and Skills factors. Each policy area can then be examined against the "framework maps" presented in Figures 2-5 – 2-10, which provide an indication of where a number of other governments are taking actions (i.e., a range of feasible options). Constructing framework maps of current policy measures in the country under review will provide a baseline for determining possible gaps and where actions would be beneficial. Because the "context" and foundations for entrepreneurship are different in each country, we would expect that the configuration of policies would also differ. This leads us to the next step of the process.

5. Configuring the E-Policy Orientation

After making this review of "context", policy foundations and framework options, government officials should have a clearer idea of their situation vis-à-vis the extent to which entrepreneurship is being supported in their economy and the possible barriers to its rising levels. Regardless of context, there are likely to be some deficiencies in the level and nature of support for new and early-stage entrepreneurs, needs that are not being met. Policymakers should be able to self-identify their entrepreneurship policy orientation, that is, which of the four Entrepreneurship Policy Typologies most aptly describes their dominant approach. At this point, they can assess whether this is where they want to be, given their current situation and their economic and social priorities for the future. From an entrepreneurship policy point of view, do they need to focus more on new firm creation policies, innovative entrepreneurship or other target group policies or should they make the transition to "holistic" entrepreneurship policy – an integrated approach? Depending on the choice, they may have to start a process of adjusting existing policy and programme delivery structures.

6. Aligning Policy and Delivery Structures

In the formulation and implementation of entrepreneurship policy, government structure matters. Government SME/entrepreneurship policy structures can be categorised as "umbrella", "silo" (vertical) or horizontal (Stevenson and Lundström, 2002). As government policy shifts more in favour of entrepreneurship policies, the interdependency of policy jurisdictions across a large number of other ministries and levels of government becomes apparent. In the case of governments with a more "holistic" entrepreneurship policy approach, we noted a tendency to move to more horizontal administrative and policy management structures. This suggests that structure follows strategy and that a realignment of structure with the entrepreneurship policy focus may be necessary. Better mechanisms may be needed for coordinating policies affecting business entry across ministries, as well as for coordinating the regional delivery of objectives, programmes and services. Entrepreneurship policy requires government-wide commitment and, therefore, integrated approaches to policy development and planning are optimal.

Some governments have set up Entrepreneurship Divisions or Directorates with the mandate to carry out an advocacy function with officials from other ministries and to interface with private sector partners and the media in support of entrepreneurship. These responsibility centers may have to solicit collaboration from other departments of government, for example, departments of education or ministries of science and technology. This networking role is an important one for these "champion units" within government. In some cases, coordination committees are established for the purposes of exchanging views and perspectives on reducing barriers to business entry and growth among representatives of the relevant government departments and agencies. The Minister responsible may put in place a Ministerial Advisory Council on Entrepreneurship and Small Business consisting of entrepreneurs and key business leaders. The Minister may also establish a Ministerial Council of state and/or provincial/regional ministers that aims to agree on a common vision for entrepreneurship and work cooperatively towards its realisation. Annual policy forums are another option.

The move to entrepreneurship policy may also mean streamlining and adjusting existing delivery structures. It was evident in our case studies that new delivery structures go hand-in-hand with the shift in focus, notably one-stops shops, campus-based incubators, community enterprise centers, and entrepreneurship units in other departments and levels of government. Much work may be required in aligning new and existing organisations to the entrepreneurship agenda, as well as the skills and knowledge of the people working in them. Special efforts may be needed to better orient business advisers and other officials (dealing with the entrepreneurial community) regarding providing services to clients at every stage of the entrepreneurial process. Part of that orientation includes attention to the "know-how" of delivering an entrepreneurship policy agenda. More of these learning networks should be considered.

7. Identifying Performance Indicators

The move to any new policy area demands new thinking about how progress will be measured. Not much is actually known about how public policy measures influence the level and quality of entrepreneurial activity. How will progress be measured? What performance indicators are needed? What types of evaluation should be undertaken? What are the appropriate benchmarks against which to monitor developments over time, or in relationship to other regions or nations? Since entrepreneurship policy is a relatively recent phenomenon, it is not surprising that efforts to measure its impacts as well as the appropriate performance indicators are not well developed. Governments are at varying levels of evaluation sophistication at this point in time, although the field is developing rapidly. With the increasing emphasis on creating "entrepreneurial economies" we notice the emergence of new categories of performance indicators. These were referred to as measurements of "general entrepreneurship trends" and "entrepreneurship climate and culture". Indicators to measure changes in the entrepreneurial climate and culture include: increases in the entrepreneurial potential of the population; improvements in social attitudes towards entrepreneurship; increases in the social value attached to entrepreneurship; increases in the preconditions for becoming an entrepreneur; and decreases in start-up obstacles. We also observe the use of new indices to measure entrepreneurial vitality in a region or country, such as:

- business formations per capita, a measure of the business start-up propensity in the population;
- enterprises or business owners per capita, a measure of the density of entrepreneurs and enterprises in the population;
- the Total Entrepreneurial Index, a measure of the prevalence rate of entrepreneurial activity in a region/country; and
- business turbulence, a measurement of the business dynamics of entries and exits.

Static and dynamic measures enable international comparisons on a country-by-country basis, which in turn, lead to international benchmarking of entrepreneurship levels. At this point, the development and adoption of "entrepreneurial activity" performance indicators and measures is at a very early stage but becoming more wide-spread as the result of enhanced ability to identify and quantify entrepreneurship activity levels.

We also observe more sophistication in the development of performance indicators for specific entrepreneurship policy/programme areas like entrepreneurship education, advisory and counseling services, start-up financing, and administrative obstacles to business entry. We are only beginning to see comprehensive evaluation frameworks for the implementation of entrepreneurship policies.

So how should a government proceed in this area? One of the first things to do is to determine what outcomes are expected from entrepreneurship policy in terms of contributing to growth in the economy. Is it employment creation, productivity improvement, innovation or something else? Secondly, it is important to identify some baseline measures that can be used to monitor progress and developments over time. Baseline measures being tracked by governments in our study include:

- The proportion of the population with positive attitudes towards entrepreneurship;
- The proportion of the population who would like to have their own business someday;

- The proportion of the population who intend to start a business within a specified time frame (for example, the next two years);
- The proportion of nascent entrepreneurs in the population;
- The actual business entry rate on an annual basis;
- The percentage of new firms that grow over a period of time.
- The number of entrepreneurs;
- The contribution of new and growth firms to employment, net sales and value-added; and
- The share of female entrepreneurs in the stock of firms.

Thirdly, it is necessary to identify what impacts are desired from each of the specific framework policy areas (e.g., entrepreneurship promotion, education, seed financing). Fourthly, it is necessary to set performance indicators for each of the micro-policies articulated through individual programmes or initiatives (e.g., micro-finance programme, youth venture programme). Finally, some governments prepare an annual review of their entrepreneurship policy programmes and benchmark their performance outcomes against international developments (e.g., EU, OECD and GEM). An annual White Paper on entrepreneurship policy or an annual report on the state of small business and entrepreneurship, including a description of entrepreneurial dynamics, should become part of the process of reporting on progress and tracking developments and changes over time.

8. Action Plan

Having carried out the various reviews, assessments and identifications enabled by the frameworks and guidelines referred to in this chapter, governments committed to pursuing the entrepreneurship policy agenda will be ready for the next steps. These will include development of the action plan, lining up budget allocations with entrepreneurship policy priorities, and organising for the implementation phase. The final policy document will include a series of tiered objectives reflecting the higher level objective(s) related to increasing the level of entrepreneurial dynamics and individual objectives for each of the framework areas contributing to the overall objective(s).

9. Budget Allocation and Implementation

Implementation of the policy requires a budget allocation and a work plan. We have seen in countries with horizontal structures that governments assign each relevant ministry with the requirement to open a budget envelope. Others allocate the budget envelope to the ministry with responsibility for implementing the overall policy.

The framework for this journey to Entrepreneurship Policy is illustrated in Figure 7-1.

CONCLUDING REMARKS

One of the objectives of this book was to share findings from our examination of the entrepreneurship policy practices of different governments. We have come to the end of that story. As we conclude, we want to stress a few key implications for the research and policymaking communities. These comments relate to the need for a systems approach to entrepreneurship
, the need to build capacity, competence and learning networks, the need for better linkages and knowledge transfer between researchers and policymakers, and the potential for further development and use of the policy tools we have described to advance knowledge about the characteristics of entrepreneurship policy and its application in different contextual environments and over time.

Entrepreneurship as a system

We are cognisant that the phenomenon of entrepreneurship is not independent of other activities taking place in the economic system. As such, it may be indirectly affected by many elements that we have not discussed. Creating a stronger and more dynamic entrepreneurial environment will be among one of the many possible solutions to economic and social problems that may exist in a society. But we believe it is an important one.

We have referred to entrepreneurship itself as a system comprised of entrepreneurs, institutions and government actions. This is a complex system with many actors, stakeholders and different behaviours. In Figure 7-2, we sketch out the extent and scope of the individuals, organisations and institutions that make up the system. It includes governments, researchers, instructors, teachers, guidance counselors, banks, chambers of commerce and trade associations, reporters and broadcasters, enterprise centers, nascent entrepreneurs, growth firms, and the list goes on. These network members exist at national, regional and local levels. There is a notable absence of research analysing the relationships between entrepreneurs, service providers, policymakers and other institutional supports in this system. A more comprehensive analysis of the interaction effects of the decision-making mechanisms of the different policy design, programme delivery and service-providing subsystems would provide useful knowledge and insight in the development of an integrated entrepreneurship policy approach.

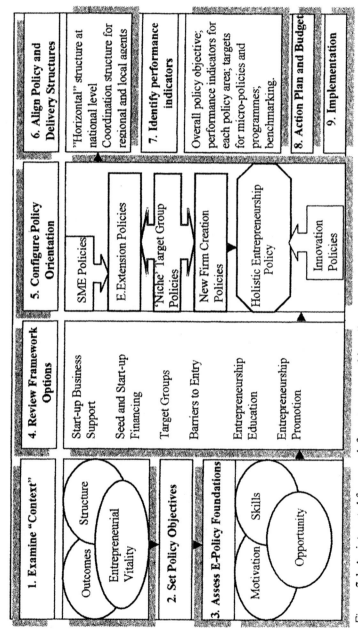

Figure 7-1. An integrated framework for entrepreneurship policy analysis

Source: Stevenson and Lundström (2002), p. 336.

Building capacity, competence and learning networks

The number of people entering the entrepreneurship system is growing. Many of them come into it without having much background knowledge or understanding of the entrepreneurial process – like entrepreneurs, they learn how to do what they do through practice. There are insufficient forums for the transfer of existing knowledge between different members of the entrepreneurship system. Many of the people and organisations working in the field are disconnected from the other parts of it, even though it is an interdependent system. What happens in one part of it affects the outcome in other parts. In measuring the effects of entrepreneurship policy, the interdependencies between actions taken by all levels of the system should be considered, including assessments of their organisational efficiency in obtaining results.

There is a need to create more "wholeness" in the system by fostering horizontal forums for the sharing of information, knowledge, perspectives and experience. A more commonly-shared understanding of the entrepreneurial process and the interconnected nature of the system that supports the movement of potential entrepreneurs through it needs to be fostered.

System members need to exchange experiences to learn from the results of their different activities and to benefit more from knowledge of what is happening at the international level (e.g., in EU, OECD and APEC countries), as well as to work actively in networks through the creation of arenas. Finally, there is a need for development of knowledge nodes, or advocacy organisations, which can promote policy positions to governments.

In recent years, there has been an observed increase in the level of competence at local and regional levels regarding the development of entrepreneurship. Many initiatives are being implemented at these levels with resources provided by local and regional organisations or other more global sources (e.g., the EU Structural Funds; private foundations like the Kauffman Foundation). As a result of such actions, a growing number of professional service providers are gaining knowledge and experience in the implementation of entrepreneurship policies. Some of the learning has been based on experimentation through pilot projects and activities. As the level and extent of this competence rises, the future role of national organisations in this area is likely to be questioned. Since officials in national organisations, internal or external to government ministries, do not normally work directly with entrepreneurs, they may have problems maintaining awareness of what is going on at the local level, even questioning the value of supporting the work of regional and local organisations.

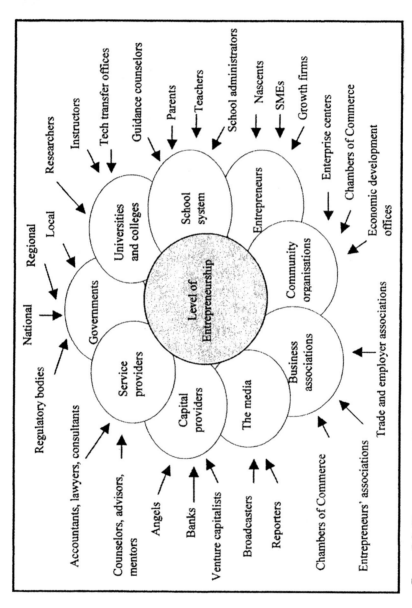

Figure 7-2. The entrepreneurship system

To avoid this, it is very important for national organisations to build networks with the different levels of the entrepreneurship support system. Such networks have developed in some countries in our study, but this is more the exception than the rule. The situation demands an answer to two questions. What type of competence will be needed at the national level and what systems will be needed to ensure all actors know what is taking place at the local and regional level and to promote mutual learning? Alternatives to top-down approaches should be adjusted so more of the bottom-up perspectives can be considered in policy design. In line with this, although a number of activities are more appropriately carried out at the national level, perhaps there should be a re-balancing of resources with more invested at the local and regional levels.

Research knowledge and policy linkages

At the moment, there are inadequate linkages between the research and the policy community and between these communities and the network of service providers. There is a growing need for more policy-oriented research. We cannot expect that decisions in the policymaking system will always be based upon knowledge generated in the research community, but hopefully, we can expect that such decisions will be made in full awareness that this knowledge exists. Policy-relevant research produces learning about how the system works and the effectiveness and efficiency of implemented policy measures.

Among researchers, there is a lot of interest in the characteristics of the individuals who start businesses, the types of firms they will create, the development of start-ups, and the survival and growth of those firms. However, there is still very little research concerning the interdependencies between start-ups and existing firms and about how the market will change in the short and long-run because of start-ups. At the same time, these factors could have a significant potential impact on the success and failure of new firms and their possibility for growth. So even if many researchers are interested in changes in individual behaviour and analysing the impact of different entrepreneurship policy measures, these interdependencies should be considered as being very important, both by policymakers and researchers. There is also an increasing need to increase the capacity for conducting independent evaluations of the overall entrepreneurship policy area. Such knowledge would provide high value to policymakers.

The context and conceptual models we have described in this book have potential to assist governments with the challenge of more strategically designing entrepreneurship policies appropriate to their unique set of circumstances. But they also raise a number of important issues, paradoxes and dilemmas that need further examination by the research community. We hope that interest in doing this research will become stimulated.

Further development of entrepreneurship policy tools

We believe there is great potential for further development of the entrepreneurship policy comprehensiveness checklist. It would be interesting to apply this policy rating tool in a larger selection of countries to test its validity and to expand its use to the measurement of policy intensity. Being able to measure policy intensity would provide a better comparison between countries because it would not only measure the scope of a government's policy but the depth of it. Even if two governments scored similarly on entrepreneurship policy comprehensiveness, the impact of the policy measures could be quite different because one had more institutionalised structures, had been implementing policy measures for a longer period of time, was investing more resources, and so on. In this study, it was not possible to take into account all of these differences. In addition, we did not include consideration of the many entrepreneurship policies and activities that might exist at the state, provincial, regional or local level (that were not part of the national policy system).

Doing a more in-depth assessment of policy intensity would require the full cooperation of participating countries in a collaborative research partnership. Annual measurements of policy comprehensiveness and intensity would enable governments to track their progress over time and to eventually be able to discern the relationship between entrepreneurship policy measures and measurable changes in the level of entrepreneurship. The entrepreneurship policy comprehensiveness checklist also has the potential to become a valuable tool for benchmarking actual entrepreneurship policy across countries, something that does not exist at the present time.

Our construction of entrepreneurship policy is based on the practices of governments in a set of developed countries that, based on GEM results, all have higher levels of opportunity entrepreneurship than necessity entrepreneurship. This is not the case in developing countries. As a next step, it would be informative and useful to apply the assessment methods and tools developed in this book to the contextually different environments of a set of countries with much lower levels of GDP and higher levels of necessity entrepreneurship. Such research would enable us to reflect on how the construction of entrepreneurship policy differs in substantially different environments.

Final comment

Baumol (1990) points out that entrepreneurship will occur in all contexts, but will only thrive when certain conditions exist. These conditions are partly shaped by the wider economic environment and partly shaped by the entrepreneurship system. It is our hope that the knowledge and insight shared in this book will enable all actors in this entrepreneurship system to create those "certain conditions" that will enable entrepreneurship to thrive in their own economic environments, whether at the national, regional or local level.

Finally, we believe that it is time to legitimate the discipline of entrepreneurship by giving it a name. We propose the term "entreprenology"; entreprenology being the study of the entrepreneurship phenomena, including dimensions of the entrepreneurial process and the behaviours and practices of the total system that leads to the emergence of entrepreneurial activity in a society.

---

[1] NUTEK (2003, p. 6) states that "Sweden needs more and many types of entrepreneurs". The business start-up rate for Sweden is 8.2 percent, low by European standards (European Observatory Study, 2002). Swedish policymakers believe that this has a negative impact on the Swedish economy and that new and small firms are not taking advantage of the structural rationalisation taking place in the large corporate sector. The Swedish government links increases in the number of businesses to actual productivity and GDP increases (NUTEK, 2003). For their evidence base of the economic impact of a national entrepreneurship policy, they developed a number of scenarios showing the result of different rates of new business formation on employment and the direct contribution of this growth to production. According to their analysis, new start-ups would immediately contribute to employment and indirectly increase demand and production. Making different assumptions about the rates of start-up growth to 2010, they were able to project employment growth based on the current average number of new jobs created in new firms. Their results for the minimum case scenario show that, from 2003-2010, an increase in the start-up rate (to the EU average) would add SEK 21 billion to the economy. They were able to make further predictions about the future dynamic of the economy based on knowing the annual start-up rate, the annual exit rate, the average number of new jobs created by a new firm, and first year survival rates. The result? The number of start-ups will have to increase from an average of 36,000 new businesses a year to over 45,000 a year by 2010 to compensate for projected job losses due to decreases in large firm employment and other structural rationalisations. The government's stated goal is now to have 150,000 new businesses over the next four years.

[2] To do these kinds of estimates and projections depends on good national data. This extent and quality of this data varies from country to country, making good analysis more possible in some countries than in others. This lack of comparable quality makes it difficult to benchmark across countries, but the idea of benchmarking start-up rates and entrepreneurial dynamics is becoming more common.

Appendix

RESEARCH METHODOLOGY

The research on which this entrepreneurship policy book is based was carried out in three phases.[1] The first phase was an exploratory study of the practices of national-level governments in ten countries. Although we decided to limit our investigation to the experiences of developed economies, we included countries with different economic and social structures, some European and non-European cases, some small countries and some large ones, some known to currently have either high or low levels of entrepreneurial activity, and some with official entrepreneurship policies already in place. They differed in population size, GDP per capita, immigration rates, political orientation, socio-economic and cultural context, size and role of government, history with SME policy, and density of SMEs, etcetera. We also selected countries that would demonstrate diversity in their reasons for identifying entrepreneurship as an economic development tool. In the 1980s and early 1990s, a major motive for focusing on entrepreneurship was to address high unemployment problems. If people became self-employed, they would create jobs. However, unemployment problems are much less severe in many countries than they were seven to ten years ago. There may be more diverse reasons for a government's decision to focus on the promotion of entrepreneurship in the year 2000. And finally, an essential criterion was a high level of certainty that some best practice entrepreneurship elements would be found in each of the chosen cases. The final selection included Australia, Canada, Finland, the Republic of Ireland, the Netherlands, Spain, Sweden, Taiwan (Republic of China), the United Kingdom and the United States. In phase 2, the entrepreneurship policy frameworks developed in phase 1 were applied to the practices of governments in a set of countries where the context was assumed to be similar. For this investigation, the five Nordic countries were selected – Denmark, Finland, Iceland, Norway and Sweden. Case studies for each of the Phase 1 and Phase 2 countries were published in Stevenson and Lundström (2001) and Lundström (ed.) (2003), respectively. In phase 3, we extended our understanding of entrepreneurship policy by conducting a 2004 update of national-level entrepreneurship policy developments in each of the 13 countries and applying further policy analysis.

Approach to Phase 1 of the Study

Site visits were organised to each country during the April 2000 – March 2001 period. We conducted a series of interviews with government officials, key academics in the study of entrepreneurship, and representatives from policy research think-tanks, key small business or entrepreneurs' associations, small business support organisations and the education community. Key areas of questioning focused on the national policy agenda, major programme measures and institutions, policies to stimulate higher levels of entrepreneurial activity, structures for policy development and implementation, and performance indicators and measures. The interview guideline is presented in Table A-1. Interviews were of an informal semi-structured nature, the primary objective being to collect information on a wide variety of issues.

For purposes of analysis, we reviewed a variety of economic and SME data for each country. These were obtained from secondary data sources such as the CIA World Fact Book, the *European Observatory on SMEs*, the *OECD Labour Force Survey*, the *OECD Small and Medium Enterprises Outlook 2000*, reports of the European Commission, and the small business statistics from each country. General country and economic data included: population; population growth; GDP; GDP per capita; average annual growth rate in GDP for the 1995-99 period; age distribution of the population; labour force participation rates (male and female); the unemployment rate; the level of employment in the public versus private sector; annual growth in the number of SMEs and SME employment; the SME share of employment; the self-employment rate; the self-employment share of women; the distribution of firms and employment by employment-size category; and firm entry, exit and survival rates.

Table A-1. Interview guide used in phase 1 of the research

A: Definitions and Data
• What is your definition of a small business? A SME?
• What is your definition of entrepreneurship or entrepreneur?
• Do you note a difference between SME development and entrepreneurship development?
• Do you keep statistics on the business start-up rate and self-employment rate, on an annual basis? What is the annual start-up rate, exit rate, percent of declining firms and expanding firms and resulting job creation; job creation from new start-ups, solo-entrepreneurs, growth companies, etc.
B: Objectives, Policies, Programmes and Structure
• How has the focus of SME policies in your country or region changed over the past 20 years and why?
• What is your economic policy development process? Is there a formal process in place? Informal process? Ad hoc process?
• What is the structure in your government for identifying SME-oriented policies and programmes? Is there a separate ministry? Do several departments have responsibility? How is co-ordination managed?
• Do you have specific policies and programmes in place to encourage people to become entrepreneurs (or self-employed)? What are the major policy measures, policy objectives, programme elements? What is the primary structure for delivering these policies and programmes?
• How do you measure the impact of your policies, programmes and approaches? What are the performance indicators, which you feel, are most important? How do you collect performance data? What is your reporting mechanism?
• What would be the ideal structure for developing and delivering the SME and Entrepreneurship Agenda in a country? What are the key success factors?
C: Entrepreneurship Focus
• How important is the creation of new businesses to your economy?
• How much government policy and programme focus is on strengthening existing SMEs versus encouraging people to start new businesses?
• What, according to you, are the major economic benefits and spin-offs to a high level of entrepreneurial activity in your economy (i.e., to a high business start-up rate)? What are the major drawbacks (if any)?
• Does your government have a White Paper that deals with "creating an entrepreneurial society"?
• What are (what should be) the major elements of a policy orientation towards the development of an entrepreneurial society?
• What specific support do you offer to help create new entrepreneurs? (Entrepreneurship training? Entrepreneurship education? Start-up financing? Advisory services? Incubators? Information?)
• Do you offer any targeted programmes to encourage entrepreneurship among particular sub-groups of the population (i.e., women, youth, aboriginals, the unemployed, etc.)? What type? How? Why? With what impact?
• What kinds of entrepreneurship promotion activity take place in your country?
• Where do you feel your country or region is strongest in terms of addressing these policy or programme areas?
• Where do you feel you need to place more emphasis to stimulate more entrepreneurial activity?

We supplemented interview and statistical data with a review of SME and entrepreneurship-related policy documents, reports, programme materials, and evaluation studies that we either obtained from country officials or from the national/central governments' websites. Key collaborators in each country were used to organise country visits and to comment on draft country reports.

We were attempting to explore an area of policy development that, until recently, had not received much attention. We did not pretend to provide a complete description of what was happening in each country because of the difficulty in doing so. A lot of entrepreneurship-oriented activity takes place, a bit at a time, at the local and regional levels. It would be almost impossible to collect and summarise data to present a picture of this in its entirety. Our approach was to provide an overview of the national scene, discuss the national policy agenda, describe the major program measures and institutions, and outline the evolution from SME policy to entrepreneurship policy.

This research could be labelled as "discovery research" so we used qualitative methodologies to "make sense of" the case material and to map individual entrepreneurship policy approaches and initiatives. This formed the basis of the collective framework, which included six major policy components (Lundström and Stevenson, 2001). We further constructed collective maps for each of the six framework areas and analysed these maps for key insights about the critical elements of each one from a policy analysis perspective.

At the end of our analysis, we were able to arrive at a definition of entrepreneurship policy and to construct several analytical tools. These included: the parameters of entrepreneurship policy; a collective Framework of Entrepreneurship Policy Measures; policy measure roadmaps for each of the framework areas; a typology of entrepreneurship policy; a guideline to the critical areas of entrepreneurship policy questioning; a checklist of signs that entrepreneurship is important and taken seriously; and best practices in entrepreneurship policy measures. These tools are presented in Stevenson and Lundström (2001), Lundström and Stevenson (2001, 2002) and Stevenson and Lundström (2002). These tools were meant to be used by government's aiming to adopt a more strategic and integrated approach to the development of entrepreneurship policy.

Approach to Phase 2 of the Research

In the second study, research teams were mobilised in each of the five Nordic countries to carry out country studies according to a standardised research approach based on the methodologies and frameworks developed in

Phase 1. This included gathering of economic data, interviewing of key informants from government, educational institutions, policy think-tanks, and business support agencies, and content analysis of policy and programme documents (Lundström (ed.), 2003). Sixteen regional seminars were also held to gain input and comments on entrepreneurship policy actions in the Nordic government system.

Approach to Phase 3 of the Research

For the final stage of this research process, we included all 13 countries. We started with the country case studies developed in the first two phases, supplementing this data with an inventory of recent developments in entrepreneurship policy activity. To obtain this updated information, we reviewed government websites for new policy documents and information on recent programmes and initiatives, as well as policy-relevant documents and research reports prepared by the European Commission, the OECD and country-specific think-tanks. We also updated the statistical data for each country relevant to the parameters of our context model. We then reclassified the inventory of 2004 policy measures according to the original entrepreneurship policy typology and collective framework and compared countries in terms of the scope of policy measures in each area. In order to do this, we developed an instrument to analyse the comprehensiveness of a government's entrepreneurship policy.[2] We started with the list of policy questions we initially presented as a "checklist of signs that entrepreneurship is important and taken seriously" in Lundström and Stevenson (2001) and Stevenson and Lundström (2002). We refined and expanded this list based on our 2004 update of current developments in the 13 countries. Following this review, we added new items in the framework areas and included measures for three additional aspects: (i) general policy approach/ commitment to entrepreneurship policy; (ii) policy structure for entrepreneurship; and (iii) performance tracking. Using this revised checklist as the benchmark, we then analysed each government's policy documents, action plans and programme information noting how many of the cumulative policy measures and actions were being implemented (at the central/national level).

The final policy comprehensiveness scoring sheet included 107 items. Ninety of these related to the six framework areas. See Table A-2. The remaining 17 items scored: (i) commitment to entrepreneurship policy (six items); (ii) entrepreneurship policy structure (five items); and (iii) performance tracking (six items).

Table A-2. Construct of the entrepreneurship policy comprehensiveness scale

Policy areas	Number of items
Commitment to entrepreneurship policy/general policy approach	6 items
Policy structure for entrepreneurship	5 items
Promotion of entrepreneurship	8 items
Entrepreneurship in the education system	19 items
Easing entry, early-stage growth, and exit	22 items
Access to start-up, seed and early-stage financing	15 items
Start-up and early-stage growth – business support	16 items
Target group policies/measures	10 items
Tracking performance	6 items
Total	107 items

We used quantitative (frequency counts) and qualitative (document analysis) techniques to develop and score policy comprehensiveness. In some cases, a government was taking some actions in a framework area; in others, evidence indicated that they were planning to launch initiatives, but had not yet started implementation; and in others, we found a lack of evidence that anything was being done. If there was evidence that the government was implementing a policy measure/ action, we gave them a score of 1 on that item. If there was no evidence of any action on the item, the score was 0. In cases where the government had made a review of a policy issue and was underway with concrete plans to launch an initiative, announce a programme or complete a restructuring, we allotted half a point (0.5).

If a government was implementing actions related to each item in the nine areas, their total score would be 107. The completed scoring sheet on the 107 items is a proxy measure of the entrepreneurship policy comprehensiveness of each government (the number of a given set of policy actions they are taking). The average number of policy actions taken by these governments was 72. This scoring of policy comprehensiveness offered a way to examine patterns across countries and to note similarities and differences in policy approaches and emphasis. Because our policy scoring approach is a simplification of a complex phenomenon, our interpretation of the scope of policy activity in each country is somewhat subjective. In some cases, initiatives may be underway in a country but documented evidence of this does not exist. In other cases, government reports may indicate that certain actions are being taken but what they say they are doing may not match their actions. In future research of entrepreneurship policy comprehensiveness, governments could be involved in a validation phase.

Study Limitations

Apart from the problems of presenting a complete picture of what is being done in a country because of the diversity of national, regional and local activity and the constantly changing landscape, work of this nature is also impeded by diverse social and economic contexts and data limitations. There are more than a few problems in trying to compare the SME sector across countries. Countries are using different employment thresholds to define what constitutes a SME; they use different employment-size breakdowns to monitor developments in subsets of the SME population of enterprises (e.g., some define a micro-enterprise as one with fewer than 10 employees, others with fewer than five); some include the agricultural sector in their statistics, others do not; some include own-account self-employed people and employer-businesses in their data, others only report on employer-firms; some have SME statistical databases that enable them to track the SME sector and individual firms over time, while others do not; some have integrated databases that combine self-employment labour force survey data (people) with data on incorporated businesses (firms), and others do not.

When examining the business entry and exit rates across economies, similar problems arise. Some governments are using new VAT registrations as a proxy for new business entries which, in many cases, eliminates the smallest of new firms from being counted; others are using new company registrations, which could eliminate a significant number of sole proprietorships from the count; others are able to track entries and exits of people into self-employment, which results in a higher rate than for new VAT entries, new company registrations, or new employer-firms. Some countries have better statistics on business exit than others. Counting the number of business bankruptcies is not a good indicator of the exit rate because the majority of firm exits are voluntary closures. Research indicates that less than 12 percent of business exits are bankruptcies (depending on the country and the timeframe). Countries with the capacity to track their SME sector longitudinally can present a more accurate picture of the business exit rate (e.g., Canada, the US, Sweden and the Netherlands). A similar problem exists in reporting on survival rates across economies, although the European Observatory is able to make approximations of survival rates from EU country data. And finally, there are, of course, many problems in trying to compare employment trends in firms by size and sector over time. Data quality varies, time series are not consistent, and enterprises are grouped differently within sector classification codes, etcetera.

It is also difficult to make cross-country comparisons because of the different social and economic contexts in each country. A set of more qualitative factors, historical, cultural, political, ideological, attitudinal and structural, may influence a country's level of entrepreneurial activity, to name a few of the major ones. The number of levels of government, the delineation of constitutional, jurisdictional responsibilities between levels of government, and the relative roles of the public and private sector differ among countries. This can impact on how entrepreneurship measures are developed and implemented.

Finally, although we were primarily interested in the features of entrepreneurship policy, we recognise that a number of other areas of economic and social policy impact on this, for example, tax policy, science and technology policy, labour market policy, regulatory policy and regional development policy. Of course, countries may differ considerably in these policy orientations. Apart from noting the linkages individual governments make between these other areas and the development and implementation of entrepreneurship policy measures, we do not make any detailed comparisons of their specific features across countries.

Governments are not using the same lexicons to describe their focus in this ambiguous field of SME/enterprise/entrepreneurship development. In the United States, the Small Business Administration (SBA) refers to the whole sector as the "small business sector" (including all firms with fewer than 500 employees) while the Small and Medium Enterprise Administration (SMEA) in Taiwan refers to the whole sector as the "SME sector", rarely using the term "small business" by itself; even Taiwan entrepreneurs are referred to as "SMEs". Spain and Sweden use "SME sector" and Ireland and the UK more commonly refer to the "enterprise sector". The Australian government most often refers to the "small business sector", although the government is beginning to make explicit references to entrepreneurship. In terms of policy references, Taiwan, Sweden and Spain refer to their SME policies; in the United States, Australia and Canada it is generally small business or SME policy; in the UK and Ireland it is "enterprise policy", and most recently, Denmark, Finland and the Netherlands refer to "entrepreneurship policy", now only rarely making references to "SME policy". However, there is considerable overlap in the meanings attached to these terms and a general lack of precision regarding the differences between them.

The use of language, to some extent, reflects cultural attitudes towards entrepreneurship (either positive or negative) that find their way into distinct policy areas. Where this is most evident is in the area of education. Increasingly, it is recognised that if countries want to become more "entrepreneurial" (an adjective that most countries do seem to be comfortable with), students should be exposed to entrepreneurship in the school system. However, educators and policymakers debate whether it is enterprise education or entrepreneurship education, often preferring to adopt the "enterprise education" label and making a distinction between the two. This has important implications for how curriculum is developed, what concepts are introduced, where in the curriculum it is introduced, how teachers are trained, and how impact will be measured. Perspectives on the use of these terms may also affect policy targets – can governments really move beyond the rhetoric of "building a more entrepreneurial economy" to policy actions oriented to increase the overall supply of entrepreneurs in the economy if they are reluctant to use the word? A discussion of some of these definitional issues is pursued further in Stevenson and Lundström (2001).

There are a number of limitations when trying to score entrepreneurship policy comprehensiveness. First of all, few governments have coherent entrepreneurship policy frameworks in place. In some cases, the entrepreneurship policy map is difficult to piece together because, in practice, relevant policies may be fragmented in a number of government policy documents. Policies and measures fitting within our entrepreneurship policy framework may be found under the rubric of SME policy, enterprise policy, innovation policy, growth policy, business environment policy, employment policy, and etcetera. Initiatives to stimulate entrepreneurship tend to be scattered among a number of ministries at the national/central government level and between levels of national, regional, and local governments. The map of this is not easy to construct.

In addition, we were not able to completely measure the relative degree to which governments were implementing actions in each of the six framework areas. The policy comprehensiveness scale as applied provides an estimation of the multiplicity of actions in each area and, to some extent, how far along the government appears to be in their implementation plans, but lack of readily available measures of reach and penetration does not allow for a comparison of the extent to which policy measures are impacting on a large number of potential and early-stage entrepreneurs. This will be affected by the length of time the government has been implementing actions. Governments that started earlier to implement policy measures have had more time to implement and therefore, would rate higher if the measurement was to include "intensity". It takes time to implement a range of policy actions within each of the policy framework areas to develop "depth" and achieve reach.

Our main interest was in assessing national-level activity but we appreciate that the actions of state, provincial, regional and local governments are also a part of the picture. In future studies, it would be interesting to include an assessment of the scope and intensity of all entrepreneurship policy initiatives in a country. This would require a comprehensive systems approach with collaboration from all levels of government.

This study included countries at a higher level of economic development (minimum GDP per capita of over US$20,000). The formulation and application of entrepreneurship policy would undoubtedly assume a different character in developing countries because the economic context of these countries and the challenges to be overcome are markedly different from those in developed countries. These differences should be explored in a future study.

---

[1] Phase 1 of the research was supported with funding from the Swedish Foundation of Small Business Research, NUTEK, and the Swedish Ministry of Industry, Employment and Communications. Phase 2 of the research was funded by the Nordic Industrial Fund (Centre for Innovation and Commercial Development). Phase 3 of the research was financially assisted by the Swedish Foundation of Small Business Research.

[2] The concept of measuring "policy comprehensiveness" was applied to the area of SME policy in ASEAN and APEC countries (Hall, 2002; 2003a). Hall's scale consisted of 35 policy questions in seven policy areas: (i) general policy approach; (ii) information access; (iii) finance; (iv) technology and technology transfer; (v) HRD and training; (vi); market access; and (vii) administrative burden, women and minorities. He used this tool to identify patterns in the SME policy approaches adopted by ASEAN and APEC governments and to provide a basis for comparing SME policy and programmes amongst these economies over two time periods: 1990-1994 and 2000-2001.

References

Acs, Zoltan J. and Catherine Armington (2003). Endogenous Growth and Entrepreneurial Activity in Cities. CES Version. January.

Acs, Zoltan J. and Catherine Armington (2002). Entrepreneurial Activity and Economic Growth: An Empirical Analysis. (Version B4g). Baltimore, Maryland: Merrick School of Business, University of Baltimore. August.

Acs, Zoltan J. and David B. Audretsch (eds.) (2003). *The Handbook of Entrepreneurship Research*. Dordrecht: Kluwer Academic Publishers.

Acs, Zoltan J., Bo Carlsson and Charlie Karlsson (1999). The Linkages Among Entrepreneurship, SMEs and the Macroeconomy. In Z. Acs, B. Carlsson and C. Karlsson (eds.), *Entrepreneurship, Small and Medium-Sized Enterprises and the Macroeconomy*, 3-42. UK: Cambridge University Press.

Acs, Zoltan J. and David B. Audretsch (1990). *Innovation and Small Firms*. Cambridge: MIT Press.

Ahl, Helene (2004). *The Scientific Reproduction of Gender Inequality. A Discourse Analysis of Research Texts on Women's Entrepreneurship*. Jönköping International Business School. Sweden: Liber Ltd.

Aldrich, Howard (1999). *Organizations Evolving*. London: Sage Publications.

APEC (2003a). Strengthening an APEC Entrepreneurial Society. Joint Ministerial Statement APEC Small and Medium Enterprises Ministerial Meeting. Chiang Mai, Thailand. 7-8 August Singapore: APEC Secretariat.

APEC (2003b). Strengthening an APEC Entrepreneurial Society: Policies for Growth and Enterprise Development – Defining Evaluation Parameters. Prepared by the Ministry of Economic Development, New Zealand for the Small and Medium Enterprises Working Group Meeting, Genting Highlands, Malaysia, 24-25 February. Singapore: APEC Secretariat.

APEC (2003b). Cultivating Entrepreneurship: The Experience of Chinese Taipei. Prepared for the Small and Medium Enterprises Ministerial Meeting, Chiang Mai, Thailand, 7-8 August. Singapore: APEC Secretariat.

APEC (1999). *Women Entrepreneurs in SMEs in the APEC Region*. Singapore: APEC Secretariat.

Arenius, Pia and Erkko Autio (2001). *GEM 2000 Finnish Executive Report*. Helsinki.

Audretsch, David B. (2002). Entrepreneurship: A Survey of the Literature. Prepared for the European Commission, Enterprise Directorate-General. Brussels. July.

Audretsch, David B. and Max Keilbach (2003). Entrepreneurship, Capital and Economic Growth. Research Series 005. UK: Durham Business School.

Audretsch, David B. and Roy Thurik (2001a). What is new about the new economy? Sources of growth in the managed and entrepreneurial economies. *Industrial and Corporate Change*, 10, 267-315.

Audretsch, David B. and Roy Thurik (2001b). Linking Entrepreneurship to Growth. STI Working Paper 2001/2. Paris: OECD.

Audretsch, David B., Roy Thurik, Ingrid Verheul and Sanders Wennekers (eds.) (2002). *Entrepreneurship: Determinants and Policy in a European-US Comparison.* Boston/Dordrecht/London: Kluwer Academic Publishers.

Australian Bureau of Statistics (ABS) (2004) *Characteristics of Small Business in Australia.* Canberra. April.

Autio, Erkko (2002). Bottlenecks and Catalysts of Entrepreneurial Growth: What is Known about Entrepreneurial Growth and How it Can be Promoted. Report submitted to the European Commission (draft manuscript).

Baldwin, John (1999). A Portrait of Entrants and Exits. Research Paper No. 121. Micro-Economic Analysis Division. Ottawa: Statistics Canada. June.

Balje, S.H. and P.M. Waasdorp (2001). Entrepreneurship in the 21st Century: The role of public policy. In *Entrepreneurship in the Netherlands. New Economy: new entrepreneurs!* Zoetermeer: EIM Business & Policy Research and the Ministry of Economic Affairs.

Balje, Sander and Pieter Waasdorp (1999). Fast Growing Enterprises: Discoverers and Innovators. In *Entrepreneurship in the Netherlands: Ambitious entrepreneurs: the driving force for the next millennium.* The Hague: EIM and Ministry of Economic Affairs. January, 37-54.

Banco Interamericano de desarrollo fundes internacional (2004). *Desarrollo Emprendedor: América Latina y las experiencia internactional.* Washington, DC.

Barclays (2002). Profiting from Support. Available at: http://www.barclays.co.uk/articles/tracking_study.pdf.

Bartelsman, Eric, Stefano Scarpetta and Fabiano Shivardi (2003). Comparative Analysis of Firm Demographics and Survival: Micro-Level Evidence for the OECD Countries. Economic Development Working papers No. 348. Paris: OECD. January. http://www.oecd.org/eco/.

Baumol, William (2002). *The Free-Market Innovation Machine – Analyzing the Growth Miracle of Capitalism.* Princeton and Oxford: Princeton University Press.

Baumol, William (1993). Formal Entrepreneurship Theory in Economics: Existence and Bounds. *Journal of Business Venturing* 8, 197-210.

Baumol, William (1990). Entrepreneurship, Productive, Unproductive and Destructive. *Journal of Political Economy*, 98(5), 893-921.

Becattini, Giacomo (2002). From Marshall's to the Italien 'Industrial Districts': A Brief Critical Reconstruction. In Curzio & Fortis (eds.), *Complexity and Industrial Clusters: Dynamics and Models in Theory and Practice.* New York: Physica Verlag.

Birch, David (1987). *Job Creation in America.* NY: Free Press.

Birch, David (1979). The job generation process. Unpublished report. Massachusetts Institute of Technology (MIT) Program on Neighbourhood and Regional Change. Prepared for the Economic Development Administration, Washington, DC: US Department of Commerce.

Birch, David, Anne Haggerty and William Parsons (1999). *Entrepreneurial Hot-Spots: The Best Places in America to Start and Grow a Company.* Boston: Cognetics, Inc.

Blees, Jasper, Ron Kemp, Jeroen Maas and Marco Mosselman (2003). Barriers to Entry: Differences in barriers to entry for SMEs and large enterprises. Research Report H200301 (SCALES (Scientific Analysis of Entrepreneurship and SMEs). Zoetermeer: EIM Business & Policy Research. May.

Bosma, Neils and Henry Nieuwenhuijsen (2000). *Turbulence and productivity in the Netherlands*. Zoetermeer: EIM Small Business Research & Consultancy. March.

Bosma, Neils, Heleen Stigter and Sanders Wennekers (2002). *The Long Road to the Entrepreneurial Society, Global Entrepreneurship Monitor 2001: The Netherlands*. Zoetermeer: EIM Business & Policy Research.

Bosma, Neils, Mirjam Van Praag and Gerrit de Wit (2002). Entrepreneurial venture performance and initial capital constraints – An Empirical Analysis. EIM Research Report H200205. Zoetermeer: SCALES. November.

Bosma, Neils and Sander Wennekers (2004). *Entrepreneurial Attitudes Versus Entrepreneurial Activities: Global Entrepreneurship Monitor 2003, The Netherlands*. Zoetermeer: EIM Business & Policy Research. April.

Bosma, Neils, Gerrit de Wit and Martin Carree (2003). Modelling Entrepreneurship: Unifying the Entry/Exit Approach. Research Report 200305 (SCALES). Zoetermeer:. EIM Business & Policy Research. September.

Boston Consulting Group (2002). *Setting the Phoenix Free: A Report on Entrepreneurial Restarters*. Germany: The Boston Consulting Group.

Boter, Hakan, Dan Hjalmarsson and Anders Lundström (1999). *Outline of a Contemporary Small Business Policy*. Stockholm: Swedish Foundation for Small Business Research.

Branchflower, David G. (2000). Self-Employment in OECD Countries. Working Paper 7486. NBER Working paper Series. Cambridge, MA: National Bureau of Economic Research. http://www.nber.org/papers/w/7486.

Branchflower, David G. (1998). Entrepreneurship and the Youth Labour Market Problem: A Report for the OECD. Paris: OECD.

Branchflower, David G. and B. Meyer (1994). A Longitudinal Analysis of Young Entrepreneurs in Australia and the United States. *Small Business Economics*, 6(1), 1-20.

Bridge, Simon, Ken O'Neill and Stan Cromie (1998). *Understanding Enterprise, Entrepreneurship and Small Business*. London: MacMillan Business.

Brockhaus, Robert H. (1980). Risk Taking Propensity of Entrepreneurs. *Academy of Management Journal* Vol. 23, No. 3, 509-520. September.

Brockhaus, Robert H. (1979). An Exploration of Factors Affecting the Entrepreneurial Decision: Personal Characteristics vs Environmental Characteristics. *Proceedings of the Academy of Management*.

Bygrave, William (2003). Financing Entrepreneurs and Their Ventures. In P. Reynolds, W. Bygrave and E. Autio. *GEM 2003 Global Report*. Babson College, the London Business School and the Ewing Marion Kauffman Foundation.

Carree, M. and J. Nijkamp (2001). Deregulation in retailing: The Dutch experience. *Journal of Economics and Business, 53.* 225-235.

Carree, Martin A. and A. Roy Thurik (2003). The Impact of Entrepreneurship on Economic Growth. In Zoltan J. Acs and David B. Audretsch (eds.), *The Handbook of Entrepreneurship Research*. Dordrecht: Kluwer Academic Publishers, 437-471.

Carree, Martin A., André van Stel, Roy Thurik and Sander Wennekers (2002). Economic Development and Business Ownership: An analysis using data of 23 OECD countries in the period 1976-1996. *Small Business Economics, 19, 271-290.*

Casson, Marc (2003). Entrepreneurship, Business Culture and the Theory of the Firm. In Zoltan J. Acs and David B. Audretsch (eds.), *The Handbook of Entrepreneurship Research*. Dordrecht: Kluwer Academic Publishers, 223-246.

CIA (2004). The World Factbook.

Central Statistics Office (CSO) (2003). *Census 2002 Volume 6 Occupations.* Stationary Office: Dublin, December.

Centre for Entrepreneurial Management and Innovation (CEMI) (2003). *Communities of Enterprise: Future Strategies for the Business Enterprise Centres Network of Western Australia.* Prepared for the Small Business Development Corporation. University of Western Australia.

Chell, Elizabeth (1985). The Entrepreneurial Personality: A Few Ghosts Laid to Rest? *International Small Business Journal,* Spring.

Charney, Alberta and Gary D. Libecap (2000). The Impact of Entrepreneurship Education. Missouri: Kauffman Foundation Center for Entrepreneurial Leadership.

Chung-Hua Institution for Economic Research (CHIER) (2002). Proposal for Improving the Funding Environment for Start-up Businesses. Taipei.

Churchill, Neil C. and Virginia Lewis (1983). The Five Stages of Small Business Growth. Cambridge: Harvard Business School Press.

Clarysse, Bart, Ans Heirman and Jean-Jacques Degroof (2000). An Institutional and Resource-Based Explanation of Growth Patterns of Research Based Spin-offs in Europe. *Frontiers of Entrepreneurship Research.* Wellesley: Babson College.

Commission of the European Communities (2004). *Report from the Commission to the Council and the European Parliament on the implementation of the European Charter for Small Enterprises.* COM(2004) 64 final. Brussels, 11.02.

Cooper, Arnold (2003). Entrepreneurship: The Past, the Present, the Future. In Zoltan J. Acs and David Audretsch (eds.), *The Handbook of Entrepreneurship Research.* Dordrecht: Kluwer Academic Publishers, 21-34.

Cowling, Marc (2003). The Contribution of the Self-Employed to Employment in the EU. Report to the Small Business Service, URN 03/539. London: Department of Trade and Industry. January.

Cowling, Marc and William D. Bygrave (2003). Entrepreneurship and Unemployment: Relationships between unemployment and entrepreneurship in 37 countries participating in the Global Entrepreneurship Monitor (GEM) 2002. Wellesley: Babson College.

Danish National Agency for Enterprise and Housing, Danish Ministry of Economic and Business Affairs, FORA; ART; and Monitor Company Group (2004). Dynamic Benchmarking of Entrepreneurship Performance and Policy in Select Countries: Entrepreneurship Index Initiative. Discussion Paper. Copenhagen. May.

Davidsson, Per (1989). Continued Entrepreneurship and Small Firm Growth. Doctoral dissertation. Sweden: Stockholm School of Economics.

Davidsson, Per, Frédéric Delmar and Johan Wiklund (2001). *Growing firms in Sweden.* Stockholm: FSF/SNS. (In Swedish).

Davidsson, Per and Magnus Henrekson (2000). Institutional Determinants of the Prevalence of Start-ups and High-Growth Firms: Evidence from Sweden. *Small Business Economics.*

Davidsson, Per, Leif Lindmark and Christer Olofsson (1994). New Firm Formation and Regional Development in Sweden. Regional Studies. *Journal of the Regional Studies Association,* Vol. 28, No 4.

De, Dennis (2001). Fostering Entrepreneurship in Europe. In A. Lundström and L. Stevenson, *Entrepreneurship Policy for the Future.* Stockholm: Swedish Foundation for Small Business Research, 107-128.

Delmar, Frédéric (1996). Entrepreneurial Behaviour and Business Performance. Doctoral dissertation. Sweden: Stockholm School of Economics.

Delmar, Frédéric and Per Davidsson (2000). Where do they come from? Prevalence and characteristics of nascent entrepreneurs. *Entrepreneurship and Regional Development* 12, 1-23.

Delmar, Frédéric, Karin Sjöberg and Johan Wiklund (2003). *The involvement in self-employment among the Swedish science and technology labour force between 1990 and 2000*. Stockholm: Swedish Institute for Growth Policy Studies.

Department of Enterprise, Trade and Employment (DETE) (2003). *National Employment Development Plan Ireland 2003-2005*. Dublin: DETE. October.

Department of Industry, Tourism and Resources (ITR) (2004a). *Backing Australia's Ability – Building our Future through Science and Innovation*. Canberra: Commonwealth Government of Australia. May.

Department of Industry, Tourism and Resources (ITR) (2004b). *Australian Government's Innovation Report 2003-04: Real Results/Real Jobs*. Canberra: Commonwealth Government of Australia.

Department of Industry, Tourism and Resources (ITR) (2003a). Capital Availability: Views of COMET companies. Canberra: Commonwealth Government of Australia. July.

Department of Industry, Tourism and Resources (ITR) (2003b). Annual Review of Small Business 2002-2003. Canberra: Commonwealth Government of Australia.

Department of Trade and Industry (2004). *A Government Action Plan for Small Business*. London.

Department of Trade and Industry (2002). *Competing in the Global Economy: The Innovation Challenge*. London. December.

Department of Trade and Industry (2001). *Opportunity for All in a World of Change – White Paper on Enterprise, Skills and Innovation*. London.

Djankov, S., R. LaPorta, F. Lopez-de-Silanes and A. Schleiler (2000). The Regulation of Entry. Harvard Institute of Economic Research. Cambridge: Harvard University. September.

EIM (n.d). BLISS COMPENDIA Data set. http://www.eim.net/compendia_Inter/.

EIM (1999). Nascent Entrepreneurship: A Study of People Setting Up Their Own Business. Zoetermeer: EIM Business & Policy Research.

Eliasson, Gunnar (2001). The Role of Knowledge in Economic Growth. In J. Helliwell (ed.), *The Contribution of Human and Social Capital in Sustained Economic Growth and Well-being*. Paris: OECD (and HRDC, Canada).

Eliasson, Gunnar (2000). Industrial Policy, Competence Blocks and the Role of Science in Economic Development. *Evolutionary Economics*. Springer Verlag.

EnterpriseFinland (2003). The New Business Centres gain popularity as starting points for entrepreneurship. 31.3.2003. Helsinki. http://www.enterprisefinland.fi .

Enterprising Nation (1995). The Report of the Industry Task Force on Leadership and Management Skills. Canberra, Commonwealth Government of Australia.

ESRN (1995). *European Observatory for SMEs, Third Annual Report*. Zoetermeer: EIM. Business & Policy Research.

European Commission (2004a). Promoting entrepreneurship amongst women. Best Reports, No 2 – 2004. Brussels: Enterprise Directorate-General.

European Commission (2004b). Report on the implementation of the European charter for small enterprises in acceding and candidate countries. SEC(2004) 187. Commission staff working paper. Brussels: 12.02.

European Commission (2004c). *Education for Entrepreneurship: Making progress in promoting entrepreneurial attitudes and skills through Primary and Secondary education*. Final Report of the Expert Group. Brussels: Enterprise Directorate-General. February.

European Commission (2004d). *Action Plan: The European Agenda for Entrepreneurship.* COM(2004) 70 final. Communication from the Commission to the Council, the European Parliament, the European Economic and Social Committee and the Committee of the Regions. Brussels: 11.02.

European Commission (2004e). *Good Practice in the Promotion of Women Entrepreneurship.* Brussels: Enterprise Directorate-General. http://www.prowomen-eu.net.

European Commission (2004f). Consultation Document for a Community Support Programme for Entrepreneurship and Enterprise Competitiveness (2006-2010). Brussels.

European Commission (2003a). *A Pocketbook of Enterprise Policy Indicators 2003 Edition: How Member States and Candidates Countries Rank in the 2003 Enterprise Policy Scoreboard.* Brussels: Enterprise Directorate-General.

European Commission (2003b). Benchmarking enterprise policy: Results from the 2003 Scoreboard. Commission Staff Working Document SEC(2003)1278. Brussels. 04.11. http://europa.eu.int/comm/enterprise/enterprise_policy/competitiveness/doc/scoreboard_2 003_en.pdf.

European Commission (2003c). *Green Paper Entrepreneurship in Europe.* COM(2003) 27 final. Brussels. 21.01.

European Commission (2003d). Thinking Small in an Enlarging Europe. COM(2003) 26 final. Communication from the Commission to the Council and the European Parliament. Brussels. 21.1.

European Commission (2003e). *Benchmarking business angels.* BEST Report No. 1. Luxembourg: Office for Official Publications of the European Communities.

European Commission (2003f). Multi-annual Programme for enterprise and entrepreneurship, and in particular for small and medium-sized enterprises (2001-2005) – MAP Intermediate Evaluation Final Report. EPMC Doc, No. 14-2003-EN. Brussels: Enterprise Directorate-General.

European Commission (2002a). *The European Charter for Small Enterprises.* Endorsed by the Member States at the Feira European Council on 19 and 20 June 2000. Brussels: Enterprise Publications.

European Commission (2002b). *Good Practices in the Promotion of Female Entrepreneurship: Examples from Europe and the other OECD Countries.* Vienna: Austrian Institute for Small Business Research (IfGH). December.

European Commission (2002c). *Benchmarking the Administration of Start-ups.* Brussels: Center for Evaluation Studies, Enterprise Directorate-General. January.

European Commission (2002d). Final report of the expert group on transfers of SMEs. Brussels: Directorate-General Enterprises. May.

European Commission (2001). Creating Top-Class Business Support Services. Commission Staff Working Paper, 28.11.2001 SEC(2001) 1937. Brussels.

European Commission (1998a). Fostering Entrepreneurship in Europe: Priorities for the Future. Communication from the Commission to the Council. Brussels, 07.04.

European Commission (1998b). *Report of the Business Simplification Task Force (BEST), Volume 1.* Luxembourg: Office of Official Publications of the European Communities.

European Policy Centre (EPC) (2004). *Lisbon Revised – Finding a New Path to European Growth.* Brussels.

Evans D.S. and L.S. Leighton (1990). Small business formation by unemployed and employed workers. *Small Business Economics*, 2(4), 319-330.

Evans E. and L. Leighton (1989). The determinants of changes in U.S. self-employment, 1968-1987. *Journal of Small Business Economics*, 1(2), 111-120.

Finnie, Ross, Christine Laporte and Maud-Catherine Rivard (2002). Setting up Shop: Self-Employment Amongst Canadian College and University Graduates. No. 11F0019 No. 183. Ottawa: Analytical Studies Branch. March.

Fitzpatrick Associates (2003). *Review of the Role of County and City Enterprise Boards in the Development of Micro-Enterprises.* Dublin. November.

Fitzpatrick Associates (2001). Small Business Failures in Ireland. Report to the Department of Enterprise, Trade and Employment. Dublin.

Fitzsimons, Paula and Colm O'Gorman (2003). *How Entrepreneurial is Ireland? The Global Entrepreneurship Monitor Irish Report.* Sponsored by Enterprise Ireland and Inter*Trade*Ireland. Dublin.

Fitzsimons, Paula, Colm O'Gorman and Frank Roche (2001). *Global Entrepreneurship Monitor: The Irish Report.* Dublin: University College of Dublin.

Forfas (2004). *Ahead of the Curve: Ireland's Place in the Global Economy.* Prepared by the Enterprise Strategy Group. Dublin: Republic of Ireland. July.

Foster, Richard (1986). *Innovation: The Attacker's Advantage.* Summit Books.

Friis, Christian, Thomas Paulsson and Charlie Karlsson (2002). Entrepreneurship and Economic Growth: A critical review of Empirical and Theoretical Research. Stockholm: Swedish Institute for Growth Policy Studies.

Frontiers of Entrepreneurship Research 1981-2003. Wellesley: Babson College. Series of volumes.

Gartner, W.B. (1988). Who is an entrepreneur? Is the wrong question. *American Journal of Small Business*, 12(4), 11-32.

Gartner, William B. and Nancy M. Carter (2003). Entrepreneurial Behaviour and Firm Organizing Processes. In Zoltan J. Acs and David B. Audretsch (eds.), *The Handbook of Entrepreneurship Research.* Dordrecht: Kluwer Academic Publishers, 195-221.

Gibb, Alan (2001). Entrepreneurship and Small and Medium Enterprise Development: Guide to a Strategic Policy Review Process and Guide to the Development of a Strategic Plan. OECD Centre for Co-operation with Non-Members in Co-operation with the United Nations Industrial Development Organization (UNIDO). Paris: OECD.

Gillen, M., M. Powe, M. Dews and W.E. McMullan (1996). An Empirical Assessment of the Returns to Investment in Entrepreneurial Education. Presented at the Babson College Kauffman Foundation Entrepreneurship Conference, Seattle. March.

Goodbody Economic Consultants (2002). Entrepreneurship in Ireland. Prepared for FORFÁS, the National Competitiveness Council, Enterprise Ireland and the Department of Enterprise, Trade and Employment. Dublin. August.

Government of Iceland (2004). Budget Proposal Highlights 2004. Reykjavik, Iceland.

Hall, Chris (2003). The SME Policy Framework in ASEAN and APEC: Benchmark comparisons and analysis. Paper for the Small Enterprise Association of Australia and New Zealand 16th Annual Conference. Ballarat, Australia. 29 September – 1 October.

Hall, Chris (2002a). *Profile of SMEs and SME Issues in APEC 1990-2000.* APEC Small and Medium Enterprises Working Group. Singapore: APEC Secretariat.

Hall, Chris (2002b). Entrepreneurship Densities in APEC and Europe: How many entrepreneurs *should* there be in China or other developing economies? Presented at the Small and Medium Enterprise Working Group Meeting, Valparaiso, Chile, April.

Hallgrímsdóttir, Berglina and Charlotte Sigurdardóttir (2003). The Case of Finland. In Lundström (ed.), *Towards an Entrepreneurship Policy – A Nordic Perspective.* Stockholm: Swedish Foundation for Entrepreneurship, 145-173.

Harding, Rebecca (2003). *Global Entrepreneurship Monitor United Kingdom 2003.* London: London Business School.

Harding, Rebecca (2002). *Global Entrepreneurship Monitor (GEM) Report*. London: London Business School.

Hart, David (ed.) (2003). *The Emergence of Entrepreneurship Policy*. Cambridge: Cambridge University Press.

Havunen, Jouko (1996). Curriculum for Entrepreneurial Education. Presented at the ICSB World Conference, Stockholm.

Hellman, Thomas (2002). When Do Employees Become Entrepreneurs? Research Paper No. 1770. Research Paper Series, Stanford Graduate School of Business. June.

Hindle, Kevin and Susan Rushworth (2003). *Westpac GEM Australia: A Study of Australian Entrepreneurship in 2003*. Melbourne: Swinburne University Press.

Hindle, Kevin and Susan Rushworth (2002b). *Entrepreneurship – A Policy Primer*. Commissioned by the Queensland Innovation Council and Department of Innovation and the Information Economy. Melbourne: Australian Graduate School of Enterprise, Swinburne University of Technology.

Hisrich, R.D. and M. O'Brien (1982). The Woman Entrepreneur as a reflection of the type of business. In K.H. Vesper (ed.), *Frontiers of Entrepreneurship Research*, 54-67. Wellesley, MA: Babson College.

Hjalager, Anne-Mette (1989). Why No Entrepreneurs? Life Modes, Everyday Life, and Unemployment Strategies in an Underdeveloped Region. *Entrepreneurship and Regional Development*, January – March.

Hjalmarsson, Dan. and Anders W. Johansson (2003). Public advisory services – theory and practice. *Entrepreneurship and Regional Development*, 15, 83-98.

Hjalmarsson, Dan (1998). Program theory for public business support. Doctoral Dissertation, no 71. Department of Business Studies. Sweden: Uppsala University. (In Swedish).

HMS Treasury and Small Business Service (2003). Bridging the financing gap: a consultation on improving access to growth capital for small businesses. London.

Hofstede, Geert (2001). *Culture's Consequences: Comparing Values, Behaviours, Institutions and Organizations Across Nations*. 2nd edition. Thousand Oaks: Sage.

Holmquist, Carin and Elisabeth Sundin (1988). Women as entrepreneurs in Sweden: Conclusions from a survey. *Frontiers of Entrepreneurship Research*. Wellesley, MA: Babson College, 626-642.

Hult, Merja (2003). Business demography in 9 Member States: Results for 1997-2000. Brussels: European Communities.

Industry Canada (2003). *Making a Difference: Contributing to the Quality of Life of Canadians*. Ottawa: Government of Canada.

Industry Canada (2002). Canadian Venture Capital Activity: An Analysis of Trends and Gaps. Ottawa.

International Management Development Network (INTERMAN) (1991). *Profiles of Entrepreneurship Development Programmes*. The International Labour Office and the United Nations Development Programme. Geneva.

Kantis, Hugo (2002). *Entrepreneurship in Emerging Economies: The Creation and Development of New Firms in Latin America and East Asia*. Washington, DC: Inter-American Development Bank.

Katz, J.A. (2003). The Chronology and Intellectual Trajectory of American Entrepreneurship Education. *Journal of Business Venturing* 18(2), 283-300.

Kauffman Foundation (2001). The Growth and Advancement of Entrepreneurship in Higher Education: An Environmental Scan of College Initiatives Kansas City, Missouri: Kauffman Center for Entrepreneurial Leadership. Winter.

Kauffman Foundation (2000). K-14 Entrepreneurship Education Market Analysis. Prepared by the Kauffman Foundation Staff. Kansas City, Missouri: Kauffman Foundation. Fall.

Kayne, Jay (1999). State Entrepreneurship Policies and Programs. Missouri: Kauffman Center for Entrepreneurial Leadership at the Ewing Marion Kauffman Foundation. http://www.entreworld.com.

Kets de Vries, M.F.R. (1977). The Entrepreneurial Personality: A Person at the Crossroads. *The Journal of Management Studies*, 34-57. February.

Kim, Philip, Howard Aldrich and Lisa Keister (2004). Access (not) denied: The Impact of Financial, Human and Cultural Capital on Becoming a 'Nascent Entrepreneur'. Draft presented at the FSF International Council Meeting in Antwerp. Stockholm: Swedish Foundation for Small Business Research. March.

Kirchhoff, B. A. (1994). *Entrepreneurship and Dynamic Capitalism: The Economics of Business Firm Formation and Growth*. CT: Praegar Publishers.

Kristensen, Frank Skov and Søren Qvist Eliassen (2003). The Case of Denmark. In Lundström (ed.), *Towards an Entrepreneurship Policy – A Nordic Perspective*. Stockholm: Swedish Foundation for Entrepreneurship, 49-79.

Kirzner, I. (1982). The theory of entrepreneurship in economic growth. In C. Kent, D. Sexton and K. Vesper (eds.) *The Encyclopaedia of Entrepreneurship*. Englewood Cliffs, NJ: Prentice Hall, 272-276.

Kuratko, Donald F. (2003). Entrepreneurship Education: Emerging Trends and Challenges for the 21st Century. 2003 Coleman Foundation White Paper Series for the U.S. Association of Small Business and Entrepreneurship. Maurice, Indiana: College of Business, Ball State University.

Landström, Hans (forthcoming, 2005). *Pioneers in Entrepreneurship Research*. Dordrecht: Kluwer Academic Publishers.

Landström, Hans (ed.) (2003). Small Business and Capital: Swedish research concerning financing of SMEs. Stockholm: Swedish Foundation for Small Business Research and SNS. (In Swedish).

Lowrey, Ying (2003). The Entrepreneur and Entrepreneurship: A Neoclassical Approach. Presented at the ASSA Annual Meeting. 5 January. Washington, DC: Office of Advocacy, Small Business Administration.

Lundström, Anders (ed.) (2003). *Towards an Entrepreneurship Policy – A Nordic Perspective*. Stockholm: Swedish Foundation for Small Business Research.

Lundström, Anders and Lois Stevenson (2002). *On the Road to Entrepreneurship Policy*. Stockholm: Swedish Foundation for Small Business Research.

Lundström, Anders and Lois Stevenson (2001). *Entrepreneurship Policy for the Future*. Special Edition for the SME Forum, Vaxjö, Sweden. Stockholm: Swedish Foundation for Small Business Research. March.

Lundström, Anders, Anneli Kjellberg, Tommy Andersson, Einar Bullvåg, Tor Korneliussen, Tommy Salonsaari, E Varumäki, and Jukka Vesalainen (1998). *Europartenariat Northern Scandinavia 1996: Effects and experiences*. Stockholm: FSF/NUTEK.

Mazzarol, T.W. (2003). Regional Enterprise – Developing a Holistic Framework for Stimulating Regional Enterprise. Regional South Australia – Growing the State, Regional Development SA Annual Conference. Victor Harbour, South Australia. 10-12 September.

McClelland, David (1971). The Achievement Motive in Economic Growth. In Kilby, Peter (ed.), *Entrepreneurship and Economic Growth*. New York: The Free Press.

McClelland, David (1961). *The Achieving Society*. Princeton, NJ: Van Nostrand.

McGrath, R. G. (2003). Connecting the Study of Entrepreneurship and Theories of Capitalist Progress. In Zoltan J. Acs and David B. Audretsch (eds.), *The Handbook of Entrepreneurship Research*. Dordrecht: Kluwer Academic Publishers, 515-531.

MICRONOMICS Inc. (1998). Business Failure and Entrepreneurship in the US. Prepared on behalf of EIM International. Zoetermeer: EIM. Business & Policy Research. September 20.

MCEETYA Task Force on Transition from School (2002). Action Plan to implement the Ministerial Declaration STEPPING FORWARD – improving pathways for all young people. Canberra, Australia.

Ministerial Council on Education, Employment, Training and Youth Affairs (MCEETYA) (2002). STEPPING FORWARD – improving pathways for all young people. A Joint Declaration by Commonwealth, State and Territory Ministers for Education, Training, Employment, Youth and Community Services. Canberra, Australia. Available at: http://www.mceetya.edu.au/forward/index.htm

Ministeriet Beskæftigelses (2003). NAP 2003: Denmark's national action plan for employment 2003. Copenhagen.

Ministry of Economic Affairs (2004). Action for Innovation: Annual Report 2003. The Hague. May.

Ministry of Economic Affairs (2003a). Action for Entrepreneurs! The Hague: Enterprise Directorate. December.

Ministry of Economic Affairs (2003b). Progress Report on the Implementation of the Charter of Small and Medium Sized Enterprises in the Netherlands. The Hague. October. http://www.europa.eu/int/comm/enterprise_policy/charter/charter2004.htm

Ministry of Economic Affairs (2000a). The Entrepreneurial Society: More opportunities and fewer obstacles for entrepreneurship. The Hague. February (English version; Dutch version published in September 1999).

Ministry of Economic Affairs (2000b). Benchmarking the Netherlands 2000: on the threshold of the new millennium. The Hague. March.

Ministry of Economic Affairs (1998). Get Set! A Discussion of new entrepreneurship. The Hague.

Ministry of Economic Affairs (1987). Create Room for Entrepreneurs. White Paper. The Hague.

Ministry of Economic Affairs, Ministry of Social Affairs and Employment and Ministry of Finance (1995). Jobs Through Enterprise. Policy paper. The Hague. 28 June.

Ministry of Economy and Business Affairs (2003). European Charter for Small Enterprises. Copenhagen. 29 September. http://www.europa.eu/int/comm/enterprise_policy/charter/charter2004.htm

Ministry of Economy and Business Affairs (2003). Promoting Entrepreneurship – A plan of action. Copenhagen. August.

Ministry of Economy and Business Affairs (2002). The Danish Growth Strategy. Copenhagen. August.

Ministry of the Economy (2003). Fourth Implementation Report on the European Charter for Small Enterprises. Madrid. October. http://www.europa.eu/int/comm/enterprise_policy/charter/charter2004.htm

Ministry of Education and the Ministry of Science, Knowledge and Innovation (n.d). Implementing Innovation, Entrepreneurial Motivation, and a Culture of Independence in the Education System. Copenhagen.

Ministry of Industry, Employment and Communications (2003a). The European Charter for Small Enterprises: A review of relevant actions and measures in Sweden. Stockholm. September. http://www.europa.eu/int/comm/enterprise_policy/charter/charter2004.htm

Ministry of Industry, Employment and Communications (2003b). Sweden's Action Plan for Employment 2003. Stockholm (with Ministry of Finance).

Ministry of Trade and Industry (2004). Entrepreneurship Policy Programme: An enterprising society in view. Helsinki. 17 June. http://www.ktm.fi

Ministry of Trade and Industry (2003). Finland's input to the Implementation Report on the European Charter for Small Enterprises. Helsinki. 30 September. http://www.europa.eu/int/comm/enterprise_policy/charter/charter2004.htm

Ministry of Trade and Industry (2003). From Ideas to Value: The Government's Plan for a Comprehensive Innovation Policy. Oslo.

Minniti, Maria and William B. Bygrave (2004). *National Entrepreneurship Assessment: United States of America. 2003 Executive Report*. GEM Global Entrepreneurship Monitor. Babson College and Kauffman Foundation. Wellesley, Mass: Babson College.

Minniti, Maria and Pia Arenius (2003). Women in Entrepreneurship: The Enterprise Advantage of Nations. United Nations Headquarters, United Nations. April.

Morris, Michael H. (1996). Sustaining the Entrepreneurial Society. Working paper 96-01. The Small Business Foundation of America: The Research Institute for Small and Emerging Business. Washington, DC.

Moulin, H. (1988). *Axioms of Cooperative Decision Making*. MA: Cambridge University Press.

National Commission on Entrepreneurship (2002). *American Formula for Growth: Federal Policy & the Entrepreneurial Economy, 1958-1998*. Washington, DC: NCOE. October.

National Commission on Entrepreneurship (2001). *High-Growth Companies: Mapping America's Entrepreneurial Landscape*. Washington, DC: NCOE, July.

National Commission on Entrepreneurship (2000). Embracing Innovation: Entrepreneurship and American Economic Growth. Washington, DC: NCOE.

National Federation of Independent Business (NFIB) (2000). *Small Business Policy Guide*. Washington, DC: NFIB Research Foundation. November.

National Governors Association (2004). *A Governor's Guide to Strengthening State Entrepreneurship Policy*. Washington, DC: NGA Center for BEST PRACTICES.

National Women's Business Council (2004). Key Facts About Women Business Owners and Their Enterprises. Washington, DC: NWBC. March.

National Women's Business Council (2003). Mentoring in the Business Environment. Washington, DC: NWBC. http://www.mwbc.gov/pressroom/documents/mentoringfinalreport.pdf

National Youth Commission (2003). Free & Young Program. Chinese Taipei.

Noorderhaven, Neils G., Roy Thurik, Sander Wennekers and André van Stel (2003). Self-employment across 15 European countries: the role of dissatisfaction SCALES -paper N200223. Zoetermeer: EIM Business & Policy Research.

NUTEK (2003). Stronger Entrepreneurship: a policy report about new perspectives, changed pre-requisites and positive attitudes. Stockholm. April.

OECD (2004a). Venture Capital: Trends and Policy Recommendations. Science Technology Industry. Paris: OECD. Available at: http://www.oecd.org/sti/micro-policies/

OECD (2004b). *Employment Outlook*. Paris: OECD.

OECD (2004c). Women's Entrepreneurship: Issues and Policies. Prepared for the Second OECD Conference of Ministers Responsible for Small and Medium-Sized Enterprises (SMEs), Istanbul, June. Paris: OECD.

OECD (2004d). Fostering Entrepreneurship as a Driver of Growth in a Global Economy. Prepared for the Second OECD Conference of Ministers Responsible for Small and Medium-Sized Enterprises (SMEs), Istanbul, June. Paris: OECD.

OECD (2004e). Evaluation of SME Policies and Programmes. Prepared for the Second OECD Conference of Ministers Responsible for Small and Medium-Sized Enterprises (SMEs), Istanbul, June. Paris: OECD.

OECD (2003a). Evaluating SME Policies and Programmes. In progress draft background report DSTI/IND/PME2003/4/REV1. Paris: OECD.

OECD (2003b). *OECD in Figures 2003 Edition: Statistics on Member Countries*. Paris: OECD Observer.

OECD (2002a). *OECD Small and Medium Enterprise Outlook, 2002 Edition*. Paris: OECD.

OECD (2002b). Policy Benchmarks for Fostering Firm Creation and Entrepreneurship. DSTI/IND(2002), 13. Paris: OECD.

OECD (2001a). The Roadmap for Benchmarking Business Policies. Oct. 12. Directorate for Science, Technology and Industry, Paris.

OECD (2001b). *Entrepreneurship, Growth and Policy*. Paris: OECD.

OECD (2001c). Drivers of Growth: Information Technology, Innovation and Entrepreneurship. Paris: OECD.

OECD (2000a). *Small and Medium Enterprise Outlook, 2000 Edition*. Paris: OECD.

OECD (2000b). The Bologna Charter on SME Policies. Paris: OECD (adopted on 15 June 2000).

OECD (1999). *Regulatory Reform for Smaller Firms*. Science Technology Industry. Paris: OECD.

OECD (1998). *Fostering Entrepreneurship*. Paris: OECD.

OECD (1997). *Small Businesses, Job Creation and Growth: Facts, Obstacles and Best Practices*. Paris: OECD.

OECD (1995). *Thematic Overview of Entrepreneurship and Job Creation Policies*. Paris: OECD.

Orr, D. (1974). The Determinants of Entry: A Study of Canadian Manufacturing Industries. *Review of Economics and Statistics*, Vol. 58, 58-66.

Pages, Erik R. and Kenneth Poole (2003). *Understanding Entrepreneurship Promotion as an Economic Development Strategy: A Three-State Survey*. A joint project of the National Commission on Entrepreneurship and the Center for Regional Economic Competitiveness. January.

Parsley, Chris and Erwin Dreessen (2004). Growth Firms Project: Key Findings. Revised 27 August. Small Business Policy Branch. Ottawa: Industry Canada. Available at: http://strategis.ic.gc.ca/epic/internet/insbrp-rppe.nsf/en/rd008i6c.html

Penrose, Edith. (1959). *The Theory of the Growth of the Firm*. UK: Oxford University Press.

Picot, Garnett, Zgebgxi Lin and Janice Yates (1999). The entry and exit dynamics of self-employment in Canada. Analytical Studies Branch. Ottawa: Statistics Canada. March.

Prime Minister's Task Force on Women Entrepreneurs (2003). *Report and Recommendations*. Ottawa. October. http://www.liberal.parl.gc.ca/entrepreneur

Purrington, C.A. and K.E Bettcher (2001). *From the garage to the boardroom: The entrepreneurial roots of America's largest corporations*. Washington, DC: The National Commission on Entrepreneurship.

Rettab, Belaid (2001). The Emergence of Ethnic Entrepreneurship: A conceptual framework. Research Report 0103. Zoetermeer: EIM Business & Policy Research.

Reynolds, Paul D. (2004) Understanding Business Creation: Serendipity and Scope in Two Decades of Business Creation Studies. Remarks on Receiving the FSF-NUTEK Award 2004. Stockholm: Swedish Foundation for Small Business Research.

Reynolds, Paul D., William D. Bygrave and Erkko Autio (2004). *GEM 2003 Global Report*. Babson College, the London Business School, and the Ewing Marion Kauffman Foundation.

Reynolds, Paul D., S. Michael Camp, William D. Bygrave, Erkko Autio and Michael Hay (2001). *Global Entrepreneurship Monitor: 2001 Executive Report*. London Business School and Kauffman Center for Entrepreneurial Leadership.

Reynolds, Paul D., Nancy M. Carter, William B. Gartner, Patricia G. Greene and Larry W. Cox (2002). *The Entrepreneur Next Door: Characteristics of Individuals Starting Companies in America.* An Executive Summary of the Panel Study of Entrepreneurial Dynamics. Missouri: The Ewing Marion Kauffman Foundation.

Reynolds, Paul D., M. Hay, W. D. Bygrave, S. M. Camp and E. Autio (2000). *Global Entrepreneurship Monitor: 2000 Executive Report.* Missouri: Kauffman Center for Entrepreneurial Leadership.

Reynolds, Paul D., M. Hay and S.M. Camp (1999). *Global Entrepreneurship Monitor, 1999 Executive Report.* Babson College, Kauffman Center for Entrepreneurial Leadership and the London Business School.

Reynolds, Paul D. and Sammis B. White (1997). *The Entrepreneurial Process.* Quorum Books.

Robson, Martin, T. and Colin Wren (1999). Marginal and average tax rates and the incentive for self-employment. *Southern Economic Journal. 65/(4). 757-774.*

Rotefoss, Beate, Eirik Pedersen, Svenn Are Jenssen and Lars Kolvereid (2003). The Case of Norway. In A. Lundström (ed.), *Towards an Entrepreneurship Policy – A Nordic Perspective.* Stockholm: Swedish Foundation for Entrepreneurship, 177-215.

Royal Ministry of Trade and Industry (2003). European Charter for Small Enterprises: Norwegian Report 2003. Oslo. 10 October. http://www.europa.eu/int/comm/enterprise_policy/charter/charter2004.htm

Routamaa, Vesa (2003). The Case of Finland. In A. Lundström (ed.), *Towards an Entrepreneurship Policy – A Nordic Perspective.* Stockholm: Swedish Foundation for Entrepreneurship, 83-142.

Sabel, Charles (2001). Diversity, Not Specialisation: The Ties That Bind the (New) Industrial District. In Curzio & Fortis (eds.), *Complexity and Industrial Clusters. Dynamics and Models in Theory and Practice.* New York: Physica Verlag.

Sarasvathy, Saras (2001). Causation and Effectuation: Toward a theoretical shift from economic inevitability to entrepreneurial contingency. *Academy of Management Review* 26(2), 243-288.

Sarasvathy, Saras, Nicholas Dew, Romakristina Velamuri and Sankavan Venkataraman (2003). Three Views of Entrepreneurial Opportunity. In Zoltan J. Acs and David Audretsch (eds.), *The Handbook of Entrepreneurship Research.* Dordrecht: Kluwer Academic Publishers.

Scarpetta, Stefano, Philip Hemmings, Thierry Tressel and Jaejoon Woo (2002). The Role of Policy and Institutions for Productivity and Firm Dynamics: Evidence from Micro and Industry Data. Working Paper No. 329, Economic Development Department. Paris: OECD. April.

Schumpeter, Joseph (1934). *The Theory of Economic Development.* Cambridge: Harvard University Press.

Shane, Scott and Jonathan Eckhardt (2003). The Individual-Opportunity Nexus. In Zoltan J. Acs and David Audretsch (eds.), *The Handbook of Entrepreneurship Research.* Dordrecht: Kluwer Academic Publishers, 161-191.

Shaver, Kelly, G. (2003). The Social Psychology of Entrepreneurial Behaviour. In Zoltan J. Acs and David Audretsch (eds.), *The Handbook of Entrepreneurship Research.* Dordrecht: Kluwer Academic Publishers, 331-357.

Shapero, Albert (1984). The Entrepreneurial Event. In C. Kent (ed.), *The Environment for Entrepreneurship.* Mass: Lexington Books, 21-40.

Shapero, Albert and Lisa Sokol (1982). The Social Dimensions of Entrepreneurship. In C. Kent, D. Sexton and K. Vesper (eds.), *Encyclopaedia of Entrepreneurship.* Englewood Cliffs. New Jersey: Prentice Hall.

Schramm, Carl F. (2004). Building Entrepreneurial Economies. *Foreign Affairs*, Vol 83, No. 4, 104-115.

Small and Medium Enterprise Administration (SMEA) (2003). *White Paper on Small and Medium Enterprises in Taiwan 2003*. Taipei: Ministry of Economic Affairs. September.

Small Business Administration (2003). SBA Budget Request & Performance Plan FY 2004. Congressional Submission. Washington, DC. 10 February.

Small Business Service (2004a). *A government action plan for small business: Making the UK the best place in the world to grow a business*. London, England: Department of Trade and Industry.

Small Business Service (2004b). *A government action plan for small business: The evidence base*. London, England: Department of Trade and Industry.

Small Business Service (2004c). Annual Small Business Survey 2003: Executive Summary. London, England: Department of Trade and Industry. July.

Small Business Service (2004d). Household Survey of Entrepreneurship 2003: Executive Summary. London, England: Department of Trade and Industry. July.

Small Business Service (2003). *A Strategic Framework for Women's Enterprise: Sharing the Vision – a collaborative approach to increasing female entrepreneurship*. London, England: Department of Trade and Industry. December.

Small Business Service (2002). *Small Business and Government – The Way Forward*. London, England: Department of Trade and Industry.

Small Business Service (2001). A Review of relevant actions and measures in force in the United Kingdom: The European Charter for Small Business. London, England: Department of Trade and Industry. October. http://www.sbs.gov.uk

Small Business Service (2000). Think Small First: A National Strategy for Supporting Small and Medium Sized Enterprises in the UK. London: Department of Trade and Industry. 2 October.

Statistics Canada (2003). Business Register. Ottawa. June.

Statistics Finland. Business Register. Helsinki.

Statistics Sweden (2003). Sweden's Business Register. Stockholm.

Stevenson, Lois (2002). Innovation and Entrepreneurship: a Dutch policy perspective in an international context. In *Innovative entrepreneurship. New policy challenges!* Zoetermeer: EIM Business & Policy Research. February, 43-66.

Stevenson, Lois (1996). *Implementation of an Entrepreneurship Development Strategy in Canada: The Case of the Atlantic Region*. Territorial Services Division. Paris: OECD/ACOA.

Stevenson, Lois (1986). Against all odds: The entrepreneurship of women. *Journal of Small Business Management*, 24(4), 30-36.

Stevenson, Lois and Anders Lundström (2002). *Beyond the Rhetoric: Defining Entrepreneurship Policy and its Best Practice Components*. Stockholm: Swedish Foundation for Small Business Research.

Stevenson, Lois and Anders Lundström (2001). *Patterns and Trends in Entrepreneurship/SME Policy and Practice in Ten Countries*. Stockholm: Swedish Foundation for Small Business Research.

Storey, David (2003). Entrepreneurship, Small and Medium Sized Enterprises and Public Policies. In Zoltan J. Acs and David Audretsch (eds.), *The Handbook of Entrepreneurship Research*. Dordrecht: Kluwer Academic Publishers, 473-511.

Storey, David (2000). Six Steps to heaven: evaluating the impact of public business in developed economies. In D.L. Sexton and Hans Landström (eds.), *Handbook of Entrepreneurship*. Oxford, UK: Blackwells, 176-194.

Storey, David (1994). *Understanding the Small Business Sector*. London/New York: Routledge.

The Curriculum Corporation (2002a). *Enterprise Education in Primary Schools*. Canberra, Australia: Commonwealth Department of Education, Science & Training.

The Curriculum Corporation (2002b). *Enterprise Education in Secondary Schools*. Canberra, Australia: Commonwealth Department of Education, Science & Training.

The Curriculum Corporation (2002c). *The Enterprising School: A guide for the development of Enterprise education in the schools*. Canberra, Australia: Commonwealth Department of Education, Science & Training.

The Curriculum Corporation (1996). Enterprise Education in Australia – the school context. Presented at the ICSB World Conference, Stockholm. June.

Thomas, T. and B. Landry (2001). Evaluating Policy Outcomes in Federal Economic Development Programs in Atlantic Canada. New Brunswick: The Atlantic Canada Opportunities Agency.

Thurik, Roy (2004). Entrepreneurship and growth. Keynote paper presented at Small Business Days in Örebro. Stockholm. Swedish Foundation for Small Business Research. January.

Uhlaner, Lorraine and Roy Thurik (2003). Post-Materialism: A Cultural Factor influencing Total Entrepreneurial Activity across Nations. SCALES-paper N200321. Zoetermeer: EIM Business & Policy Research. February.

United Nations Development Programme (2004). *Unleashing Entrepreneurship: Making Business Work for the Poor*. Report to the Secretary-General of the United Nations by the Commission on the Private Sector & Development. New York: UNDP. 1 March.

UK Treasury (2003). Bridging the finance gap: A consultation on improving access to growth capital for small businesses. London. Available on the internet at http://www.sbs.gov.uk/content/consultations/bridgingthefinancegap.pdf

Van Stel, André (2003). COMPENDIA 2000.2: a harmonized data set of business ownership rates in 23 OECD countries. Research Report H200302 (SCALES). Zoetermeer: EIM Business & Policy Research. May.

Van Stel, André and Martin Carree (2002). Business Ownership and Sectoral Growth. Research Report H200206. Zoetermeer: EIM Business & Policy Research. December.

Van Stel, André and Bart Diephius (2004). Business dynamics and employment growth: a cross-country analysis. Research Report H200310. Zoetermeer: EIM Business & Policy Research. March.

Van Stel, André and Viktor Stunnenberg (2004). Linking Business Ownership and Perceived Administrative Complexity: An Empirical Analysis of 18 OECD Countries. SCALES-paper N200409. Zoetermeer: EIM Business & Policy Research. July.

Van Stel, André, Sander Wennekers, Roy Thurik, Paul Reynolds and Gerrit de Wit (2003). Explaining nascent entrepreneurship across countries. SCALES-paper N200301. Zoetermeer: EIM Business & Policy Research. May.

Verheul, Ingrid, André van Stel and Roy Thurik (2004). Explaining female and male entrepreneurship across 29 countries. SCALES-paper N200403. Zoetermeer: EIM Business & Policy Research. May.

Verheul, Ingrid, Sander Wennekers, David Audretsch and Roy Thurik (2001). *An eclectic theory of entrepreneurship: policies, institutions and culture*. EIM Research Report 0012/E. Zoetermeer: EIM Business & Policy Research. March.

Vesalainen, Jukka and Timo Pihkala (2000). Barriers to Entrepreneurship – Educational Opportunities. Proceedings of the IntEnt-conference. Tampere. July.

Vesalainen, Jukka and Timo Pihkala (1999) Entrepreneurial Identity, Intentions and the Effect of the Push-Factor. *Academy of Entrepreneurship Journal. 5:2. 1-24.*

Waldinger, R., R. Aldrich, R. Ward and Associates (1990). *Ethnic Entrepreneurs. Immigrant Business in Industrial Societies*. Newbury Park CA: Sage Publications.

Waasdorp, Pieter (2002). Innovative entrepreneurship: a Dutch perspective. In *Innovative entrepreneurship. New policy challenges*. Zoetermeer: EIM: Business & Policy Research. 27-42.

Welsh, John A. and Jeffrey F. White (1981). A Small Business is not a Little Big Business. *Harvard Business Review*.

Wennekers, Sander and Roy Thurik (2001). Institutions, entrepreneurship and economic performance. In A. Lundström and L. Stevenson, *Entrepreneurship Policy for the Future*, 51-87. Stockholm: Swedish Foundation for Small Business Research.

Wennekers, Sander and Roy Thurik (1999). Linking entrepreneurship and economic growth. *Small Business Economics, 13*, 27-55.

Wigren, Caroline (2003). The Spirit of Gnosjö – The Ground Narrative and Beyond. Doctoral dissertation. Sweden: Jönköping International Business School.

Wildeman, R.E., Geert Hofstede, N.G. Noorderheven, Roy Thurik, W.H.J. Verhoeven and Sander Wennekers (1999). Self-employment in 23 OECD countries, the role of cultural and economic factors. Research report 9811/E. Zoetermeer: EIM Business & Policy Research.

Wilken, Paul H. (1979). The Emergence of Entrepreneurship and its Significance for Economic Growth and Development. In *Entrepreneurship: A Comparative and Historical Study*. Norwood, NJ: Ablex.

Yin, R. K. (1989). *Case Study Research Design and Methods*. Sage Publications.

Zacharakis, Andrew L., William D. Bygrave and Dean A. Shepherd (2000). *Global Entrepreneurship Monitor: National Entrepreneurship Assessment, United States of America: 2000 Executive Report*. Babson College and the Kauffman Center for Entrepreneurial Leadership.

INDEX

Printed in the United States
84796LV00001B/2/A